STO

Y0-ACF-049

*A guide to film, television, and radio programs supported by the*

**National Endowment for the Humanities**
*Division of Public Programs*
*Humanities Projects in Media*

For sale by the U.S. Government Printing Office
Superintendent of Documents, Mail Stop: SSOP, Washington, DC 20402-9328
ISBN 0-16-038136-3

# INTRODUCTION

In the belief that the well-being of a democratic society depends in part on a shared understanding among its citizens of their cultural and intellectual heritage, and on the vitality of critical discourse in their common life, the Congress authorized and encouraged the Endowment to foster public understanding and appreciation of the humanities. The Division of Public Programs supports projects that convey significant scholarship to the general public and engage citizens in critical interpretation and analysis of the humanities. It does this through interpretive exhibitions, lectures, symposia, reading and discussion groups, and printed materials. Another important focus has been the development of radio, television, and film programs through the division's Humanities Projects in Media program.

This guide, with descriptions of more than 800 productions developed with NEH support, is designed to identify available materials and to stimulate their use by individuals, groups, schools, and organizations. Most of the programs, though originally produced for broadcast, can be used effectively in small discussion settings or in larger program efforts.

All film, video, and radio programs are listed in alphabetical order in one of the following eight sections:

**United States History and American Studies**
**Literature and Language**
**World Culture and History**
**History, Theory, and Criticism of the Arts**
**Archaeology and Anthropology**
**Philosophy, Religion, and Ethics**
**Children's and Family Programming**
**General Humanities**

Each program listing includes information about content, production credits, format, length, ancillary materials, and awards. Each also provides the name of the current distribution agent (as of June 1992). Unless otherwise noted, the listed distributor represents the audiovisual/educational market (libraries, schools, etc.). All distributor addresses and phone numbers can be found at the back of the book. It will be necessary to contact the distributor to determine fees.

Radio programs are noted by an (R) in the table of contents. All other programs are either films or videos.

In several instances, the number of individual programs in a radio or television series exceeds thirty. Limitations of space preclude a full listing of the individual program titles; however, general themes of the programs and some sample program titles are included.

We are grateful to the many individuals and organizations who contributed so substantially to this body of work and through it to public understanding and appreciation of the humanities. We hope that you will find this listing useful.

Donald Gibson
*Director*
*Division of Public Programs*

# THE NATIONAL ENDOWMENT FOR THE HUMANITIES

In order "to promote progress and scholarship in the humanities and the arts in the United States," Congress enacted the National Foundation on the Arts and the Humanities Act of 1965. This act established the National Endowment for the Humanities as an independent grant-making agency of the federal government to support research, education, and public programs in the humanities. Grants are made through six divisions—Education Programs, Fellowships and Seminars, Preservation and Access, Public Programs, Research Programs, and State Programs—and one office, the Office of Challenge Grants.

## The Humanities

In the act that established the National Endowment for the Humanities, the term humanities includes, but is not limited to, the study of the following disciplines: history; philosophy; languages; linguistics; literature; archaeology; jurisprudence; the history, theory, and criticism of the arts; ethics; comparative religion; and those aspects of the social sciences that employ historical or philosophical approaches.

## What the Endowment Supports

The National Endowment for the Humanities supports exemplary work to advance and disseminate knowledge in all the disciplines of the humanities. Endowment support is intended to complement and assist private and local efforts and to serve as a catalyst to increase nonfederal support for projects of high quality.

Although the activities funded by the Endowment vary greatly in cost, in the numbers of people involved, and in their specific intents and benefits, they all have in common two requirements for funding: significance to learning in the humanities and excellence in conception. In the most general terms, NEH-supported projects aid scholarship and research in the humanities, help improve humanities education, and foster in the American people a greater curiousity about and understanding of the humanities.

Further information about the Endowment as well as guidelines and application forms are available from the Office of Publications and Public Affairs, National Endowment for the Humanities, 1100 Pennsylvania Avenue, N.W., Washington, D.C. 20506, telephone 202/606-8438, (TDD for the hearing-impaired only 202/606-8282).

# Table of Contents

(R) denotes Radio Production

(R) denotes Radio Production

(R) denotes Radio Production

(R) denotes Radio Production

(R) denotes Radio Production

(R) denotes Radio Production

(R) denotes Radio Production

(R) denotes Radio Production

(R) denotes Radio Production

## LITERATURE AND LANGUAGE

(R) denotes Radio Production

(R) denotes Radio Production

(R) denotes Radio Production

(R) denotes Radio Production

(R) denotes Radio Production

(R) denotes Radio Production

(R) denotes Radio Production

(R) denotes Radio Production

(R) denotes Radio Production

## WORLD CULTURE AND HISTORY

(R) denotes Radio Production

(R) denotes Radio Production

(R) denotes Radio Production

(R) denotes Radio Production

(R) denotes Radio Production

## HISTORY, THEORY, AND CRITICISM OF THE ARTS

(R) denotes Radio Production

## PHILOSOPHY, RELIGION, AND ETHICS

(R) denotes Radio Production

## CHILDREN'S AND FAMILY PROGRAMMING

(R) denotes Radio Production

(R) denotes Radio Production

(R) denotes Radio Production

(R) denotes Radio Production

## GENERAL HUMANITIES

## DISTRIBUTORS

(R) denotes Radio Production

U.S.
History &
American
Studies

# THE ADAMS CHRONICLES

*Dramatic Series*

This series of thirteen one-hour dramas weaves together the lives of four generations of the Adams family with events that shaped American history. Spanning the years 1750 to 1900, it is based on 300,000 pages of letters, diaries, and journals written by various members of the family.

*Program 1*

**John Adams: Lawyer (1758–70)**

This program features John Adams's experiences as a young lawyer, his courting of Abigail Smith, and his emergence as a voice against unjust practices imposed by the British crown.

*Program 2*

**John Adams: Revolutionary (1770–76)**

While John Adams serves as a delegate to Philadelphia's second Continental Congress and signs the Declaration of Independence, Abigail is left alone with the young children to tend the family farm in Braintree, Massachusetts.

*Program 3*

**John Adams: Diplomat (1776–83)**

John Adams undertakes several diplomatic missions during the Revolutionary War, including negotiations with Lord Howe, commander of the British forces, and an appointment as Commissioner to France.

*Program 4*

**John Adams: Minister to Great Britain (1784–87)**

John Adams faces many problems in negotiating trade agreements with Great Britain. A brief visit from Thomas Jefferson results in their first disagreement over constitutional issues.

*Program 5*

**John Adams: Vice-President (1788–1796)**

John Adams suffers eight years of frustration as vice president under George Washington before election to the presidency, when he inherits a cabinet loyal to Hamilton.

*Program 6*

**John Adams: President (1797–1801)**

John Adams faces a new crisis with France, the futility of peace missions, and public sentiment over the XYZ Affair urging him to declare war on France. Jefferson defeats him in the election of 1800.

*Program 7*

**John Quincy Adams: Diplomat (1809–15)**

John Quincy Adams serves as minister to Russia, and heads the peace commission that negotiates the Treaty of Ghent, before becoming the second Adams to serve as minister to Great Britain.

*Program 8*

**John Quincy Adams: Secretary of State (1817–25)**

As secretary of state, John Quincy Adams drafts the Transcontinental Treaty with Spain and proposes a course in international relations, later known as the Monroe Doctrine. He becomes President in 1824.

*Program 9*

**John Quincy Adams: President (1825–29)**

John Quincy Adams faces growing opposition from states' rightists throughout his presidency, and loses the election of 1828 to Andrew Jackson.

*Program 10*

**John Quincy Adams: Congressman (1830–48)**

Despite objections from his family, John Quincy Adams serves in the U.S. House of Representatives until his death in 1848.

*Program 11*

**Charles Francis Adams: Minister to Great Britain (1861–63)**

Charles Francis Adams, son of John Quincy, is able to keep the British from recognizing the Confederacy while serving as minister to Great Britain.

*Program 12*

**Henry Adams: Historian (1870–85)**

The sons of Charles Francis Adams, Henry and Charles Francis II, pursue separate careers to fulfill their postwar vision of a reunited and revitalized America.

*Program 13*

**Charles Francis Adams II: Industrialist (1886–93)**

Charles Francis Adams II enjoys many triumphs as president of the Union Pacific Railroad but ultimately loses the battle for its control to Jay Gould. Like his brother Henry, he is dismayed by the nation's changing values in the industrial society.

4

Production Organization: WNET/13, New York, NY
Year Produced: 1976
Executive Producer: Jac Venza
Series Producer: Virginia Kassel
Coordinating Producer: Robert Costello
Producers: James Cellan Jones, Fred Coe, Robert Costello, Jac Venza, Paul Bogart
Directors: Paul Bogart, James Cellan Jones, Fred Coe, Barry Davis, Bill Glenn, Anthony Page
Writers: Jerome Coopersmith, Ian Hunter, Tad Mosel, Jacqueline Babbin, Sherman Yellan, Allan Sloane, Anne Howard Bailey, Sam Hall, Roger Hirson, Corinne Jacker, Millard Lampell, Philip Reisman, Jr.
Story Consultant: Jacqueline Babbin
Cast: George Grizzard, John Houseman, Kathryn Walker, Nancy Marchand, William Daniels, Stephen Austin, John Wylie, Albert Stratton, Robert Snively, Charles Siebert, James Broderick, Peter Brandon, Nancy Coleman, Helen Stenborg, George Hearn, Harris Yulin, Stephen Joyce, Roberta Maxwell, Keene Curtis, Robert Prosky, David Birney, John Beal
Awards/Festivals: Four Emmy awards, eleven Emmy nominations, 1976; sixteen Emmy nominations, 1977; George Foster Peabody Award; Virgin Islands International Film Festival, First Prize, Television Category; Ohio State Bicentennial Award
Print Material: Teacher, Viewer, and Study Guides no longer available
Format: 16mm
13 (60:00) programs
Distributor: Indiana University, Audio-Visual Center

## MR. ADAMS AND MR. JEFFERSON
*Dramatic Radio Series*

Based on their correspondence, this nine-part series presents the life-long personal and political relationship between John Adams and Thomas Jefferson.

Production Organization: Adams-Jefferson Project of Carleton College, Carleton College, Northfield, MN
Year Produced: 1986
Executive Producers/Writers: Michael P. Zuckert, Ruth Weiner, Charles Umbanhower
Director: Karl Schmidt
Editor: Marv Nonn
Narrator: Carol Cowan
Cast: James Lawless, John Lewin, Denise DuMaurier, Richard Riehle, Claudia Wilkins
Print Material: Study Guide available
Format: Audiocassette
9 (30:00) programs
Distributor: Adams-Jefferson Project of Carleton College

## AFTER THE CRASH
*Documentary*

After the Crash considers three significant protest groups of the early Depression years: farmers in Arkansas; auto workers in Detroit; and the "Bonus Army," an assembly of World War I veterans and their families who came to Washington, D.C., to lobby for benefits.

Production Organization: Blackside, Inc., Boston, MA
Year Produced: 1990 (first broadcast on *The American Experience*)
Executive Producer: Henry Hampton
Senior Producer: Terry Kay Rockefeller
Producer/Director: Eric Neudel
Writer: Steve Fayer
Cinematography: Joe Vitagliano
Editor: Bernice K. Schneider
Narrator: Jason Robards
Award: CINE Golden Eagle

Print Material: Study guide available through The American Experience, WNET-TV, 357 West 58th Street, New York, NY l00l9, attn: Robert Miller
Format: Video (51:30)
Distributor: Blackside, Inc.

## AMERICA AND LEWIS HINE
*Documentary*

This film examines the life and times of America's pioneer social photographer Lewis Hine (1874–1940), who documented the story of European immigrants in early industrial America.

Production Organization: Daedalus Productions, Inc., New York, NY
Year Produced: 1984
Executive Producer: David Loxton
Coproducers: Nina Rosenblum, Daniel V. Allentuck
Director: Nina Rosenblum
Writers: Daniel V. Allentuck, John Crowley, L.S. Block
Editors: Lora Hays, Gerald Donlan
Cinematography: John Walker, Robert Aachs, Kobi Kobiashi
Narration: Jason Robards, Maureen Stapleton
Awards: American Film and Video Festival, Red Ribbon; U.S. Film Festival, Special Jury Prize; CINE Golden Eagle; Baltimore Film Festival, First Prize; National Educational Film and Video Festival, First Prize; Columbus (OH) International Film Festival, Chris Statuette; International Documentary Association, Exceptional Creative Achievement; *Booklist,* Nonprint Editor's Choice (American Library Association)
Format: 16mm, Video (60:00)
Distributor: The Cinema Guild

## AMERICA LOST AND FOUND

*Documentary*

America Lost and Found is a portrait of Americans as they experienced the Great Depression.

Production Organization: Media Study Inc., Buffalo, NY
Year Produced: 1980
Producers/Directors: Lance Bird, Tom Johnson
Writers: Lance Bird, John Crowley
Editor: Kate Hirson
Narrator: Pat Hingle
Awards: American Film and Video Festival, Blue Ribbon; CINE Golden Eagle
Format: 16mm, Video (58:00)
Distributor: Direct Cinema Limited

## AMERICAN DREAM

*Documentary*

American Dream examines the Hormel meatpacking plant strike in Austin, Minnesota, in the mid-1980s and its impact on the union, community, and individuals.

Production Organization: Cabin Creek Center for Work and Environmental Studies, New York, NY
Year Produced: 1990
Producers: Barbara Kopple, Arthur Cohn
Director: Barbara Kopple
Cinematography: Peter Gilbert, Kevin Keating, Hart Perry, Mark Petersson, Mathieu Roberts
Editors: Tom Haneke, Lawrence Silk, Cathy Caplan
Music: Michael Small
Awards/Festivals: Academy Award, Best Documentary Feature; Sundance Film Festival, Grand Jury Prize, Audience Award, and Filmmakers Trophy; San Francisco Film Festival, Golden Gate Award, Current Events Category; American Film and Video Festival, Blue Ribbon; Baltimore Film Competition, Governor's Citation; New York Film Festival, premiere; U.S.A. (Dallas) Film Festival; AFI/L.A. Film Festival; Cleveland International Film Festival
Format: 35mm, 16mm, Video
Distributor: Cabin Creek Center for Work and Environmental Studies

## AMERICAN FORUM

*Documentary*

In this three-part program, professionals in constitutional law and history discuss ideas central to the development of the U.S. Constitution that have been debated since 1787.

### Program 1
**Virtue and the Constitution**
The question of conflict between the need for civic virtue and the commercial impulses in a democratic republic is examined by author George Gilder; Dr. Ernest van den Haag, Professor of Jurisprudence and Public Policy at Fordham University Law School; and Robert A. Goldwin, Director of Constitutional Studies, American Enterprise Institute.

### Program 2
**Is the Constitution Democratic?**
Vanderbilt University professor of political science, William C. Havard; The Brookings Institution's James L. Sundquist; and University of Virginia political scientist, David M. O'Brien provide various perspectives on this issue.

### Program 3
**Rights and the Constitution**
This program traces the relationship of rights to the Constitution, beginning with the Convention and Hamilton's *Federalist* papers. The ideas are discussed by Georgetown University professor of government, Richard G. Stevens; Harvey Mudd College professor of humanities, William B. Allen; and historian, Doris Kearns Goodwin.

Production Organization: World News Institute, Great Falls, VA
Year Produced: 1986
Executive Producer: Richard Bishirjian
Producer: Gerald W. Lange
Director: Chuck Martin
Program Research: Nelson Ong
Host/Narrator: Avi Nelson
Print Material: Program transcripts available
Format: Video
3 (30:00) programs
Distributor: Not currently available

## AMERICAN TONGUES

*Documentary*

American Tongues examines attitudes toward regional, social, and ethnic variations in American speech and how those attitudes reflect larger cultural issues.

Production Organization: Center for New American Media, New York, NY
Year Produced: 1986
Executive Producers: Andrew Kolker, Louis Alvarez
Coproducers/Codirectors/Cowriters: Andrew Kolker, Louis Alvarez
Cinematographer: Andrew Kolker
Editors: Andrew Kolker, Louis Alvarez, John Purcell
Narrator: Polly Holliday
Awards/Festivals: George Foster Peabody Journalism Award; CINE Golden Eagle; American Film and Video Festival, Finalist; The Margaret Mead Film Festival; National Educational Film and Video Festival, Silver Apple
Print Material: Study Guide and brochure available
Format: Video (two versions, 56:00 and 40:00)
Distributor: New Day Films

5

6

## ANARCHISM IN AMERICA
*Documentary*

This film explores the history of anarchism in the United States.

Production Organization: Pacific Street Film Projects, Inc., Brooklyn, NY
Year Produced: 1981
Producers/Directors: Joel Sucher, Steven Fischler
Production Coordinator: Elizabeth Garfield
Editor: Krishna Boden
Award: Chicago International Film Festival, Silver Plaque
Format: 16mm, Video (90:00)
Distributor: The Cinema Guild

## "...AND THE MEEK SHALL INHERIT THE EARTH"
*Documentary*

This film follows the efforts of Native Americans to maintain control of the land in Menominee County, Wisconsin, the only Indian-governed county in the nation.

Production Organization: NET (National Educational Television), New York, NY
Year Produced: 1971
Producer/Writer: Ann Delaney
Narrator: E. G. Marshall
Format: 16mm (59:00)
Distributor: Indiana University, Audio-Visual Center

## APACHE MOUNTAIN SPIRITS
*Drama*

Apache Mountain Spirits weaves an ancient legend with a modern story to illustrate the role of the mythical Apache holy figures known as the *Gaan*. The actors are all members of the tribe.

Production Organization: Silvercloud Video Productions, Inc., Tuczon, AZ
Year Produced: 1985
Producer: John Crouch
Associate Producer: Jennie Crouch
Director: Bob Graham
Editors: Tim Clark, John Crouch
Writers: Joy Harjo, Henry Greenberg
Format: Video (59:00)
Distributor: Silvercloud Video Productions, Inc.

## THE BALLAD OF GREGORIO CORTEZ
*Drama*

This film is based on the true story of a Mexican farmer in Texas in 1901 who, through a faulty translation from Spanish to English, is accused of a robbery he did not commit.

Production Organization: The National Council of La Raza, Washington, DC
Year Produced: 1982
Producers: Moctezuma Esparza, Michael Hausman
Director: Robert Young
Writer: Victor Villaseñor (from the book *With a Pistol in His Hand* by Américo Paredes)
Editors: John Bertucci, Arthur Coburn
Music: W. Michael Lewis, Edward James Olmos
Cast: Edward James Olmos, Tom Bower, James Gammon, Pepe Serna, Rosanna DeSoto
Festivals: Santa Fe Film Festival; Telluride Film Festival; Mill Valley (CA) Film Festival
Format: 16mm, Video (90:00)
Distributor: contact Moctezuma Esparza (See Distributor List); also available in video stores

## THE BEST OF FAMILIES
*Dramatic Series*

This eight-part series presents the lives of three fictional families, each typifying a different social, ethnic, and economic segment of New York City in the 1880s and 1890s.

*Program 1*
**Generations**
In 1880, each family suffers financial setbacks when the failure of the Reading Railroad causes an economic crisis.

*Program 2*
**The Bridge**
When the Brooklyn Bridge is completed and opened in 1883, the three families respond with varying degrees of optimism and skepticism to this symbol of emerging technology.

*Program 3*
**The Election—Patronage or Paradise**
The families have various encounters with city politics through connections with Tammany Hall and in the 1886 mayoral election campaign of Teddy Roosevelt.

*Program 4*
**Ambition**
In 1890, the paths of the families cross when the prominent banker Teddy Wheeler decides to pursue philanthropy to make his bank better known.

*Program 5*
**A Chill to The Bones**
The deepening recession of 1893 finds the lives of the three families converging at Morton House, the first settlement house for the poor.

*Program 6*
**The Great Trolley Battle**
Two brothers take opposite sides in a violent trolley strike in 1895.

*Program 7*
**New Times**
On New Year's Eve, 1899, the families reflect on their lives and unrealized dreams and look toward the approaching century with renewed hope.

*Program 8*
**January 17, 1977**
In this final episode, twentieth-century descendants of the original three families confront situations similar to those faced by members of their families in the late nineteenth century.

Production Organization: Children's Television Workshop, New York, NY
Year Produced: 1977
Series Creator: Naomi Foner
Executive Producer: Ethel Winant
Producer: Gareth Davies
Series Head Writer: Corinne Jacker
Cast: Guy Boyd, William Carden, Frederick Coffin, Alice Drummond, George Ede, Jill Eikenberry, Peter Evans, Clarence Felder, Pauline Flanagan, Victor Garber, Sean Griffin, George Hearn, William Hurt, Suzanne Lederer, Kate McGregor-Stewart, Julia McKenzie, Milo O'Shea, Lisa Pelikan, William Prince, Josef Sommer, Sigourney Weaver
Format: Video
Program 1 (110:00), Programs 2–8 (59:00)
Distributor: Indiana University, Audio-Visual Center

## BILL OF RIGHTS RADIO PROJECT

*Documentary Radio Series*

Each program in this fifteen-part series examines the legal, historical, and social context of a contemporary public policy issue rooted in the Bill of Rights.

*Program 1*
**Gun Control and the Second Amendment: Interpretations and Misinterpretations**

*Program 2*
**Pressure Groups, Censorship, and the First Amendment**

*Program 3*
**Of God, Land, and Nation: Native American Land Claims and the Bill of Rights**

*Program 4*
**Neutral against God: Prayer in Public Schools**

*Program 5*
**And Throw Away the Key: The Eighth Amendment and Cruel and Unusual Punishment**

*Program 6*
**Public Libraries and the First Amendment**

*Program 7*
**The Birds, the Bees, and the Constitution: Sex Education in the Public Schools**

*Program 8*
**The Politics of the Original Sin: Entrapment, Temptation, and the Constitution**

*Program 9*
**He Went and Preached unto the Spirits in Prison: Freedom of Religion in American Penal Institutions**

*Program 10*
**Abortion: A Matter of Life and Death**

*Program 11*
**Open Secrets: Technological Transfer, National Security, and the First Amendment**

*Program 12*
**Cults and the Constitution: Who's Abusing Whom?**

*Program 13*
**Television on Trial: Cameras in the Courts**

*Program 14*
**Without Due Process: Prejudice in the Application of Constitutional Rights of Citizens and Non-Citizens**

*Program 15*
**Crazy and/or Guilty as Charged: Constitutional Aspects of the Insanity Plea and Diminished Capacity Defenses**

Production Organization: Bill of Rights Educational Radio Project, Berkeley, CA
Year Produced: 1983
Executive Producer: Adi Gevins
Award: The Religious Relations Council, Inc., Wilbur Award
Format: Audiocassette
15 (30:00) programs
Distributor: Pacifica Program Service/Radio Archive

## THE BLOOD OF BARRE

*Radio Documentary*

The Blood of Barre traces the early history of the granite industry and its workforce in Barre, Vermont.

Production Organization: Vermont Public Radio, Windsor, VT
Year Produced: 1979
Executive Producers: Steve Robinson, Betty Smith
Producer/Director: Betty Rogers
Associate Producer: Art Silverman
Writer: Tom Looker
Format: Audiocassette (30:00)
Distributor: Not currently available

8

# A BOND OF IRON

*Drama*

Through a point-counterpoint dialogue, A Bond of Iron depicts the relationship between a master and slave at a Virginia ironworks foundry prior to the Civil War.

Production Organization: South Carolina Educational Television Network, Columbia, SC
Year Produced: 1979
Executive Producers: Peter Anderson, John G. Sproat
Producer/Director/Writer: William Peters
Associate Producer: Patricia Curtice
Cast: Brock Peters, Darren McGavin
Format: 16mm, Video (60:00)
Distributor: South Carolina Educational Television Marketing

# BROOKLYN BRIDGE

*Documentary*

This film focuses on the struggle to construct the Brooklyn Bridge in 1883 and on its transformation into a symbol of American strength, ingenuity, and promise.

Production Organization: Department of Records and Information, New York, NY
Year Produced: 1981
Producer/Director: Ken Burns
Cinematography: Ken Burns, Buddy Squires
Editor/Writer: Amy Stechler
Researcher: Thomas Lewis
Narrator: David McCullough
Readings: Paul Roebling, Julie Harris, Arthur Miller, Kurt Vonnegut, David McCullough, and others
Awards/Festivals: Academy Award nomination, Best Documentary Feature; CINE Golden Eagle; American Film and Video Festival, Blue Ribbon; Selected for MOMA/New Directors; FILMEX (Los Angeles); Chicago International Film Festival, Certificate of Merit; Christopher Award; Organization of American Historians, Erik Barnouw Award (for outstanding historical documentary); Festival dei Popoli, Florence, Italy, Special Mention

Format: 16mm, Video (two versions, 58:00 and 39:00; the shorter version focuses on the history and building of the bridge)
Distributor: Direct Cinema Limited

# BUFFALO SOCIAL HISTORY PROJECT

*Documentary Radio Series*

Through oral histories, music, dramatic readings, and commentary, this twelve-part series presents changing patterns in the social and cultural life of a Great Lakes city from 1825 through the 1970s.

*Program 1*
**Buffalo 100 Years Ago**
features accounts of everyday life in Buffalo 100 years ago through newspaper advertisements, features, and editorials.

*Program 2*
**Immigration**
relates the experiences of mid-nineteenth-century Irish, turn-of-the-century Polish, and contemporary Puerto Rican immigrants.

*Program 3*
**Working Life**
describes the work expectations and personal experiences of members of the Buffalo community over three generations.

*Program 4*
**Compulsory Education**
examines the development and maintenance of compulsory public education from 1874 to the 1930s.

*Program 5*
**Land and Property**
looks at the social and financial value of land in the city of Buffalo.

*Program 6*
**Social Welfare**
focuses on the problems of poverty in relation to democratic ideals of social and political equality.

*Program 7*
**Parkside Neighborhood**
profiles one of the city's residential neighborhoods from 1880 to the present.

*Program 8*
**Erie Canal**
features literary descriptions of canal boat travel, as well as information on the techniques of canal building in England and America during the early nineteenth century.

*Program 9*
**Labor and Capital**
examines the history of industrialization, unionism, and the free market economy in Buffalo.

*Program 10*
**Opportunity and Education**
explores issues of pluralism and bilingualism in nineteenth- and twentieth-century public schools.

*Program 11*
**Catholic Culture**
probes Catholicism as the religion of many of Buffalo's immigrants.

*Program 12*
**Pan American Exposition**
presents information on two local legends with national import: the Pan American Exposition of 1901 and the Larkin Company's mail order emporium (1876–1941), a distributor of household goods that collapsed during the Great Depression.

Production Organization: WBFO-FM,
Buffalo, NY
Year Produced: 1977
Producer/Director/Editor: Jo Blatti
Format: Audiocassette
12 magazine-format radio programs (2-to-3
hours)
Distributor: Pacifica Program Service/Radio
Archive
(ask for NFCB 5555-NFCB 5583)

## THE CASE OF THE LEGLESS VETERAN

### Documentary

This film documents the McCarthy-
era defense campaign of James
Kutcher, a World War II veteran
fired from his job at the Veterans
Administration in 1948 for his
socialist beliefs.

Production Organization: Film Arts
Foundation, San Francisco, CA
Year Produced: 1981
Producer/Director/Writer: Howard Petrick
Editor: Kenji Yamamoto
Cinematography: Ashley James
Format: 16mm (58:00)
Distributor: Mass Productions

## CHESAPEAKE BAY: ITS HISTORY AND HERITAGE

### Documentary Radio Series

Through interviews with residents
and regional specialists, this fifty-
part series examines the influence of
the Chesapeake Bay on the people
who have inhabited its shores from
prehistoric times to the present.

Production Organization: WRFK,
Richmond, VA
Year Produced: 1982
Executive Producer: Joe Goldenberg
Hosts: Joe Goldenberg, Fred Hopkins
Engineer: Jerry Glass
Format: Cassette, Reel to Reel 50 (15:00)
programs
Distributor: Not currently available

## THE CIVIL WAR

### Documentary Series

This nine-part series examines the
history and meaning of the American Civil War, from its complex
causes and the daily life of soldiers
to its impact on the nation's political
and social life.

### Program 1

**1861: A 90-Day War**

begins with an examination of slavery and the causes of the war, then
traces the events that led to the firing
on Fort Sumter and the rush to arms
on both sides, and concludes with
the first Battle of Bull Run.

### Program 2

**1862: A Very Bloody Affair**

explains how Lincoln's war to preserve the Union is transformed into
a war to emancipate the slaves.

### Program 3

**1862: Forever Free**

shows how as 1862 wears on, it
marks a difficult year for the Union,
leading up to the Battle of Antietam,
the bloodiest single day of the war,
and the emancipation of the slaves.

### Program 4

**1863: Simply Murder**

considers Northern opposition to
the Emancipation Proclamation, the
miseries of regimental life, the
increasing desperation of the Confederate homefront, Lee's brilliant
victory at Chancellorsviile, and
Grant's futile attempts to take
Vicksburg by seige.

### Program 5

**1863: The Universe of Battle**

opens with an account of the Battle
of Gettysburg, and goes on to
describe the fall of Vicksburg, the
New York draft riots, the first use of
black troops, and Lincoln's
Gettysburg address.

### Program 6

**1864: Valley of the Shadow of Death**

opens with a biographical comparison of Grant and Lee, recounts the
battles that pitted the two generals
against each other, traces Sherman's
Atlanta campaign, and explores the
ghastly medical practices in both
North and South.

### Program 7

**1864: Most Hallowed Ground**

considers how Union victories in
Mobile Bay, Atlanta, and the
Shenandoah Valley tilt the 1864
election toward Lincoln, and the
Confederacy's last hope for indepen-
dence dies.

### Program 8

**1865: War Is All Hell**

traces the decline of the Confederacy
from Sherman's March to the sea
through Lee's surrender at
Appomattox.

### Program 9

**The Better Angels of Our Nature**

recounts Lincoln's assassination and
the final days of the war, closing
with a look at how the Civil War
transformed the country.

Production Organizations: WETA,
Washington, DC, and Florentine Films,
Walpole, NH
Years Produced: 1986–1990
Producers: Ken Burns, Ric Burns
Director: Ken Burns

10

Writers: Geoffrey C. Ward, Ric Burns, with Ken Burns
Cinematography: Ken Burns, Buddy Squire, Allen Moore
Editors: Paul Barnes, Bruce Shaw, Tricia Reidy
Coordinating Producer: Catherine Eisele
Associate Producer/Post Production: Lynn Novick
Coproducers: Stephen Ives, Julie Dunfey, Mike Hill
Associate Producers: Camilla Rockwell, Susanna Steisel
Narrator: David McCullough
On-Camera Interviews: Shelby Foote, Barbara J. Fields, William Safire, Ed Bearss, and others
Voices: Sam Waterson, Jason Robards, Julie Harris, Jeremy Irons, Derek Jacobi, Morgan Freeman, Garrison Keillor, Kurt Vonnegut, Arthur Miller, Studs Terkel, Colleen Dewhurst, Charley McDowell, Jody Powell, George Plimpton, Philip Bosco, Horton Foote, and others
Awards/Festivals: George Foster Peabody Award; The Lincoln Prize, Lincoln and Soldiers Institute, Gettysburg College, PA; The People's Choice Award, America's Favorite Miniseries; Television Producer of the Year Award, Producers Guild of America, Documentary Category; Christopher Award; CINE Golden Eagle; Telluride Film Festival; Museum of Broadcasting, Special Honor; National Board of Review, D.W. Griffith Award for Best Television Miniseries; Dartmouth College Film Award; Civil War Round Table, Bell I. Wiley Award; Clarion Award; National Emmy (two); Angel Award, Best TV Miniseries of the Year; Advancement of Learning through Broadcasting Award, National Education Association; National Educational Film & Video Festival, Silver Apple; American Film & Video Festival, Blue Ribbon; Alfred I. du Pont-Columbia University Awards, Silver Baton, Independent Television Productions
Print Material: Educational materials (Teacher's Guide, etc.) available from Tel-Ed, Inc., 7449 Melrose Avenue, Los Angeles, CA 90046
Format: Video
Programs 1, 5 (90:00); programs 2,3,4,6,7,8,9 (60:00)
Distributors: PBS Video; Time-Life Video (home video); PBS Adult Learning Service (telecourse)

## THE COLOR OF HONOR
### Documentary

The Color of Honor documents Japanese-American experiences during World War II by examining the internment of American citizens of Japanese ancestry, the distinguished record of Japanese-American combat soldiers in the liberation of France and Italy, and the role that 6,000 Japanese Americans played in the Asian-Pacific theater as part of the U.S. Military Intelligence Service.

Production Organizations: Center for Educational Telecommunications, Inc., and Vox Productions, San Francisco, CA
Year Produced: 1988
Executive Producer/Director/Writer: Loni Ding
Editors: Loni Ding, Steve Kuever
Cinematography: Tomas Tucker, Michael Chin
Narrator: Loni Ding
Special Screenings: Smithsonian Institution; U.S. Congress
Format: Video (101:00)
Distributor: Vox Productions

## CONEY ISLAND
### Documentary

This film explores the history and meaning of Coney Island from the mid-nineteenth century to the present.

Production Organizations: Coney Island Film Project and City Lore, New York, NY
Year Produced: 1991 (first broadcast on *The American Experience*)
Producers: Ric Burns, Buddy Squires
Director: Ric Burns
Writer: Richard Snow
Cinematography: Buddy Squires, Allen Moore
Editor: Paul Barnes
Narrator: Philip Bosco

Readings: Andrei Codrescu, Vincent Gardenia, Judd Hirsch, Nathan Lane, John Mahoney, Jerry Orbach, George Plimpton, Lois Smith, Frances Sternhagen, Eli Wallach
Awards: Chicago International Film Festival, Silver Hugo; Sundance Film Festival; CINE Golden Eagle; *Time* Magazine, "Best of 1991 Television"
Format: 16mm, Video (two versions, 67:00 and 52:00)
Distributors: PBS Video (video, 67:00 only); Direct Cinema Limited (16mm and video, 67:00 and 52:00)

## CONSTITUTIONAL JOURNAL
### Radio Series (Documentary and Drama)

In 122 three-minute programs, this series recounts the proceedings of the Constitutional Convention of 1787 from the vantage point of a reporter on the convention floor at Independence Hall in Philadelphia. It also includes dramatizations of the remarks of Washington, Franklin, Madison, and other delegates.

Production Organization: Radio America, Washington, DC
Year Produced: 1987
Executive Producer: James C. Roberts
Producer: Marc A. Lipsitz
Writer/Narrator: Jeffrey St. John
Cast: Phil Nicolaides, Jim Parisi, Sarah Ban Breathnach, Jim Kelly
Print Material: Book version available through Jameson Books, Ottawa, IL
Format: Audiocassette
6 (60:00) programs
Distributor: Radio America

## CONTRARY WARRIORS: A STORY OF THE CROW TRIBE

### Documentary

Contrary Warriors tells the story of the Crow people of southwestern Montana, focusing on the leadership of 97-year-old Robert Summers Yellowtail, who began his career in 1910 defending Crow lands, rights, and tribal authority in the halls of Congress.

Production Organization: Rattlesnake Productions, Missoula, MT
Year Produced: 1986
Producers: Connie Poten, Pamela Roberts, Beth Ferris
Writers: Connie Poten, Beth Ferris
Cinematography: Stephen Lighthill
Editor: Jennifer Chinlund
Narrator: Peter Coyote
Award: American Film and Video Festival, John Grierson Award
Format: 16mm, Video (60:00)
Distributor: Direct Cinema Limited

## A COUNTRY AUCTION

### Documentary

A Country Auction examines how an estate sale in rural Pennsylvania reveals the personal, social, and economic pressures on a family and a community dealing with death.

Production Organization: Center for Visual Communication,
Philadelphia, PA
Year Produced: 1984
Producers/Directors: Robert Aibel, Ben Levin, Chris Musello, Jay Ruby
Editor: Ben Levin
Cinematography: Tom Ott
Format: 16mm, Video (58:00)
Distributor: Pennsylvania State University, Audio Visual Services

## DARROW

### Drama

This film presents the events and issues that concerned Clarence Darrow (1857–1938) and documents his transformation from a corporate lawyer to the maverick defense attorney who represented Eugene Debs, the McNamara brothers, Leopold and Loeb, and Thomas Scopes.

Production Organization: KCET, Los Angeles, CA
Year Produced: 1991 (first broadcast on *American Playhouse*)
Executive Producer: Ricki Franklin
Producers: Richard Heus, Stephen Stept
Director: John Coles
Writers: William Schmidt, Stephen Stept
Cinematography: Paul Murphy
Editor: Angelo Carrao
Cast: Kevin Spacey, Rebecca Jenkins, Christopher Cooper
Format: Video (120:00)
Distributor: contact KCET; Cypress Productions, Inc. (international broadcast)

## DATELINE 1787

### Dramatic Radio Series

Dateline 1787 is a fourteen-part series that uses modern broadcast journalism to present and examine the events, issues, and personalities surrounding the drafting of the Constitution at the Convention of 1787. Commentators William B. Allen, professor of government, Harvey Mudd College, and Jack N. Rakove, professor of history, Stanford University, discuss the issues raised in each episode.

*Program 1*
**May 27, 1787**
The National Radio Theatre News Team, situated in the "broadcast booth" of the Philadelphia State House, reports on the background and opening of the Convention called to revise the Articles of Confederation.

*Program 2*
**June 3, 1787**
Virginia Governor Edmund Randolph introduces a plan for wholesale reform.

*Program 3*
**June 10, 1787**
Elements of the Randolph Plan are debated as differences emerge on questions of representation.

*Program 4*
**June 17, 1787**
Tension mounts between the federalists and nationalists regarding legislative representation.

*Program 5*
**June 24, 1787**
National response to the confederal argument of the New Jersey Plan is aired; a final vote is taken to choose between the Randolph and Paterson plans.

*Program 6*
**July 1, 1787**
Delegates reach an impasse over methods of apportioning representation.

*Program 7*
**July 8, 1787**
The controversy over representation is turned over to a committee.

12

*Program 8*
**July 15, 1787**
The debate turns to differences between the North and South over slavery.

*Program 9*
**July 22, 1787**
A vote temporarily settles the representation issue; the delegates turn their attention to the presidency and powers of federal government.

*Program 10*
**August 4, 1787**
Methods of electing the president are debated, as the controversies between large and small states continue.

*Program 11*
**August 12, 1787**
Committee reports are followed by particularly rapid progress.

*Program 12*
**September 2, 1787**
Delegates reach a compromise on the slavery issue; the presidency takes final form; property requirements for suffrage are thrown out.

*Program 13*
**September 16, 1787**
The Committee on Postponed Matters reports as the convention draws to a close. There is a discussion of defection, an interview with George Washington, and presentation of the final draft of the Constitution.

*Program 14*
**September 17, 1787**
The News Team captures Benjamin Franklin's "rising sun" remark and buttonholes other delegates after adjournment for their closing impressions.

Production Organization: National Radio Theatre, Chicago, IL
Year Produced: 1986
Producer/Director: Yuri Rasovsky
Writers: Michelle Damico, Denise Jiménez, Yuri Rasovsky
Format: Audiocassette
14 (30:00) programs
Distributor: Pacifica Program Service/Radio Archive

## DAWN'S EARLY LIGHT: RALPH MCGILL AND THE SEGREGATED SOUTH
*Documentary*

Dawn's Early Light examines journalist Ralph McGill, as he emerged during the 1950s and 1960s to become an influential Southern white opponent of racial segregation.

Production Organization: Center for Contemporary Media, Inc., Atlanta, GA
Year Produced: 1988
Producers/Directors: Kathleen Dowdey, Jed Dannenbaum
Editor: Kathleen Dowdey
Cinematography: Edwin Myers
Host/Narrator: Burt Lancaster
Interviews: Julian Bond, Tom Brokaw, Jimmy Carter, John Lewis, Vernon Jordan, Herman Talmadge, Sander Vanocur, Andrew Young, Harry Ashmore, Eugene Patterson, Claude Sitton, and others
Awards/Festivals: Chicago International Film Festival, Silver Plaque; National Educational Film and Video Festival, Bronze Apple
Format: Video (two versions, 88:00 and 58:00)
Distributor: New Day Films

## THE ELECTRIC VALLEY
*Documentary*

The Electric Valley presents the history of the Tennessee Valley Authority, a federal agency with a broad mission to tame the forces of nature, create energy, and produce lasting prosperity in the Tennessee Valley.

Production Organization: James Agee Film Project, Johnson City, TN
Year Produced: 1983
Associate Producer: Jude Cassidy
Writers: Ross Spears, Dick Couto, Melanie Maholick
Editor: Melanie Maholick
Cinematography: Anthony Forma
Narrator: Wilma Dykeman
Awards/Festivals: American Film and Video Festival, Finalist; National Emmy nomination, Public Affairs Documentary; FILMEX (Los Angeles); U.S. Film Festival; American Studies Association, Special Screening
Format: 16mm, Video (90:00)
Distributor: James Agee Film Project Library

## EMPIRE OF THE AIR
*Documentary*

This film tells the story of three men whose role in the creation of radio transformed American culture: Lee de Forest, Edwin Howard Armstrong, and David Sarnoff.

Production Organizations: Florentine Films, NH, in association with WETA, Washington, DC
Year Produced: 1991
Executive Producer: Ken Burns
Producers: Ken Burns, Morgan Wesson, Tom Lewis, Camilla Rockwell, Susanna Stelsel
Writer: Geoffrey C. Ward
Cinematography: Ken Burns, Buddy Squires, Allen Moore
Editors: Yaffa Lerea, Paul Barnes
Narrator: Jason Robards
Format: Video (116:00)
Distributor: Florentine Films

## EPHRAIM MCDOWELL'S KENTUCKY RIDE
*Drama*

In 1809, Dr. Ephraim McDowell performs America's first successful abdominal surgery on Jane Dodd Crawford, who is suffering from an undiagnosed ovarian tumor.

Production Organization: WGBH
Educational Foundation, Boston, MA
Year Produced: 1979
Executive Producer: Peter McGhee
Producer: Jo Gladstone
Director: Francis Gladstone
Writer: Milan Stitt
Cinematography: Peter Hoving
Editor: Elvido Abella
Cast: Paul Guilfoyle, Elizabeth Perry, John
Seitz, Mark Winkworth, Judith Harkness,
Maryce Carter, Jack Davison, Max Deitch,
Ellin Ruskin, Eric Tull, Eileen Sokol, Clifton
Powell, Martin R. Anderson, William Dean,
Jenny Applegate, Elwyn Gladstone, Sally
Bohl
Format: 16mm (60:00)
Distributor: Not currently available

## THE EXILES

### Documentary

The Exiles tells the story of the European artists, intellectuals, and scientists who escaped to America before
the outbreak of World War II, and
of their far-reaching contributions
to culture and scholarship in their
adopted country. Among those fea-
tured are Billy Wilder, Bruno
Bettelheim, Erich Leinsdorf, Hanna
Gray, Edward Teller, and Alfred
Eisenstaedt.

Production Organization: Exiles Project,
New York, NY
Year Produced: 1989
Coproducers/Cowriters: Richard Kaplan,
Lou Potter
Director/Cinematography: Richard Kaplan
Editors: Anne Borin, Walter Hess, Richard
Kaplan
Host/Narrator: Vartan Gregorian
Festivals: Montreal International Film
Festival; Nyon (Switzerland) International
Film Festival
Print Material: Viewer's Guide available
Format: Video (116:00)
Part I, 1931–42 (63:00); Part II, 1942–
Present (53:00)
Distributor: Filmakers Library

## EXPRESSIONS: BLACK AMERICAN FOLK ART AND CULTURE

### Documentary Radio Series

Expressions is a ten-part series of
radio programs about African-
American art forms which derive
from folk culture. The programs
supported by NEH are designated by
an asterisk; the other programs were
funded by the National Endowment
for the Arts.

### *Program 1
### Authentic Afro-American Legends

traces the origin, evolution, and
transmittal of African-American
legends.

### *Program 2
### Afro-American Proverbs

explores the use of short sayings that
express simple, common-sense
truths based on practical experience.

### *Program 3
### Arabing

considers the art of "arabing" as
practiced in Baltimore, Maryland.
"Arabers" are street vendors who sell
their wares by walking through city
streets with calls derived from the
same source as blues, gospel, and
other traditional black American
music genres.

### *Program 4
### A Capella

explores the African-American tradition of singing without instrumen-
tal accompaniment.

### Program 5
### Song Making

looks at the development of the African-American song tradition, spe-
cifically how it may be used to

record history and how melodies,
rhythms, and lyrics are reshaped
through the oral tradition.

### Program 6
### Hair Sculpture

examines the history and significance of the popular urban and rural
art of African-American hair design.

### Program 7
### The Party

compares historical slave rituals and
their cultural connection with
present-day house, rent, and card
parties.

### Program 8
### Street Cheers

analyzes the contemporary urban art
form called street cheers, popular
among African-American youth.

### *Program 9
### Rhythms

looks at the beat and style of black art.

### *Program 10
### Preaching

treats the musical, dramatic, and
oratorical preaching styles in the traditional black church and considers
the black preacher as artist.

Production Organization: Judi Moore Smith
Productions,
Temple Hills, MD
Year Produced: 1983
Producer/Director/Writer/Narrator: Judi
Moore Smith
Awards: National Association of Black
Journalists; Federation of Community
Broadcasters, Outstanding Radio
Production; Ohio State Achievement Award
Format: Audiocassette
10 (30:00) programs
Distributor: Judi Moore Smith-Latta

14

# FIRST PERSON AMERICA: VOICES FROM THE THIRTIES

*Radio Series (Documentary and Drama)*

Based on interviews collected by the Federal Writers' Project during the late 1930s, this six-part series recreates the experiences of Americans from diverse walks of life in the decade of the Great Depression.

*Program 1*
**Troupers and Pitchmen: A Vanishing World**
considers a time when itinerant salesmen and traveling entertainers regaled America with their performances.

*Program 2*
**When I First Came to This Land**
describes how immmigrants struggled to preserve their ethnic identity.

*Program 3*
**Making Ends Meet**
suggests some of the ways women sustained themselves during the hard times of the 1930s.

*Program 4*
**Talking Union**
focuses on the fierce struggle for unionization in the 1930s.

*Program 5*
**Smoke and Steel**
portrays the human cost of building America and describes how industrial work became a legitimate literary theme.

*Program 6*
**Harlem Stories**
centers around the dramatized narrative of a Pullman porter who lamented his move north to Harlem in a conversation with federal writer Ralph Ellison.

Production Organization: WGBH-Radio, Boston, MA
Year Produced: 1980
Coproject Directors: Ann Banks, Barbara Sirota
Executive Producer: Robert Montiegel
Producer: Knute Walker
Director: Joan Micklin Silver
Editor: Ann Banks
Writer: Tom Looker (based on the book *First Person America* by Ann Banks)
Host/Narrator: Oscar Brand
Award: CPB Award, Best Arts and Humanities Documentary
Print Material: The series is based on the book *First Person America* edited by Ann Banks, published by Alfred A. Knopf
Format: Audiocassette
6 (30:00) programs
Distributor: WGBH-Radio

# FIT: EPISODES IN THE HISTORY OF THE BODY

*Documentary*

This film looks at the scientific theories and cultural values underlying the American fascination with physical fitness and the body over the past 150 years.

Production Organization: Straight Ahead Pictures, Inc., Conway, MA
Year Produced: 1991
Producer/Director: Laurie Block
Writers: Laurie Block, John Crowley
Editor: Howard Sharp
Narrator: Linda Hunt
Format: 16mm, Video (two versions, 73:00 and 57:30)
Distributor: Straight Ahead Pictures, Inc.

# FOR US, THE LIVING: THE MEDGAR EVERS STORY

*Drama*

Based on Myrlie Evers's book, *For Us, The Living,* this film tells the story of assassinated civil rights leader Medgar Evers and his efforts at ending segregation.

Production Organization: Charles Fries Productions, Inc., Studio City, CA, and Public Television Playhouse, Inc., New York, NY
Year Produced: 1983 (first broadcast on *American Playhouse*)
Executive Producer: Charles W. Fries
Producer: J. Kenneth Rotcop
Director: Michael Schultz
Adaptation: Ossie Davis, J. Kenneth Rotcop
Cinematography: Alan Kozlowski
Cast: Howard Rollins, Jr., Irene Cara, Margaret Avery, Roscoe Lee Browne, Larry Fishburne, Janet MacLaughlan, Dick Anthony Williams, Paul Winfield, Thalmus Rasulala
Award: NAACP Image Award
Format: 16mm, Video (90:00)
Distributor: contact Charles Fries Entertainment

# THE FORWARD: FROM IMMIGRANTS TO AMERICANS

*Documentary*

This film documents the history of the Jewish *Forward*, a Yiddish-language daily newspaper based in New York City, which was for many years the most successful and widely read Yiddish paper in the United States.

Production Organization: Jewish Forward Film Project, Amherst, MA
Year Produced: 1987
Producers/Writers: Marlene Booth, Linda Matchan
Director: Marlene Booth
Cinematography: Nancy Schreiber
Editor: Eric W. Handley
Narrator: Tim Sawyer
Print Material: Program transcript available
Format: Video (58:00)
Distributor: Direct Cinema Limited

## FUNDI: THE STORY OF ELLA BAKER

*Documentary*

This film presents the life and career of little-known civil rights activist Ella Baker, who was friend and adviser to Martin Luther King, Jr.

Production Organization: Fundi
Productions, Inc., New York, NY
Year Produced: 1981
Producer/Director: Joanne Grant
Directorial Consultant: Saul Landau
Cinematography: Judy Irola
Editor: Hortense Beveridge
Consulting Editor: John Carter
Music: Bernice Johnson Reagon
Awards: London Film Festival, Film of the Year; San Francisco International Film Festival, Best of Category; Black Filmmakers Hall of Fame, First Prize Documentary
Format: 16mm, Video (two versions, 60:00 and 45:00)
Distributor: First Run/Icarus Films

## GEORGE MARSHALL AND THE AMERICAN CENTURY

*Documentary*

This is a biography of General George C. Marshall who as U.S. Army chief of staff led the Allied Victory in World War II and as secretary of state helped create the Marshall Plan.

Production Organization: Great Projects Film Company, Inc., New York, NY
Year Produced: 1991
Producers: Daniel B. Polin, Kenneth Mandel
Directors: Kenneth Mandel, Ken Levis
Writer: Geoffrey C. Ward
Cinematography: Phil Abraham
Editor: Ken Levis
Awards: Cine Golden Eagle; Educational Film and Vido Festival, Silver Apple; Worldfest (Houston, TX), Silver Award; American Film and Video Association, Red Ribbon
Format: Video (88:00)
Distributors: Great Projects Film Company
Devillier Donegan Enterprises (international)

## THE GOLDEN CRADLE: IMMIGRANT WOMEN IN THE UNITED STATES

*Documentary Radio Series*

Through a blend of music, drama, archival material and interviews, this ten-part series examines the social history of America's women immigrants from the 1840s to the present.

### *Program 1*
**The Journey**
looks at diaries and other accounts from immigrant women who survived the journey to America.

### *Program 2*
**The Half-Open Door**
recalls how several generations of immigrants faced the realities of the quota system, exclusion laws, detainment, and deportation.

### *Program 3*
**The Alley, The Acre, and Back a' the Yards**
is the story of women who established ethnic communities that continue today despite changing economic and social pressures.

### *Program 4*
**In America, They Say Work Is No Shame**
relates the experiences of immigrant laborers and union organizers in American factories and sweatshops.

### *Program 5*
**Three Tunes for an American Songbook**
explains how and why three women emigrated from Russia, Greece, and Italy in the early 1900s.

### *Program 6*
**Daily Bread**
examines the working experience of immigrant women who served as domestic servants, farm wives, shopkeepers, and boardinghouse operators.

### *Program 7*
**English Lessons**
records the difficulties that immigrant women have faced in trying to educate their children and themselves.

### *Program 8*
**My Mother Was a Member of the Rumanian Ladies Aide Society**
explores the history of societies and organizations, originally formed as support systems, that affected the socio-political fabric of America.

### *Program 9*
**Tapestries**
expresses the way immigrant women artists responded to life in a new world.

### *Program 10*
**In America, We Wear a New Name**
features Russian, Cuban, Japanese, and Hungarian women speaking of conflicting identities in their new homeland.

Production Organization: Soundscape, Inc., Alexandria, VA
Year Produced: 1984
Coproducers: Deborah George, Louise Cleveland
Research Director: Jane M. Deren
Administrative Coordinator: Karen Getman
Narrator: Mandy I. Bynum
Print Material: Loan of cassettes with detailed discussion leader's guide available to senior citizen groups from: Discovery through the Humanities Program, The National Council on Aging, 409 Third Street, S.W., Washington, D.C. 20024, 202-479-1200
Format: Audiocassettes
10 (30:00) programs on 5 (60:00) cassettes
Distributor: Pacifica Program Service/Radio Archive

15

16

## THE GOOD FIGHT: THE ABRAHAM LINCOLN BRIGADE IN THE SPANISH CIVIL WAR

*Documentary*

Through the recollections of eleven veterans, The Good Fight tells the story of the 3,200 Americans of the Abraham Lincoln Brigade who fought against the armies of France, Hitler, and Mussolini in the Spanish civil war.

Production Organization: Abraham Lincoln Brigade Film Project, New York, NY
Year Produced: 1984
Producers/Directors: Noel Buckner, Mary Dore, Sam Sills
Cinematography: Stephen Lighthill, Peter S. Rosen, Joe Vitagliano, Renner Wunderlich
Editor: Noel Buckner
Narration Coauthor: Robert A. Rosenstone
Narrator: Studs Terkel
Awards: American Film Festival, Blue Ribbon; National Educational Film and Video Festival, First Prize, History
Format: 16mm, Video (98:00)
Distributor: First Run/Icarus Films

## HARD WINTER

*Drama*

Based on primary sources, the drama focuses on conflicting public attitudes toward the Revolutionary war in Morris County, New Jersey, during the winter of 1779–80, when George Washington's troops were encamped there.

Production Organization: Morris County Historical Society, Morristown, NJ
Year Produced: 1984
Executive Producer: Chiz Schultz
Associate Producer: Valerie Shepherd
Director: Mat Brauchitsch
Editors: Victor Kanefsky, Les Mulkey
Cinematography: Judith Irola, Joseph Friedman

Cast: Alfred De Quoy, Janet Scott, Wil Buchanan, Tony Carlin, Steve Orlouski, Chuck Portz
Award: American Film and Video Festival, Finalist
Format: 16mm, Video (58:00)
Distributor: Great Plains National Instructional Television Library

## HARRY HOPKINS: AT FDR'S SIDE

*Documentary*

This is a film about the life and work of Harry Hopkins, with special emphasis on his role as domestic and foreign policy adviser to President Franklin D. Roosevelt.

Production Organization: Educational Film Center, Annandale, VA
Year Produced: 1989
Executive Producer: Ira Klugerman
Producers: Verne Newton, Frank Nesbitt
Director/Editor: Frank Nesbitt
Writer: Verne Newton
Script Editor: Ruth Pollak
Cinematography: Chris Li, Greg Larsen
Narrator: Walter Cronkite
Awards: National Emmy nominee, Outstanding Historical Documentary; American Film and Video Festival, Blue Ribbon; CINE Golden Eagle; National Educational Film and Video Festival, Silver Apple; Columbus (OH) International Film Festival, Bronze Plaque
Format: 16mm, Video (87:41)
Distributor: Educational Film Center

## HEARTLAND

*Drama*

Heartland is based on the experiences of a widow homesteading near Burntfork, Wyoming, in the early twentieth century.

Production Organizations: Filmhaus and Wilderness Women Productions, Inc., Bonner, MT
Year Produced: 1979
Executive Producer: Annick Smith
Producers: Beth Ferris, Michael Hausman

Director: Richard Pearce
Writers: Beth Ferris, William Kittredge
Cinematography: Fred Murphy
Cast: Rip Torn, Conchata Ferrell, Barry Primus, Lilia Skala, Megan Folsom, Amy Wright
Awards: U.S. Film Festival, Best Independent Film, Co-winner; Berlin Film Festival, Grand Prix Golden Bear, Co-winner
Format: 16mm, Video (95:00)
Distributors: The Pickman Film Corporation and Thorn EMI (available in video stores)

## HEARTS AND HANDS

*Documentary*

This film chronicles how, through their quilting and sewing, nineteenth-century women responded to the major events and developments of their times, such as abolitionism, the Civil War, industrialization, westward expansion, and the temperance and suffrage movements.

Production Organizations: Ferrero Films and Film Arts Foundation, San Francisco, CA
Year Produced: 1987
Executive Producer/Producer/Director: Pat Ferrero
Associate Producer: Julie Silber
Writer: Beth Ferris
Cinematography: Emiko Omori
Editor: Jennifer Chinlund
Narrator: Nancy Houfek
Print Material: Companion book available through Quilt Digest Press, 955 14th Street, San Francisco, CA 94114
Format: Video (63:00)
Distributor: Hearts and Hands Media Arts

## THE HOMEFRONT

*Documentary*

The Homefront explores the impact of World War II on American civilians, with an emphasis on changes in agriculture, industry, labor, and the status of minorities.

Production Organization: The University of Southern California, Los Angeles, CA
Year Produced: 1985
Executive Producer: Jack Kaufman
Producer/Director/Writer: Steve Schechter
Coproducer: Mark Jonathan Harris
Associate Producer: Franklin D. Mitchell
Cinematography: Don Lenzer
Editor: Ron Brody
Narrator: Leslie Nielson
Awards: American Film and Video Festival, Blue Ribbon, History; National Educational Film and Video Festival, Best of Festival; Baltimore Independent Filmmakers' Competition, First Prize, Documentary; Columbus (OH) International Film and Video Festival, Chris Award; Houston International Film Festival, Gold Special Jury Award, History; Chicago International Film Festival, Bronze Hugo; New York International Film and Television Festival, Silver Medal
Format: 16mm, Video (90:00)
Distributor: Churchill Films, Inc.

## A HOUSE DIVIDED

*Dramatic Series*

Each drama in this three-part series considers the actions and experiences of an important but little-known African American who addressed the problems of slavery and inequality during the nineteenth century.

### Program 1

**Denmark Vesey's Rebellion**

In 1822, a prosperous free black carpenter in Charleston, South Carolina, leads an abortive rebellion to free the city's slaves.

Production Organization: WPBT/Community Television Foundation of South Florida, Inc., Miami, FL
Year Produced: 1981
Executive Producer: Robert S. Morgan
Producer: Yanna Kroyt Brandt
Director: Stan Lathan
Writer: William Hauptman
Editors: John Carter and Paul Evans
Cinematography: Larry Pizer
Cast: Yaphet Kotto, Ned Beatty, Cleavon Little, Antonia Fargas, Donald Moffat, Brock Peters, William Windom, Mary Alice, Bernie Casey
Awards: Ohio State Award; Freedom Foundation Award; National Black Programming Consortium, Best Drama; Black Filmmakers Hall of Fame, Best Drama; NAACP Image Award
Format: Video (90:00)
Distributor: Not currently available

### Program 2

**Solomon Northup's Odyssey**

A free black man from Saratoga, New York, struggles for twelve years to regain his freedom after being kidnapped and sold into slavery in 1841.

Production Organization: Past America, Inc.
Year Produced: 1984
Executive Producer: Robert S. Morgan
Producer: Yanna Kroyt Brandt
Director: Gordon Parks
Writers: Lou Potter and Samm-Art Williams
Editor: John Carte
Cinematography: Hiro Narita
Cast: Avery Brooks, Petronia Paley, Rhetta Greene, John Saxon, Mason Adams, Lee Bryant, Janet League, Joe Seneca, Kent Broadhurst, J.C. Quinn, Michael Tolan
Awards: CINE Golden Eagle; Organization of American Historians, Erik Barnouw Award (for outstanding historical drama)
Format: Video (113:00)
Distributor: SVS, Inc. (retitled Half Slave, Half Free)

### Program 3

**Experiment in Freedom: Charlotte Forten's Mission**

In 1861, the daughter of a wealthy black family gives up her comfortable life in Philadelphia to teach and help freed slaves build a new society on the Sea Islands of South Carolina.

Production Organization: Past America, Inc.
Year Produced: 1985
Executive Producer: Robert S. Morgan
Producer: Yanna Kroyt Brandt
Director: Barry Crane
Writer: Samm-Art Williams
Editor: John Carter
Cinematography: Joseph Wilcots
Cast: Melba Moore, Ned Beatty, Glynn Turman, Mary Alice, Moses Gunn, Carla Borelli, Micki Grant, Anna Marie Horsford, Bruce McGill, Jay Paterson, Vyto Reginis, Roderick Wimberly
Format: Video (120:00)
Distributor: Not currently available

## H.R. 6161: AN ACT OF CONGRESS

*Documentary*

This film follows the process by which a bill becomes a law by tracing the activities of Representatives Paul G. Rogers (D-Fla) and John D. Dingell (D-Mich) as they and others work for and against the Clean Air Amendments of 1977 (H.R. 6161).

Production Organization: WVIA, Pittston, PA
Year Produced: 1979
Producer: Jerry Colbert
Director: Charles Guggenheim
Awards: American Film and Video Festival, Honorable Mention; San Francisco International Film Festival, Political Documentary, Best of Category
Format: 16mm, Video (59:00)
Distributor: Coronet/MTI Film and Video

18

## HUEY LONG

*Documentary*

Through archival footage and interviews with opponents, allies, and scholars, this film documents Huey Long's impact on the state of Louisiana and the nation at large.

Production Organization: Florentine Films, Inc., Walpole, NH
Year Produced: 1985
Coproducers: Ken Burns, Richard Kilberg
Director: Ken Burns
Cinematography: Buddy Squires
Narrator: David McCullough
Awards: American Film and Video Festival, Red Ribbon; Organization of American Historians, Erik Barnouw Award (for outstanding historical documentary)
Format: 16mm, Video (88:00)
Distributor: Direct Cinema Limited

## INHERITANCE

*Documentary*

Inheritance examines the meaning of work and the role it plays in human happiness through consideration of three contemporary traditional craftsmen—a tinsmith, a blacksmith, and a lacrosse-stick maker—whose work and lives are reminiscent of the independent worker of a century ago.

Production Organizations: Bowling Green Films and WMHT-TV, Schenectady, NY
Year Produced: 1975
Producer/Director: Jack Ofield
Writer: Helen-Maria Erawan
Format: 16mm (two versions, 60:00 and 43:00)
Distributor: University of Michigan, Film and Video Library
(ask for title #: 027-64-F)

## ISHI, THE LAST YAHI

*Documentary*

This film tells the story of Ishi, the last Yahi Indian in North America, who became a source of valuable information and a friend of anthropologist Alfred Kroeber, who brought him to San Francisco for study.

Production Organization: Rattlesnake Productions, Inc., Berkeley, CA
Year Produced: 1991
Producers/Directors: N. Jed Riffe, Pamela Roberts
Additional Location Direction: Steven Okazaki
Writers: Anne Makepeace with Jenifer Hood and Louise Steinman
Cinematography: Stephen Lighthill
Editor: Jennifer Chinlund
Print Material: Viewers Guide, Curriculum Guide, Anthology forthcoming
Format: Video, 16mm (56:00)
Distributor: Rattlesnake Productions, Inc.

## KEEPING ON

*Drama*

Keeping On portrays the changes in community structures and social relationships in a Southern textile community during a campaign to unionize the local mill.

Production Organization: Many Mansions Institute/Cabin Creek Center, New York, NY
Year Produced: 1982
Executive Producer/Director: Barbara Kopple
Producer: Coral Hawthorne
Writer: Horton Foote
Editor: Lora Hayes
Cinematography: Larry Pizer
Cast: James Broderick, Danny Glover, Dick Anthony Williams, Carol Kane
Format: 16mm, Video (72:00)
Distributor: Caridi Entertainment

## THE KILLING FLOOR

*Drama*

The Killing Floor tells the story of a Southern black sharecropper who moves to Chicago and becomes involved in the organization of workers in the stockyards between 1917 and 1919.

Production Organizations: KERA-TV, Dallas and Public Forum Productions
Year Produced: 1984
Executive Producer: Elsa Rassbach
Producer: George Manasse
Director: Bill Duke
Writers: Leslie Lee, Ron Milner, Elsa Rassbach
Editor: John Carter
Cinematography: Bill Birch
Cast: Damien Leake, Alfre Woodward, Clarence Felder, Moses Gunn
Awards: U.S.A. (Dallas) Film Festival, Special Jury Award; U.S. Film Festival (Sundance), Special Jury Award; International Film and Television Festival of New York, Silver Medal; Hemisfilm International Festival, Best Feature; National Black Consortium, First Place, Drama; NAACP Image Award nominations for Best Television Movie, Best Actor and Best Actress; Critics' Week, Cannes Film Festival
Format: 16mm, Video (120:00)
Distributor: Films Inc./P.M.I.; Orion-Nelson Entertainment (home video)

## KING OF AMERICA

*Drama*

King of America tells of the struggles of a Greek immigrant seeking success in America in the early twentieth century.

Production Organization: Center for Television in the Humanities, Inc., Atlanta, GA
Year Produced: 1980
Producer: David Horwatt
Director: Dezso Magyar
Writer: B.J. Merhoiz
Editor: Jay Freund
Cinematography: Michael Fash
Musical Director: Elizabeth Swados
Cast: Barry Miller, Andreas Katsulas, Olympia Dukakis
Format: Video (74:00)
Distributor: Caridi Entertainment

# LaGuardia, the Dreamer and the Doer

## Documentary Radio Series

Using original sound footage, this seven-part series examines the life and times of New York City's legendary mayor, Fiorella H. LaGuardia (1882–1947).

### Program 1
**LaGuardia and Reform**

describes the mayor's war with Tammany Hall and his fights against gamblers, racketeers, and "tin horns."

### Program 2
**Health and Housing**

explains how LaGuardia made the availability of proper housing a function of city government and established the largest public health effort in the city's history.

### Program 3
**LaGuardia and Organized Labor**

traces LaGuardia's shifting stance *vis à vis* unions and unionization.

### Program 4
**LaGuardia and the Physical City**

shows how LaGuardia's public works brought about government-sponsored municipal transformation in New York City.

### Program 5
**LaGuardia and Aviation**

discusses the mayor's lifelong support for aviation.

### Program 6
**LaGuardia and Relief**

recounts how LaGuardia made public assistance a reality in New York.

### Program 7
**World War II**

looks at LaGuardia's third term as mayor and his emergence as a radio personality.

Production Organization: LaGuardia Archives, LaGuardia Community College/ CUNY, Long Island City, NY
Year Produced: 1990
Executive Producer/Director: Richard K. Lieberman
Producer/Editor: Tom Vitale
Writer: Dick Worth
Narrator: Tony LoBianco
Format: Audiocassette
7 (30:00) programs
Distributor: LaGuardia Archives, LaGuardia Community College

# LBJ

## Documentary Series

This four-part documentary series traces the political career of America's thirty-sixth president, Lyndon Baines Johnson.

### Program 1
**Beautiful Texas**

chronicles Johnson's youth in rural Southwest Texas, his early political campaigns, and his years as Senator and Vice President. It concludes with his assumption of the Presidency upon the assassination of John F. Kennedy in 1963.

### Program 2
**My Fellow Americans**

traces the formation of Johnson's civil rights agenda, his vision of the Great Society, and the events leading to the Gulf of Tonkin resolution.

### Program 3
**We Shall Overcome**

traces the developing war in Vietnam and its effects on the Great Society.

### Program 4
**The Last Believer**

chronicles the remaining year's of Johnson's presidency, his decision not to seek reelection in 1968, and his final days on his Texas ranch.

Production Organizations: KERA-TV, Dallas, TX, and David Grubin Productions, New York, NY
Year Produced: 1991 (first broadcast on *American Experience*)
Executive Producer: Patricia P. Perini
Producer/Director/Writer: David Grubin
Senior Producer: Chana Gazit
Editors: Geof Bartz, Tom Haneke
Associate Producers: Hillary Dann, Sam Sills
Cinematography: William McCullough
Music: Michael Bacon
Narrator: Will Lyman
Format: Video
4 (60:00) programs
Distributors: PBS Video; Pacific Arts Video (home video)

# The Life and Times of Rosie the Riveter

## Documentary

Through newsreel footage and the testimonies of five women, this film examines the experiences of the eighteen million women who were brought into factories and plants during World War II.

Production Organization: Clarity Educational Productions, Emeryville, CA
Year Produced: 1980
Producer/Director: Connie Field
Associate Producers: Ellen Geiger, Lorraine Kahn, Jane Scantlebury, Bonnie Bellow
Editors: Lucy Massie Phenix, Connie Field
The Women in the Film: Wanita Allen, Gladys Belcher, Lyn Childs, Lola Weixel, Margaret Wright

20

Awards: Chicago International Film Festival, Gold Hugo, Documentary; Houston International Film Festival, Special Jury Gold Award, Best in Category; Festival dei Popoli, Florence, Italy, Gold Marzocco (First Prize); Athena International Film Festival, Gold Athena (First Prize)
Format: 16mm, Video (60:00)
Distributor: Direct Cinema Limited/Clarity Educational Productions

## LINCOLN AND THE WAR WITHIN

*Drama*

This is the story of Abraham Lincoln's handling of the Fort Sumter crisis of 1861, as he assumed the office of the presidency.

Production Organizations: WGBY-TV, Springfield, MA, and Lumiere Productions, Inc., New York, NY
Year Produced: 1992
Executive Producer: Mark Erstling
Producer/Director: Calvin Skaggs
Associate Producer: Robert Brent Toplin
Co-Producer: Paul Marcus
Writers: Frederic Hunter, Thomas Babe
Cinematography: Michael Spiller
Editor: Jay Freund
Cast: Chris Sarandon, Tom Aldredge, Will Patton, Remak Ramsay, Dylan Baker, Alan North, Joan Macintosh, Tony Carlin, Jack Gilpin, Pirie MacDonald, Veronica Cartwright
Format: Video (73:30)
Distributor: WGBY-TV

## LINDBERGH

*Documentary*

This film examines the life of Charles A. Lindbergh, including his family background, solo flight across the Atlantic Ocean in 1927, his isolationist crusade, his shattered faith in technology, and his final commitment to environmental causes.

Production Organization: Insignia Films, New York, NY
Year Produced: 1990
Executive Producer: Judy Crichton
Producers: Stephen Ives, Ken Burns
Director: Stephen Ives
Writer: Geoffrey C. Ward
Cinematography: Buddy Squires
Editor: Juliet Weber
Award: CINE Golden Eagle
Format: Video (56:00)
Distributor: PBS Video

## LIVING ATLANTA

*Documentary Radio Series*

This fifty-part series illustrates aspects of Atlanta's history between the two World Wars, focusing on the experiences of blacks and whites in a segregated city. Among the program topics are: The Depression in Atlanta; the Great Atlanta Fire of 1917; Atlanta's church life; Atlanta's Jewish community; the Ku Klux Klan in Atlanta; white liberals and interracial organizations; blacks in politics; Atlanta's progressive mayors; the death of Mary Phagan and the lynching of Leo Frank; public education, health, and welfare; Atlanta's five black colleges; black newspapers; black baseball in the South; domestic workers of Atlanta; and Atlanta's blues and country musicians.

Production Organization: WRFG Radio, Atlanta, GA
Year Produced: 1979
Producer: Harlan E. Joye
Associate Producer: Cliff Kuhn
Print Material: A book titled *Living Atlanta: An Oral History of the City from 1914 to 1948* (University of Georgia Press, 1990) is available
Format: Audio
50 (30:00) programs
Distributor: WRFG Radio-Atlanta, attn: Harlan Joye

## LONG SHADOWS

*Documentary*

Long Shadows examines the modern echoes of the American Civil War, documenting how repercussions of the war still influence the American psyche.

Production Organization: James Agee Film Project, Johnson City, TN
Year Produced: 1987
Executive Producer/Director: Ross Spears
Writers: Ross Spears, Jamie Ross
Cinematography: Anthony Forma
Editor: Neil Means, Grahame Weinbren
Narrator: Ross Spears
Interviews: Robert Penn Warren, Jimmy Carter, Robert Coles, Studs Terkel, Tom Wicker, C. Vann Woodward, John Hope Franklin, and others
Special Screenings: Museum of Modern Art; Kennedy Center; American Studies Association
Format: Video (88:00)
Distributor: James Agee Film Project Library

## METROPOLITAN AVENUE: COMMUNITY WOMEN IN A CHANGING NEIGHBORHOOD

*Documentary*

This film examines the changing roles of contemporary working-class women in the Williamsburg-Greenpoint neighborhood of Brooklyn, New York.

Production Organization: Metropolitan Avenue Film Project, New York, NY
Year Produced: 1985
Producer/Director/Narrator: Christine Noschese
Editor: Stan Salfas
Associate Editor: Kirk LaVine
Cinematography: John Bonanno
Awards/Festivals: American Film and Video Festival, John Grierson Award; Film Forum, Premiere; Leipzig International Film Festival, Special Jury Prize; Mannheim International Film Festival; Festival dei Popoli, Florence, Italy
Format: 16mm (58:00), Video (two versions, 58:00 and 49:00)
Distributor: New Day Films

## MIDDLETOWN

*Documentary Series*

Building on the sociological study of the town by Robert and Helen Merrill Lynd, this six-part series examines fundamental elements of life in Muncie, Indiana.

### *Program 1*
### Second Time Around

looks at the issues and complexities surrounding a contemporary marriage, especially as contrasted to those of fifty years ago.

Producer/Director: Peter Davis
Editor: Tom Haneke
Cinematography: John Lindley
Award: Emmy nomination (for editing)

### *Program 2*
### Family Business

examines the idea of personal freedom through economic independence as it follows the struggles of a family of ten to save their pizza parlor from bankruptcy.

Executive/Producer: Peter Davis
Producer/Director: Tom Cohen
Editor: Bob Brady
Cinematography: Tom Hurwitz
Award: Emmy nomination (for directing)

### *Program 3*
### The Campaign

follows the personalities, strategies, and pressures involved in Muncie's mayoral race.

Producer: Peter Davis
Director: Tom Cohen
Editor: Bob Brady
Cinematography: John Lindley
Awards: Two Emmy's (for sound and editing), Emmy nomination (producer)

### *Program 4*
### Community of Praise

examines the influence of faith on a family of evangelical Christian fundamentalists.

Producer: Peter Davis
Directors/Editors: Richard Leacock, Marisa Silver
Cinematography: Richard Leacock
Award: Emmy nomination (for editing)

### *Program 5*
### The Big Game

looks at the role of sports and how basketball games between two local high schools provide outlets for community tension.

Executive Producer: Peter Davis
Producer/Director: E.J. Vaughn
Editor: Ruth Newald
Cinematography: Paul Goldsmith, Mark Benjamin
Award: American Film and Video Festival, Blue Ribbon

### *Program 6*
### Seventeen

focuses on Muncie high school seniors as they face the tensions and uncertainties of growing up. (Some viewers may find the language in the film objectionable.)

Producer: Peter Davis
Directors: Joel DeMott, Jeff Kreines
Editors/Cinematography: Joel DeMott, Jeff Kreines
Award: U.S. Film Festival, First Prize
Series Production Production: The Middletown Film Project, New York, NY
Years Produced: 1979–1982

Series Producer: Peter Davis
Format: 16mm, Video
Programs 1,4,5 (60:00), Program 2 (90:00), Program 3 (80:00), Program 6 (120:00)
Distributors: First Run/Icarus Films (program 6, Seventeen);
Programs 1–5 not currently available

## MIDDLETOWN REVISITED

*Documentary*

This film examines the relationship of the documentary series (see above) to Robert and Helen Merrill Lynd's original sociological study of Muncie, Indiana, in the late 1920s.

Production Organization: WIPB/49, Muncie, IN
Year Produced: 1982
Executive Producer: Larry A. Dyer
Production Assistants: Tim Merriweather, Linda Furnish
Director: Richard Roffman
Editors: John Prager, Steve Singer, Ralph Cassano
Camera Operators: Debra Steele, Richard Collins, Gary Valente
Narrator: Ben Wattenburg
Format: Video (58:55)
Distributor: Ball State University, University Libraries, Educational Resources/Public Services (on-site viewing only)

## MISSISSIPPI TRIANGLE

*Documentary*

This film explores the emergence of the Chinese community in the Mississippi Delta and examines economic and civil rights issues, education, labor, and class in the Delta.

Production Organization: Film News Now Foundation, New York, NY
Year Produced: 1984
Producer/Director: Christine Choy
Codirectors: Worth Long, Allan Siegel
Awards/Festivals: Berlin International Film Festival; FILMEX (Los Angeles); Dorothy Arzner Film Festival, Critics' Award
Format: 16mm, Video (110:00)
Distributor: Third World Newsreel

## MITSUYE AND NELLIE:
## ASIAN-AMERICAN POETS

*Documentary*

This film portrays the experience of two poets, Mitsuye Yamada, Japanese-American, and Nellie Wong, Chinese-American. Among the issues explored are Japanese-American internment, Chinese immigration, intergenerational conflict in Asian-American families, and the dispelling of Asian-American stereotypes.

Production Organization: Mitsuye and Nellie Film Project, San Francisco, CA
Year Produced: 1981
Producer: Allie Light
Director: Irving Saraf
Cinematography: Emiko Omori
Cast: Mitsuye Yamada, Nellie Wong
Format: 16mm, Video (60:00)
Distributor: Light-Saraf Films

## MOLDERS OF TROY

*Drama*

From 1859 to 1876, Brian Duffy, resisting pressure from his fellow Irish immigrants, organizes Troy's iron molders into one of the country's strongest unions.

Production Organizations: Bowling Green Films, Inc. and WMHT, Schenectady, NY
Year Produced: 1979
Producer/Director: Jack Ofield
Writers: W.W. Lewis, Paul Wilkes
Project Director: Daniel J. Walkowitz
Research Director: Barbara Abrash
Format: 16mm (90:00)
Distributor: PBS Video

## MY PALIKARI

*Drama*

Greek immigrant Pete Panakos, the proprietor of a small cafe in Yonkers, New York, returns to Greece with his son. There they reshape their conceptions of the village and each other.

Production Organization: Center for Television in the Humanities, Inc., Atlanta, GA
Year Produced: 1982
Executive Producer: David Horwatt
Producers: Sue Jett, Tony Mark
Director: Charles S. Dubin
ScriptWriter: George Kirgo
Storywriter: Leon Capetanos
Editor: Richard Bracken
Cinematography: Ennio Guarnieri
Music: John Cacavas
Cast: Telly Savalas, Keith Gordon, Edye Byrde, Lori-Nan Engler
Format: 16mm, Video (90:00)
Distributor: Caridi Entertainment

## NIAGARA FALLS: THE
## CHANGING NATURE OF A
## NEW WORLD SYMBOL

*Documentary*

This film explores the changing cultural and historical significance of Niagara Falls.

Production Organization: Florentine Films, Northampton, MA
Year Produced: 1985
Producers/Directors/Writers: Diane Garey, Larry R. Hott
Editor: Steve Alves
Narrator: Adolph Caesar
Award: American Film and Video Festival, Blue Ribbon
Format: 16mm, Video (29:00)
Distributor: Direct Cinema Limited

## ONE ON EVERY CORNER:
## MANHATTAN'S GREEK-
## OWNED COFFEE SHOPS

*Documentary*

This film examines Manhattan's neighborhood coffee shops and their role as a means of support and social mobility for new Greek immigrants who run them.

Production Organization: International Women's Film Project, Washington, DC
Year Produced: 1984
Coproducers: Doreen Moses, Andrea Hull
Editor: Andrea Hull
Cinematography: Tom Siegel
Award: CINE Golden Eagle
Format: 16mm, Video (48:00)
Distributor: Doreen Moses

## THE OTHER SIDE OF
## VICTORY

*Drama*

The Other Side of Victory dramatizes the problems facing ordinary American soldiers during the Revolutionary War, explaining why most ultimately chose to stay and fight.

Production Organization: New York State Bicentennial Commission
Year Produced: 1976
Producer: Ira Barmak
Director: Bill Jersey
Writers: Richard Wormser, Ira Barmak
Cast: Josh Clark, William Sanderson, Tom Waite, Jamie Ross, David Naughton, Roberta Maxwell, Mark Margolis, Steve Simpson
Format: Video (58:00)
Distributor: Bill Jersey Productions/Quest Productions

## PARADOX ON 72ND STREET

*Documentary*

Through observations of passersby in a New York neighborhood over a three year period, this film examines the paradox of how we can be "our individual separate selves and, at the same time, the working part of others."

Production Organizations: Equinox Films and WNET/13, New York, NY
Year Produced: 1982
Producer/Director/Writer: Gene Searchinger
Format: 16mm, Video (60:00)
Distributor: Equinox Films, Inc.

## PEARL HARBOR: SURPRISE AND REMEMBRANCE

*Documentary*

This film examines Japanese-American relations and the events leading to the attack on Pearl Harbor, with special emphasis on the way in which various interpretations of events and evidence arise from conflicting national purposes and personal insights.

Production Organization: American Studies Film Center, Inc., New York, NY
Year Produced: 1991 (premiere on *American Experience*)
Producers/Directors: Lance Bird, John Crowley, Tom Johnson
Writer: Tom Johnson
Cinematography: Mead Hunt
Editors: Victor Kanefsky, Julianna Parroni
Narrator: Jason Robards
Format: Video (85:00)
Distributor: Direct Cinema Limited

## THE PERFORMED WORD

*Documentary*

This film explores the structure and style of African-American preaching, the sermon as performance, and the nature of oral performance in secular and sacred environments.

Production Organization: Anthropology Film Center Foundation, Santa Fe, NM
Year Produced: 1981
Producer: Gerald Davis
Codirectors: Carlos de Jesus, Ernest Shinagawa
Editors: Ernest Shinagawa, Paul Grindrod
Writers: Gerald Davis, Ernest Shinagawa
Cinematographers: Hiroaki Tanaka, Rick Butler
Narrator: Gerald Davis
Format: 16mm, Video (60:00)
Distributor: Center for Southern Folklore

## THE PROBABLE PASSING OF ELK CREEK

*Documentary*

This film considers the impact of a government-funded dam on two communities north of San Francisco, both of which are to be flooded: the predominantly white community of Elk Creek which opposes it, and the Nomlaki Indians of the Grindstone Creek Indian Reservation who are ambivalent.

Production Organizations: Tocayos Films and KTEH, San Jose, CA
Year Produced: 1983
Executive Producers: John W. Bloch, Elie Abel, Peter Baker
Producer/Director/Writer/Narrator: Rob Wilson
Cinematography: Mahlon Picht, William Zarchy, David Ambriz
Editors: Susan Slanhoff, Richard Chasen
Format: 16mm, Video (60:00)
Distributor: The Cinema Guild

## THE PUEBLO REVOLT

*Radio Drama*

This two-part program dramatizes the Peublo Revolt of 1680, during which the Peublo Indians attacked Santa Fe and drove the Spanish out of New Mexico until 1692.

Production Organization: The Wheelwright Museum, Santa Fe, NM
Year Produced: 1980
Producer: Mel Lawrence
Director: Phil Austin
Writer: Peggy Schneider
Format: Audiocassette
2 (60:00) programs
Distributor: Not currently available

## REBUILDING THE TEMPLE: CAMBODIANS IN AMERICA

*Documentary*

This film examines the influence of traditional Khmer Buddhism and culture on the adjustment of Cambodian refugees to life in America.

Production Organization: Florentine Films, Haydenville, MA
Year Produced: 1990
Producers/Directors: Claudia Levin, Lawrence R. Hott
Cinematography: Buddy Squires, Allen Moore, Bruce Jacoby
Editor: Sharon Sachs
Narrator: Linda Hunt
Format: Video (60:00)
Distributor: Direct Cinema Limited

## ROANOAK

*Dramatic Series*

This three-part drama covers the period 1584–1590 and examines the first prolonged contact between English explorers and the Algonquian-speaking Indians on Roanoke Island. Drawing on the perspectives of both peoples, it considers the relationship between "Lost Colony" governor John White and two Native Americans. The series concludes with the disappearance of the colony, which remains a mystery.

Production Organizations: First Contact Films, Inc., and The South Carolina ETV Network, Spartanburg, SC
Year Produced: 1986
Executive Producer: Lindsay Law
Producers: Timothy Marx, James K. McCarthy
Coproducers: Robin C. Maw, Dina Harris
Director: Jan Egleson
Writers: Dina Harris, James K. McCarthy
Editor: Bill Anderson
Cast: Victor Garber, Joseph Running Fox, Tino Juarez, Will Sampson
Print Material: Viewer's Guide available
Format: Video (120:00)
Distributor: PBS Video

23

24

## Seasons of a Navajo

*Documentary*

This film documents a year in the life of the Neboyias, a Navajo couple who farm, weave, and tend sheep from a traditional hogan (dwelling) in Arizona.

Production Organizations: Peace River Films and KAET, Tempe, AZ
Year Produced: 1985
Executive Producer: Anthony Schmitz
Associate Producer: Joana Hattery
Director: John Borden
Editor: Michel Chalufour
Cinematography: John Borden, Doug Shaffer
Narrator: Will Lyman
Awards: American Film and Video Festival, Red Ribbon; CINE Golden Eagle
Format: Video (60:00)
Distributor: PBS Video

## Seeing Red

*Documentary*

Seeing Red looks at the American Communist Party's goals, organization, and eventual decline in light of McCarthyism and revelations about Stalinism.

Production Organization: Heartland Productions, Dayton, OH
Year Produced: 1984
Codirectors/Coproducers: James Klein, Julia Reichert
Associate Producer: Aaron Ezekiel
Awards/Festivals: Academy Award nominee, Best Feature Documentary; American Film and Video Festival, Blue Ribbon; Chicago International Film Festival, Bronze Hugo; New York Film Festival
Format: 16mm, Video (100:00)
Distributor: New Day Films

## Seguin

*Drama*

The film dramatizes the story of Juan Seguin, a Mexican who joined the Texans in their war for independence from Mexico. After building a successful political career, ethnic rivalries forced him from office, causing him to flee to Mexico, where he later joined the Mexican forces in the Mexican-American war (1846–1848) and fought against former neighbors and constituents.

Production Organization: KCET, Community Television for Southern California, Los Angeles, CA
Year Produced: 1981
Executive Producer/Director/Writer: Jesus S. Trevino
Producer: Severo Perez
Cast: Enrique Castillo, Henry Darrow, Danny De La Paz, A Martinez, Julio Medina, Edward James Olmos, Lupe Ontiveros, Rose Portillo, Pepe Serna
Format: 16mm (60:00)
Distributor: Not currently available

## Sentimental Women Need Not Apply

*Documentary*

This film chronicles the emergence and evolution of professional nursing, and explores the realities and myths that have characterized the field.

Production Organization: Florentine Films, Haydenville, MA
Year Produced: 1988
Producers/Directors/Writers: Diane Garey, Lawrence R. Hott
Cinematography: Buddy Squires, Allen Moore
Editor: Sharon Sachs
Narrator: Elaine Princi
Music: Richard Einhorn
Awards/Festivals: National Educational Film and Video Festival, Silver Apple, Women's Issues Category; Sigma Theta Tau International Honor Society of Nursing, Award of Excellence
Format: Video (60:00)
Distributor: Direct Cinema Limited

## Shannon County

*Documentary*

This two-part film examines the economic, cultural, and psychological expectations of the inhabitants of the Ozarks region of southern Missouri, and juxtaposes those expectations against past experiences and present reality.

Production Organizations: Center for Ozarks Studies of Southwest Missouri State University, Springfield, MO, and Veriation Films, Palo Alto, CA
Year Produced: 1982
Executive Producer: Robert Flanders
Producer/Director: Robert Moore
Editors: Robert Moore, Lise Rubinstein, David Espar
Awards/Festivals: American Film and Video Festival, Blue Ribbon; CINE Golden Eagle; The Margaret Mead Festival
Format: 16mm, Video
Part 1, Shannon County: Home (67:00),
Part 2, Shannon County: The Hearts of the Children (57:00)
Distributors: Veriation Films (16mm); Center for Ozarks Studies, Southwest Missouri State University (video)

## The Silence at Bethany

*Drama*

In 1939, a young man returns to his Mennonite roots in Pennsylvania farm country, where he is accepted into the community. However, because of external pressures on the church, he and his wife soon become the focus of a power struggle between orthodox and liberal members of their community.

Production Organization: Keener
Productions, Los Angeles, CA
Year Produced: 1987
Executive Producers: Lindsay Law, Joyce
Keener
Producer: Tom Cherones
Director: Joel Oliansky
Writer: Joyce Keener
Cinematography: Charles Minsky
Editor: Pasquale Buba
Music: Lalo Schifrin
Cast: Tom Dahlgren, Richard Fancy, Dakin
Matthews, Mark Moses, Susan Wilder
Format: 35mm, Video (88:23)
Distributor: Keener Productions

## STORIES FROM THE SPIRIT WORLD: LEGENDS OF NATIVE AMERICANS

### Radio Series (Documentary and Drama)

This four-part series presents the
mythology and heritage of the
Cahuilla and Chumash Indians of
southern California and of the
Nahuatl-speaking (Áztec) peoples of
pre-Columbian Mexico. The programs feature dramatizations of episodes from the myths as well as
discussions of their themes and role
in traditional tribal cultures.

### Program 1
### The Old Ways Are Gone: The Cahuilla Indians of Southern California

introduces the Cahuilla creation
myth, featuring contemporary
native songs, dances, and games,
with historic Cahuilla language
recordings.

### Program 2
### The Legend of the Sun: Aztec Mythology

considers creation cycle stories
popular among the Nahuatl-speaking people of Mexico, especially the
Aztecs.

### Program 3
### December's Child: Chumash Mythology

is adapted from a book of the same
name, which presents a collection of
Chumash oral narratives.

### Program 4
### Confrontation of Mythologies

features a dialogue between Aztec
priests and European missionaries
that took place in 1524, an exchange
that was reconstructed in 1564 by a
Catholic priest and a group of Aztec
informants in a document known as
*Colloquios y Doctrina Christiana.*

Production Organization: Voices
International, New York, NY
Years Produced: 1985–86
Producer/Director/Writer: Everett C. Frost
Associate Producer/Writer: Faith Wilding
Narrators: Marcos Gutierrez (Program 1);
Katherine Siva Saubel (2); Jimmie Skaggs
(3); Tony Amendola (4)
Format: Audiocassette
Program 1 (two versions, 60:00 and 90:00);
Programs 2 & 3 (60:00);
Program 4 (30:00)
Note: In the three-part *Soundplay* series
package, Program 1 has been cut to 60:00
and Program 4 is excerpted in Program 2
Distributor: Pacifica Program Service/Radio
Archive

## STORM OF STRANGERS

### Documentary Series

Storm of Strangers looks at the experiences of three different ethnic
groups that came to America: the
Chinese, the Irish, and the Italians.

### Program 1
### Jung Sai: Chinese American

follows a young, fourth-generation
Chinese-American journalist as she
interviews members of the West
Coast Chinese community about its
history.

Directors: Frieda Lee Mock, Terry Sanders

### Program 2
### The Irish

combines photographs, illustrations,
and a fictional oral autobiography to
portray the immigration of the Irish
to America.

Director: Chris Jenkyns
Narrator: Edmund O'Brien

### Program 3
### Italian American

Based on interviews with his parents, Martin Scorsese profiles the
experiences of Italian-American
immigrants through their eyes.

Director: Martin Scorcese
Production Organization: National
Communications Foundation, Los Angeles,
CA
Year Produced: 1975

Series Producers: Saul Rubin, Elaine Attias
Awards: CINE Golden Eagle; American Film
and Video Festival, First Prize & Red
Ribbon; Association of Visual
Communicators (formerly IFPA), Cindy
Award
Format: 16mm
3 (30:00) programs
Distributor: Pennsylvania State University,
Audio-Visual Center
(Jung Sai, #34831; The Irish, #32261; Italian-
American, #34830)

## STRANGERS AND KIN

### Documentary

Strangers and Kin examines the history of stereotypes associated with
people living in the Appalachian
Mountains.

Production Organization: Appalshop Films,
Whitesburg, KY
Year Produced: 1984
Executive Producer/Director: Herb E. Smith
Writers: Herb E. Smith, Helen Lewis, Don
Baker
Format: 16mm, Video (58:00)
Distributor: Appalshop Films

## THE SUPREME COURT'S HOLY BATTLES

*Documentary*

This program explores the history of the First Amendment's clauses on religion, from colonial thought and culture through significant Supreme Court decisions regarding the separation of church and state.

Production Organization: Film Odyssey, Inc., Washington, DC
Year Produced: 1988
Producer/Director: Karen Thomas
Coproducer: George Wolfe
Writers: Karen Thomas, George Wolfe
Cinematography: Erich Roland, Terry Hopkins, Judy Irola, Don Sellars
Editor: Mark Muheim
Correspondent: Roger Mudd
Print Material: Companion Guide available
Format: Video (60:00)
Distributor: PBS Video

## THREE SOVEREIGNS FOR SARAH

*Drama*

Three Sovereigns for Sarah is a three-part drama that depicts the Salem witch trials of 1692 by focusing on the story of three sisters, distinguished matrons in the community, who were caught up in these events. The script is based on existing trial manuscripts and on the writings of Sarah Cloyce, the youngest sister and the only one to escape the hanging tree.

Production Organization: NightOwl Productions, Nahant, MA
Year Produced: 1985
Executive Producer: Michael Uslan
Producers: Ben Melniker, Victor Pisano
Director: Philip Leacock
Writer: Victor Pisano
Cinematography: Larry Pizer
Editor: Stan Salfas

Cast: Vanessa Redgrave, Patrick McGoohan, Phyllis Thaxter, Kim Hunter, Ronald Hunter, Will Lyman
Format: Video
3 (56:00) programs
Distributors: PBS Video; NightOwl Productions (for large groups or special events)

## THROUGH ALL TIME: THE AMERICAN SEARCH FOR COMMUNITY

*Documentary*

These two films explore the contemporary American search for community by examining the dilemmas and challenges facing small towns.

### Program 1
**Traditional Small Towns**
features research sociologists and residents of numerous towns throughout America commenting on small-town life.

### Program 2
**Pleasure Domes and Money Mills**
examines resort and recreation towns, a new kind of American boomtown, in contrast with the traditional company town.

Production Organization: KPBS/15, San Diego State University,
San Diego, CA
Year Produced: 1977
Producer/Director: James Case
Writer: Margaret Cort Clifford
Format: 16mm, Video
2 (28:00) Programs
Distributor: Not currently available

## THE TRIAL OF STANDING BEAR

*Drama*

The Trial of Standing Bear dramatizes an 1879 case adjudicated in the U.S. District Court in Omaha, Nebraska, establishing that Native Americans have protection under the Constitution.

Production Organization: Nebraskans for Public Television, Inc., Lincoln, NE
Year Produced: 1983
Executive Producer: Eugene Bunge
Line Producer: Dan Jones
Director: Marshall Jamison
Assistant Director: Bob Hicks
Story: Adapted from *The Ponca Chiefs* by Thomas Tibbles
Cinematography: Robert Schoenhut
Editor: Michael Farrell
Narrator: William Shatner
Cast: Ivan Naranjo, George Ede, Carmen de Lavallade, George Riddle
Format: Video (90:00)
Distributor: Nebraska ETV

## THE TWO WORLDS OF ANGELITA (LOS DOS MUNDOS DE ANGELITA)

*Drama*

Told through the eyes of a nine-year-old girl, this drama portrays the dilemmas faced by a Puerto Rican family as they migrate from the island to the barrios of New York's Lower East Side.

Production Organization: Casa del Autor Puertorriqueño, San Juan, PR
Year Produced: 1982
Producer/Director: Jane Morrison
Associate Producer: Lianne Halfon
Writer: José Manuel Torres Santiago
Editor: Suzanne Fenn
Cinematography: Alfonso Beato
Music: Dom Salvador

Cast: Marien Perez Riera, Rosalba Rolón, Angel Domenech Soto, Delia Esther Quiñones
Awards/Festivals: American Film Festival, Red Ribbon; U.S. Film Festival; Festival dei Popoli, Florence, Italy
Format: 16mm, Video (73:00)
In Spanish with English subtitles
Distributor: First Run/Icarus Films

## UNDER ALL IS THE LAND

*Documentary Radio Series*

This five-part series considers land issues within a historical and social context and examines how changes in land tenure patterns have affected people's lives.

*Program 1*
**Cycles: The Physical Centrality of the Land**
explores the physical limits of the universe, the capacity for development, and the frontiers of scientific knowledge.

*Program 2*
**Down to Earth: Culture and the Centrality of the Land**
discusses the relationship between land and the development of cultural institutions.

*Program 3*
**Useful Trees: Culture and Land**
looks at the concept of land as expressed in the creative imagination, with a focus on music and literature.

*Program 4*
**Get Big or Get Out: Small Farmers**
examines the history of small farmers in the United States.

*Program 5*
**The Way the Land Is Worked**
evaluates the conditions and trends of land use in America, from the dangers of soil erosion to the use of migrant farm workers.

Production Organization: Sound and Print United, Inc., Warrenton, NC
Year Produced: 1983
Director: Willa Blackshear
Producer/Writer: Phaye Poliakoff
Music: Si Kahn, Bernice Johnson Reagon
Format: Audiocassette
5 (30:00) programs
Distributor: Not currently available

## UNDER THIS SKY

*Drama*

This film portrays the campaign of Elizabeth Cady Stanton and Susan B. Anthony to establish women's suffrage in Kansas, where the issue was on the state ballot in 1867. Financial troubles and other difficulties lead them to accept the assistance of George Francis Train, an eccentric reformer, excellent speaker, and white supremacist.

Production Organization: Red Cloud Productions, Cambridge, and WGBY, Springfield, MA
Year Produced: 1979
Executive Producer: Christine M. Herbes
Producer: Phylis Geller
Director: Randa Haines
Writer: Sherry Sonnett
Cast: Irene Worth, Collin Wilcox-Paxton, W. B. Brydon, John Glover
Format: 16mm (60:00)
Distributor: Not currently available

## VILLAGE OF NO RIVER

*Documentary*

Featuring a mix of old and new footage, this film explores the impact of modern life and technology on Kwigillingok, a small Eskimo village of 200 people located one mile from the Bering Sea in southwestern Alaska.

Production Organization: The Newark Museum Association, Newark, NJ
Year Produced: 1981
Executive Producer/Writer: Barbara Lipton
Producer/Director: Stuart Hersh
Editor: Vincent Stenerson

Cinematography: Craig Makhitarian
Narrator: Elsie Jimonie
Festival: Margaret Mead Film Festival
Format: Video (58:00)
Distributor: The Newark Museum

## VISIONS OF THE CONSTITUTION

*Documentary Series*

Visions of the Constitution is a three-part series that probes the constitutional foundations of several issues in the American legal system.

*Program 1*
**The Search for Equality**
explores the principle of equal protection under the law, from the efforts to abolish slavery through the suffragette and civil rights movements, to affirmative action.

Executive Producer: Tom Skinner
Producer/Writer: Peggy Zapple
Associate Producers: John Boyer, Lisa Cantini-Seguin, Vicki Johnson-Cherney
Cinematography: Norris Brock, William Wegert, Allen Rosen, Mark Knobil
Editor: Gary J. Hines
Host: Andrea Mitchell
Law Correspondent: Tom Gerety

*Program 2*
**The Judges**
explores the nature and role of the Supreme Court, its justices, and its landmark cases.

Executive Producer: Tom Skinner
Producer/Writer: Peggy Zapple
Associate Producers: John Boyer, Lisa Cantini-Seguin, Vicki Johnson-Cherney
Cinematography: Norris Brock, William Wegert, Allen Rosen, Mark Knobil
Editor: Patricia Yarborough
Host: Andrea Mitchell
Law Correspondent: Tom Gerety

28

*Program 3*
**Crime and the Bill of Rights**
looks at the right against self-in-
crimination and broader issues
raised by the Christian Burial Case
of 1968 in which the suspect was
asked to locate the body of a 10-
year-old girl he allegedly murdered.

Executive Producer: Dan Fales
Producer: Gordon Hyatt
Associate Producers: Shirley J. Saldamarco
Writer/Law Correspondent: Tom Gerety
Cinematography: Joe Seamans, Richard
Kahn, John Connors, Art Vogel,
Bruce Drummon
Editor: Christine Ochtum
Host: Andrea Mitchell

Production Organization: Metropolitan
Pittsburgh Public Broadcasting (WQED),
Pittsburgh, PA
Years Produced: 1985–1989
Series Executive Producer: Tom Skinner
Format: Video
3 (57:00) programs
Distributor: WQED

## WASHINGTON: CITY OUT OF WILDERNESS

*Documentary*

Combining historical photographs
and motion picture footage with
current photography, this film
studies the city of Washington, D.C.,
past and present.

Production Organization: United States
Capitol Historical Society,
Washington, DC
Year Produced: 1974
Project Director: William M. Maury
Producer: Francis Thompson Company
Award: CINE Golden Eagle
Format: 35mm (28:00)
Distributor: Not currently available

## WASHINGTON'S NEIGHBORHOODS: A HISTORY OF CHANGE

*Documentary Radio Series*

**Washington's Neighborhoods: A
History of Change**
is an eleven-part radio series tracing
the development of the nation's
capital.

*Program 1*
**Washington: The Capital City—
Part 1**
traces the development of the
nation's capital from its beginning as
a swampland village through the
mid-nineteenth century.

*Program 2*
**Washington: The Capital City—
Part 2**
looks at further settlement of the
federal city, particularly during the
Civil War when Washington's residents were ambivalent about their
loyalties.

*Program 3*
**Georgetown and Alexandria**
considers the evolution of both
towns from competitive seaports,
through decline, to their present
status as fashionable residential
areas.

*Program 4*
**Anacostia: The Land across
the River**
chronicles how the Anacostia community became Washington's first
suburb for working people of mod-
est means.

*Program 5*
**Streetcars and Streetcar Suburbs**
examines the impact of the trolley,
especially as it contributed to socio-
economic divisions within the city.

*Program 6*
**Monumental Washington**
portrays the well-known sites and
attractions of the city.

*Program 7*
**LeDroit Park: Washington's Black
Community**
focuses on the desegregation of
LeDroit Park, once a fashionable
suburb for well-to-do white Wash-
ingtonians.

*Program 8*
**The Interwar Period: 1920–1940**
examines the growth of the city during the Interwar Years.

*Program 9*
**Automobile Suburbs**
describes how the automobile led to
the development of distant suburbs
which, by the end of World War II,
were spilling over the city's bound-
aries into neighboring Maryland and
Virginia.

*Program 10*
**In the Capitol's Shadow: Two
Neighborhoods**
explores the divergent histories and
lifestyles of Capitol Hill and southwest Washington.

*Program 11*
**The Death and Life of a Great
American Downtown**
presents the rise and fall of downtown Washington, and the new life
that is returning to it.

Production Organization: The Washington
Ear, Inc., Silver Spring, MD
Year Produced: 1981
Executive Director: Margaret W. Rockwell
Producers: Larry Massett, Deborah Amos,
Thomas Looker, Carol Malmi
Writers: Luther Spoeher, Larry Massett,
Thomas Locker, Carol Malmi
Narrator: Noah Adams
Print Material: A set of fourteen braille and
large-type maps of the city, with alphabetical
index, is also available.
Format: Audiocassette
11 (60:00) programs
Distributor: The Metropolitan Washington
Ear, Inc.

## WATER AND THE DREAM OF THE ENGINEERS
*Documentary*

This film considers the troubled
relations between engineering and
environmentalism, with attention
given to California's "water wars,"
river contamination in New Orleans,
and the modern use of old sewage
systems.

Production Organization: Cine Research
Associates, Boston, MA
Year Produced: 1983
Executive Producer/Director: Richard
Broadman
Coproducer: John Grady
Writers: Richard Broadman, John Grady
Cinematography: Nick Doob
Format: 16mm, Video (80:00)
The film is also available in two parts, Water
History (40:00) and The Shape of a Crisis
(40:00)
Distributor: Cine Research Associates

## WE SHALL OVERCOME
*Radio Documentary*

The history of the song "We Shall
Overcome" is recounted through
archival tapes and interviews with
cultural historian and musician
Bernice Johnson Reagon and
folksingers Pete Seeger and Guy
Carawan.

Production Organization: The Public Affairs
Media Center, Madison, WI
Year Produced: 1983
Producer/Writer: Judith L. Strasser
Format: Audiocassette (25:00)
Distributor: Kaleidoscope Media Service,
attn: Judith L. Strasser

## WE WERE SO BELOVED: THE GERMAN JEWS OF WASHINGTON HEIGHTS
*Documentary*

This film examines the experiences
of German-Jewish refugees who fled
Nazi Germany in the 1930s and
resettled in New York City's Washington Heights neighborhood.

Production Organizations: Streetwise Films
and New York Foundation for the Arts, New
York, NY
Year Produced: 1985
Producer/Director/Writer: Manfred
Kirchheimer
Cinematography: James Callanan, Steven
Giuliano
Festivals: Berlin Festival; FILMEX (Los
Angeles)
Format: 16mm, Video (145:00)
Distributor: First Run/Icarus Films

## A WEAVE OF TIME
*Documentary*

Through the photography, footage,
and observations of anthropologist
John Adair, A Weave of Time
explores change and continuity over
fifty years in a Navajo family in
Arizona.

Production Organization: New York
Foundation for the Arts, New York, NY
Year Produced: 1986
Executive Producer/Director: Susan Fanshel
Producers: Susan Fanshel, John Adair,
Deborah Gordon
Cinematographers: Robert Achs, Jack
Parsons
Editors: Susan Fanshel, Deborah Gordon
Music: Jim Pepper
Awards/Festivals: Earthwatch Film Award;
American Film and Video Festival, Blue
Ribbon; National Educational Film and
Video Festival, Silver Apple; Margaret Mead
Film Festival; Hawaii International Film
Festival; International Flaherty Film
Seminar; Festival dei Popoli, Florence, Italy;
Berlin Film Festival
Format: Video (58:00)
Distributor: Direct Cinema Limited

## THE WOBBLIES
*Documentary*

This film presents the history of the
International Workers of the World,
nicknamed the Wobblies, through
the eyes of rank-and-file members.

Production Organization: Center for
Educational Productions, New York, NY
Year Produced: 1979
Directors: Deborah Shaffer, Stewart Bird
Cinematography: Sandi Sissel, Judy Irola,
Peter Gessner, Bonnie Friedman
Editors: Deborah Shaffer, Stewart Bird
Awards/Festivals: American Film and Video
Festival, Red Ribbon; New York Film
Festival, premiere
Format: 16mm, Video (89:00)
Distributor: First Run/Icarus Films

30

## THE WOMEN OF SUMMER: THE BRYN MAWR SUMMER SCHOOL FOR WOMEN WORKERS

*Documentary*

From 1921 to 1938, seventeen hundred blue-collar women participated in an educational experiment that exposed them to a broad range of humanistic disciplines and political thought. This film blends archival materials with the individual experiences of Bryn Mawr Summer School alumnae, as recounted at a specially planned reunion fifty years later.

Production Organization: The Women of Summer, Inc., Tenafly, NJ
Year Produced: 1985
Producer/Director/Writer: Suzanne Bauman
Associate Producer: Rita Heller
Editor: Phyllis Chinlund
Cinematography: Ross Lowell
Awards: American Film and Video Festival, Red Ribbon, History; CINE Golden Eagle; San Francisco International Film Festival, Second Place; Athens (OH) International Film Festival, Golden Athena; National Educational Film and Video Festival, First Prize, Social Studies; Booklist, Editor's Choice (American Library Association)
Format: 16mm, Video (60:00)
Distributor: Filmmakers Library

## YOU MAY CALL HER MADAM SECRETARY

*Documentary*

This film traces the life and career of Frances Perkins, who became the first woman member of a presidential cabinet as secretary of labor (1933–1945) under Franklin D. Roosevelt.

Production Organization: The Frances Perkins Film Project, Inc. West Tisbury, MA
Year Produced: 1987
Producers/Writers: Robert Potts, Marjory Potts
Director: Marjory Potts
Cinematographer: Dean Gaskill
Editors: Michael Grenadier, Robert Potts
Cast: Frances Sternhagen, Robert Potts
Awards: American Film and Video Festival, Red Ribbon; CINE Golden Eagle; Columbus (OH) International Film Festival, Chris Bronze Plaque; "Outstanding Non-Print" Lists in *Booklist* and *Choice*, (American Library Association)
Format: 16mm, Video (57:40)
Distributor: Vineyard Video Productions

## ZIVELI: MEDICINE FOR THE HEART

*Documentary*

Filmed in Chicago and northern California, Ziveli examines the culture of Serbian immigrants, with emphasis on rituals of the Eastern Orthodox church and on the performance of traditional songs and dances.

Production Organization: Center for Visual Anthropology, University of Southern California, Los Angeles, CA
Year Produced: 1987
Executive Producers: Andrei Simic, Edward Levine
Producer: Vikram Jayanti
Director/Cinematography: Les Blank
Writer: Andrei Simic
Editor: Maureen Gosling
Narrator: Andrei Simic
Award: Chicago International Film Festival, Silver Plaque
Format: Video (55:00)
Distributor: Flower Films

# Literature &
# Language

# THE AMERICAN SHORT STORY

*Dramatic Series*

The American Short Story series dramatizes seventeen short stories by eminent American writers.

## *Program 1*
### Almos' a Man, by Richard Wright.
In this story a misunderstood black teenaged farm worker in the rural South of the 1930s comes of age.

Year Produced: 1977
Producer: Dan McCann
Adaptation: Leslie Lee
Director: Stan Lathan
Cinematography: Tak Fujimoto
Cast: LeVar Burton, Madge Sinclair, Robert Doqui, Chistopher Brooks,
Roy Andrews, Gary Goodnow
Awards/Festivals: American Film Festival; Columbus (OH) Film Festival, Bronze Plaque; John D. and Catherine T. MacArthur Foundation, a MacArthur Video Classics Library selection
Format: 16mm, Video (39:00)

## *Program 2*
### Barn Burning, by William Faulkner
The adolescent son of a post-Civil War sharecropper finds himself torn between trying to win his father's acceptance and his aversion to his father's unrelenting and violent nature.

Year Produced: 1979
Producer: Calvin Skaggs
Adaptation: Horton Foote
Director: Peter Werner
Editor: Jay Freund
Cinematography: Peter Sova
Cast: Tommy Lee Jones, Diane Kagan, Shawn Whittington, Jimmy Faulkner
Format: 16mm, Video (41:00)

## *Program 3*
### Bernice Bobs Her Hair, by F. Scott Fitzgerald
A girl from Eau Claire, Wisconsin, is transformed from a reticent "ugly duckling" into a successful, sought-after vamp by her manipulative cousin.

Year Produced: 1976
Producer: Paul R. Gurian
Director/Adaptation: Joan Micklin Silver
Editor: Ralph Rosenblum
Cinematography: Ken Van Sickle
Cast: Shelley Duvall, Veronica Cartwright, Bud Cort, Dennis Christopher,
Gary Springer, Lane Binkley, Polly Holliday, Mark LaMura, Murray Moston,
Patrick Byrne, Mark Newkirk, Leslie Thorsen, Claudette Warlick
Awards/Festivals: American Film Festival, Red Ribbon; CINE Golden Eagle; International Short and Documentary Film Festival Award; Columbus (OH) Film Festival, Bronze Plaque; John D. and Catherine T. MacArthur Foundation, a MacArthur Video Classics Library selection
Format: 16mm, Video (48:00)

## *Program 4*
### The Blue Hotel, by Stephen Crane
A disturbed young Swede arrives in a small Nebraska town in the l880s expecting the Wild West of popular dime novels, and projecting these fears onto the hotel keeper and his fellow guests.

Year Produced: 1975
Producer: Ozzie Brown
Director: Jan Kadar
Adaptation: Harry M. Petrakis
Editors: Barbara Marks, Richard Marks
Cinematography: Ed Lynch
Cast: David Warner, James Keach, John Bottoms, Rex Everhart,
Geddeth Smith, Thomas Aldredge, Red Sutton, Lisa Pelikan, Cynthia Wright
Format: 16mm, Video (55:00)

## *Program 5*
### The Displaced Person, by Flannery O'Connor
A conscientious but driven Polish refugee disrupts the hierarchy of power on a Georgia farm in the 1940s.

Year Produced: 1976
Producer: Matthew N. Herman
Adaptation: Horton Foote
Director: Glenn Jordan
Editor: Aaron Stell
Cinematography: Ken Van Sickle
Cast: Irene Worth, John Houseman, Shirley Stoler, Lane Smith, Robert Earl Jones
Format: 16mm, Video (58:00)

## *Program 6*
### The Golden Honeymoon, by Ring Lardner
Charlie and Lucy Tate, an elderly couple from New Jersey, celebrate their fiftieth wedding anniversary in St. Petersburg, Florida, in the 1920s. There they encounter Lucy's suitor of fifty years past, who is vacationing with his wife.

Year Produced: 1979
Producers: Don McCann, Whitney Green
Director: Noel Black
Adaptation: Frederic Hunter
Cinematography: Jonathan Else
Cast: Teresa Wright, James Whitmore, Stephen Elliott, Nan Martin
Award: American Film Festival, Finalist
Format: 16mm, Video (52:00)

## *Program 7*
### The Greatest Man in the World, by James Thurber
When an illiterate lout becomes the first man to complete a nonstop solo flight around the world, he instantly captures national attention, and the highest government officials strive to make the man into a hero worthy of the adulation they would bestow.

**34**

Year Produced: 1979
Producer: Ed Lynch
Associate Producer: Calvin Skaggs
Director: Ralph Rosenblum
Adaptation: Jeff Wanshel
Editor: Sandra Morse
Cinematography: Tony Mitchell
Cast: Brad Davis, Reed Birney, John
McMartin, Howard DaSilva, Carol
Kane, William Prince, Sudie Bond
Format: 16mm, Video (51:00)

### Program 8
### I'm a Fool, by Sherwood Anderson
At the turn of the century, a young
man from Ohio, who is serving an
apprenticeship at the Sandusky race
track, lies about his family and posi-
tion in order to impress a beautiful
woman.

Year Produced: 1975
Producer: Dan McCann
Director: Noel Black
Adaptation: Ron Cowen
Editors: Arnold Faderbush, Stan Siegel
Cinematography: Jonathan Else
Cast: Ron Howard, Santiago Gonzalez, Amy
Irving, John Light, Randi
Kallan, Otis Calef, John Tidwel
Awards: Chicago Educational Film Festival,
Golden Babe
Format: 16mm, Video (38:00)

### Program 9
### The Jilting of Granny Weatherall, by Katherine Anne Porter
On her deathbed, a proud and once
domineering matriarch reviews the
successes and failures of her life.

Year Produced: 1978
Producers: Calvin Skaggs, Phylis Geller
Director: Randa Haines
Adaptation: Corinne Jacker
Editor: Stan Warnow
Cinematography: Mike Fash
Cast: Geraldine Fitzgerald, Lois Smith,
William Swetland
Format: 16mm, Video (57:00)

### Program 10
### The Jolly Corner, by Henry James
An expatriate American who fled
from the Civil War returns thirty-
five years later to a changed and
highly commercialized America that
both attracts and repels him.

Year Produced: 1976
Producer: David B. Appleton
Director/Adaptation: Arthur Barron
Editor: Zina Voynow
Cinematography: Peter Sova
Cast: Fritz Weaver, Salome Jens, Paul
Sparer, Lucy Landau, Sudie Bond,
James Greene, George Backman
Format: 16mm, Video (43:00)

### Program 11
### The Man That Corrupted Hadleyburg, by Mark Twain
A mysterious stranger who was
slighted by the people of Hadleyburg
years ago reappears with a scheme to
test the honesty of the town's leading citizens.

Year Produced: 1980
Producer: Christopher Lukas
Director: Ralph Rosenblum
Adaptation: Mark Harris
Editor: Jay Freund
Cinematography: Mike Fash
Cast: Robert Preston, Fred Gwynne, Tom
Aldredge, Frances Sternhagen
Awards/Festivals: American Film Festival,
Finalist; Pacific Film Festival, Golden
Medallion
Format: 16mm, Video (40:00)

### Program 12
### The Music School, by John Updike
A contemporary writer struggles
during a twenty-four-hour period to
find a focus to his life.

Year Produced: 1974
Producer: Dan McCann
Director/Adaptation/Cinematography: John
Korty
Editor: Richard Chew
Cast: Ron Weyand, Dana Larsson, Tom
Dahlgren, Vera Stough, Frank
Albertson, Elizabeth Huddle Nyberg, Anne
Lawder

Awards: San Francisco Film Festival, Golden
Gate Award; CINE Golden Eagle; John D.
and Catherine T. MacArthur Foundation, a
MacArthur Video Classics Library selection
Format: 16mm, Video (30:00)

### Program 13
### Parker Adderson, Philosopher, by Ambrose Bierce
A Union spy is captured behind
enemy lines at the end of the Civil
War and confronts a weary Confederate general.

Year Produced: 1973
Producer: Ozzie Brown
Director/Adaptation: Arthur Barron
Cinematography: Paul Goldsmith
Cast: Harris Yulin, Douglass Watson,
Darren O'Connor
Format: 16mm, Video (39:00)

### Program 14
### Paul's Case, by Willa Cather
In turn-of-the-century Pittsburgh, a
desperate young man drops out of
high school and, using stolen
money, moves to New York to gain
entry to a world of refinement.

Year Produced: 1979
Producer: Ed Lynch
Director: Lamont Johnson
Adaptation: Ron Cowen
Editor: William Haugse
Cinematography: Larry Pizer
Cast: Eric Roberts, Michael Higgins, Lindsay
Crouse
Awards: American Film Festival, Red
Ribbon; American Library Association,
Selected Film for Young Adults; John D. and
Catherine T. MacArthur Foundation, a
MacArthur Video Classics Library selection
Format: 16mm, Video (55:00)

## Program 15

**Rappaccini's Daughter, by Nathaniel Hawthorne**

In eighteenth-century Padua, Italy, a young scholar falls in love with a beautiful but forbidden woman in a strange garden.

Year Produced: 1979
Producer: Calvin Skaggs
Director: Dezso Magyar
Adaptation: Herbert Hartig
Editor: Jay Freund
Cinematography: Mike Fash
Cast: Kristoffer Tabori, Kathleen Beller, Michael Egan, Leonardo Cimino
Award: Chicago Educational Film Festival, Golden Babe
Format: 16mm, Video (57:00)

## Program 16

**The Sky Is Gray, by Ernest J. Gaines**

In the 1940s, a young black boy from rural Louisiana encounters a variety of people and attitudes when he journeys to Bayonne with his mother, a struggling sharecropper.

Year Produced: 1980
Producer: Whitney Green
Associate Producer: Calvin Skaggs
Director: Stan Lathan
Adaptation: Charles Fuller
Cinematography: Larry Pizer
Cast: Olivia Cole, James Bond III, Margaret Avery, Cleavon Little, Clinton Derricks-Carroll
Awards: American Film Festival, Blue Ribbon and Emily Award; Birmingham International Education Film Festival, Best of Festival; Chicago Educational Film Festival, Golden Babe; Cleveland Instructional Film Festival, Top Twenty Award; American Library Association, Selected Film for Young Adults
Format: 16mm, Video (47:00)

## Program 17

**Soldier's Home, by Ernest Hemingway**

After service in World War I, a soldier returns to Kansas, where he struggles with a pervasive sense of alienation from his neighbors and family.

Year Produced: 1976
Producer: David B. Appleton
Director: Robert Young
Adaptation: Robert Geller
Editor: Ed Beyer
Cinematography: Peter Sova
Cast: Richard Backus, Nancy Marchand, Robert McIlwaine, Lisa Essary, Mark LaMura, Lane Binkley, Robert Hitt, Philip Oxnam, Robert Nichols, Mark Hall, Tom Kubiak, Brian Utman
Awards: Chicago International Film Festival, Silver Hugo; American Film Festival, Final Competition Selection; John D. and Catherine T. MacArthur Foundation, a MacArthur Video Classics Library selection
Format: 16mm, Video (42:00)

Series Production Organization: Learning in Focus, Inc., NY
Years Produced: 1973–80
Series Executive Producer: Robert Geller
Series Award: George Foster Peabody Award
Format: 16mm, Video (all 17 titles)
Series Distributors: Coronet/MTI Film and Video; Monterey Movie Company (home video)

# AUDIO SKETCHES OF AMERICAN WRITERS
*Radio Series (Drama and Documentary)*

This twelve-part series presents American poets, playwrights, fiction writers, and essayists through critical commentary and dramatic presentation of the authors' works.

## Program 1

**Literature of the Black Experience**

This program considers African-American writing from the deep South to New York City, from the Harlem Renaissance to today. Writers included are W.E.B. DuBois, Langston Hughes, Ralph Ellison, Richard Wright, Alice Walker, and Amiri Baraka.

Readings: Christopher Moore, Al Freeman, Amiri Baraka, Carl Lumbly
Commentaries: Julian Bond, Owen Dodson, Alice Walker, Amiri Baraka

## Program 2

**Socio-Political Literature**

This segment explores the many forms that social and political commentary has taken in American literature, including autobiographies, addresses, memoirs, fiction, and poetry. Among the works considered are those by Thomas Jefferson, Margaret Fuller, Henry Adams, Emma Goldman, W.E.B. DuBois, and Theodore Dreiser, as well as literature of the Vietnam War.

Readings: Frances Sternhagen, Jason Robards, Jr., William Hurt, Marsha Jean Kurtz, Christopher Moore, Harris Yulin, Tim O'Brien
Commentaries: Ann Douglas, Otto Freidrich, Leo Marx, Richard Drinnon, Julian Bond, Alfred Kazin, James West, Peter Marin

36

## Program 3
### Cross-Currents of American Life
As American literature has broken away from British traditions, its diversity has increased to include Native American, Jewish, Chicano, and other immigrant experiences. Among the selections are writings by Alfred Kazin, Ralph Ellison, James Welch, and Gary Soto.

Readings: Eli Wallach, Richard Bauer, Laura Esterman, June Gable
Commentaries: Irving Howe, Pietro Di Donato, James Welch, Gary Soto

## Program 4
### Four Generations of Women Poets
Spanning nearly three hundred years of American literature, this program includes sketches of Anne Bradstreet, Emily Dickinson, Marianne Moore, Muriel Rukeyser, Louise Bogan, and Denise Levertov.

Readings: Charlotte Moore, Frances Sternhagen, Diane Wiest, Muriel Rukeyser, Marian Seldes, Denise Levertov
Commentaries: Ann Stanford, Alfred Kazin, Jeffrey Kindley, Carolyn Kizer, Denise Levertov

## Program 5
### Women's Fiction
Selections from the following five writers provide a sense of the wide range of styles of women's fiction of the twentieth century: Edith Wharton, Gertrude Stein, Ellen Glasgow, Carson McCullers, Joyce Carol Oates, and Katherine Anne Porter.

Readings: Ann Stone, Frances Sternhagen, William Hurt, James Cunningham, Susan Sarandon
Commentaries: Cynthia Wolfe, Alfred Kazin, Virginia Spencer Carr, Ellen Friedman, Jane de Mouy

## Programs 6 and 7
### Modern American Poets
These two programs trace important developments in modern American poetry.

Program 6 features Emily Dickinson, James Russell Lowell, Amy Lowell, Wallace Stevens, and Adrienne Rich. Program 7 features Walt Whitman, Stephen Crane, Langston Hughes, Marianne Moore, Archibald MacLeish, and William Carlos Williams.
Readings: Frances Sternhagen, Adrienne Rich, Ed Hermann, Maureen Anderman, Sam Waterston, Mark Hammer, William Atherton, Al Freeman, Diane Wiest, Micahel Moriarty, Michael Tolan
Commentaries: Alfred Kazin, Peter Brazeau, Justin Kaplan, James Culvert, Owen Dodson, Jeffrey Kindley, Archibald MacLeish, Reed Whittemore

## Programs 8–12
### American Prose
The rest of the series surveys twenty of America's most widely read authors and discusses their significance to our literary tradition.

Program 8 features Ernest Hemingway, Stephen Crane, James Jones, and Raymond Chandler.

Program 9 concentrates on Mark Twain, John Dos Passos, Henry Miller, and Jack Kerouac.

Program 10 features Edith Wharton, Thomas Wolfe, Randall Jarrell, and Carson McCullers.

Program 11 includes Herman Melville, Theodore Dreiser, Zane Grey, and Joyce Carol Oates.

Program 12 features Jack London, Eugene O'Neill, James Agee, and Delmore Schwartz.

Readings: Peter Weller, William Atherton, James Jones, Paul Dooley, Len Cariou, Mark Hammer, William Hurt, John Heard, Sam Waterston, Ann Stone, Frances Sternhagen, Tammy Grimes, George Hearn, Harris Yulin, James Cunningham, Henderson Forsythe
Commentaries: Leslie Fiedler, James Culvert, Gloria Jones, Willie Morris, Frank McShane, Alfred Kazin, Dennis McNally, Townsend Luddington, James Atlas, Cynthia Wolfe, Virginia Spencer Carr, Ruth Matthewson, Mary Jarrell, James West, Ellen Friedman, Barbara Gelb, Mia Agee

Series Production Organization: National Public Radio, Washington, DC
Year Produced: 1981 (first broadcast on NPR's *Morning Edition*)
Executive Producer: Joe Gwathmey
Producer/Director: Jo Ellyn Rackleff, Wendy Blair
Writer: Jo Ellyn Rackleff
Narrator: Bob Edwards
Format: Audiocassette
12 (45:00) programs
Distributor: Not currently available

# BECKETT DIRECTS BECKETT: WAITING FOR GODOT AND KRAPP'S LAST TAPE
*Dramatic and Documentary Series*

Beckett Directs Beckett is a three-part program that features dramatizations of *Waiting for Godot* and *Krapp's Last Tape* by Nobel laureate Samuel Beckett (1906–1989). It includes behind the scenes footage, interviews, and a roundtable discussion with scholars and theater professionals.

## Program 1
### Waiting for Godot (1955)
dramatizes the human condition through the plight of Vladimir and Estragon, who pass the time on the road as they wait in vain for the arrival of Godot.

Year Produced: 1988
Producers: Mitchell Lifton, Jean-Pierre Cottet
Associate Producer: John Fuegi
Writer: Samuel Beckett
Director: Walter D. Asmus from the Mise-en-Scène by Samuel Beckett
Writer: Samuel Beckett
Director of Photography: Daniel Vogel
Cinematography: Luc Hervè, Guy Kartagener, Jean-Louis Angelini, Roger Wrona
Editors: Jacques Audoir, Christian Martin
Cast: The San Quentin Drama Workshop, featuring Rick Cluchey, Lawrence Held, Bud Thorpe, Alan Mandell, Louis Beckett Cluchey
Award: American Film and Video Festival, Blue Ribbon
Print Material: Study Guide forthcoming from Smithsonian Press
Format: Video (150:00) on two cassettes
French version with different cast also available

## Program 2
### Krapp's Last Tape (1958)
concerns an old man, who reviews his life by listening to a recording he made at age 39 summarizing another tape made ten or fifteen years earlier. At each stage, Krapp sees the foolishness of his earlier self but not the fool he presently is.

Year Produced: 1988
Executive Producer: John Fuegi
Producers: Mitchell Lifton, Jean-Pierre Cottet
Director: Walter D. Asmus from the Mise-en-Scène by Samuel Beckett
Director of Photography: Daniel Vogel
Cinematography: Tom Arnold, Francis Guilbert, Jean-Marc Zilbering
Editor: Christian Martin
Cast: Rick Cluchey
Print Material: Study Guide available
Format: Video (60:00)
French version with different cast also available

## Program 3
### Beckett and the Television
This is a roundtable discussion with scholars about Beckett's ideas for the staging of the plays and about the nature of "television texts."

Year Produced: 1988
Producers: Mitchell Lifton, John Fuegi, Jean-Pierre Cottet
Director: Jacques Audoir
Director of Photography: Daniel Vogel
Cinematography: Luc Hervé, Guy Kartagener, Jean-Louis Angelini, Roger Wrona
Editor: Christian Martin
Moderator: John Fuegi, University of Maryland, College Park
Participants: Herbert Blau, theater director, University of Wisconsin-Milwaukee; Dr. Martin Esslin, Stanford University; Dr. Robert Corrigan, University of Texas, Dallas; and Dr. Kathleen Woodward, University of Wisconsin-Milwaukee
Print Material: Study Guide available
Format: Video (27:00)
Available only as part of Beckett Directs Beckett package

Production Organizations: University of Maryland Visual Press, College Park, MD, in association with WGBH, Boston, MA; Camèras Continentales, La SEPT, Société Française de Production (SFP), and FR3, Paris, France; and Radioteleviseo Portuguesa-E.P. (RTP), Lisbon, Portugal
Series Producers: Mitchell Lifton, Jean-Pierre Cottet, John Fuegi
Format: Video (see individual listings)
Distributor: Smithsonian Institution Press

# THE BECKETT FESTIVAL OF RADIO PLAYS
## Radio Series (Drama and Documentary)
This five-part series presents American premiere productions of all the extant radio plays of Samuel Beckett (1906–1989). Each drama is introduced by a host and accompanied by a short interpretive documentary that includes interviews and discussions.

## Program 1
### All That Fall (1957)
describes Maddy Rooney's laborious trip to the Boghill railway station to meet her blind husband and their return home together.

Production Organizations: Soundscape, Inc., Alexandria, VA; Voices International, New York, NY; and RIAS, Berlin, Germany
Year Produced: 1986
Project Director: Louise Cleveland
Project Originator: Martha Fehsenfeld
Director/Producer: Everett C. Frost
Associate Producer: Faith Wilding
Writer: Samuel Beckett
Studio Sound Effects: Charles Potter
Recording Engineer: Mike Moran
Production Engineer: David Rapkin
Host: Henry Strozier
Cast: Billie Whitelaw, David Warrilow, Alvin Epstein, Jerome Kilty, George Bartenieff, Susan Willis
Commentary: Desmond Briscoe, Everett Frost, Billie Whitelaw, Richard Ellman, Linda Ben-Zvi, Enoch Brater, Hersh Zeifman, David Hesla
Awards: New York International Radio Festival, Gold Medal, Best Drama Special; Corporation for Public Broadcasting, Honorable Mention, Arts and Humanities Programming
Format: Audiocassette (120:00)
2 (60:00) tapes: drama (89:00); documentary (31:00)

## Program 2
### Embers (1959)
Henry sits on the beach talking to his dead father who has drowned and does not answer, and to his wife Ada, who does.

Production Organization: Voices International, New York, NY
Year Produced: 1989
Director/Producer: Everett C. Frost
Documentary Producer: Charles Potter
Associate Producer: Faith Wilding
Writer: Samuel Beckett
Panel Engineer: Peter Novis
Sea Sound Effects: Liam Saurin
Recorded Sound Effects: Bert Coules

38

Sound Effects: Mike Etherden
Production Engineer: Stephen Erickson
Host: Henry Strozier
Cast: Barry McGovern, Billie Whitelaw
Commentary: Barbara Bray, Barry
McGovern, Ruby Cohn, Linda Ben-Zvi
Award: New York International Radio
Festival, Gold Medal
Format: Audiocassette (60:00)
1 tape: drama (48:00); documentary (12:00)

### Program 3
### Words and Music (1962)
Words, called Bob, and Music,
called Joe, are forced to collaborate
by the club-wielding Croak and
under duress they produce two
exquisite lyric poems.

Production Organizations: Voices
International, New York, NY, and WDR,
Cologne, Germany
Year Produced: 1986
Director/Producer: Everett C. Frost
Documentary and Sound Effects Producer:
Charles Potter
Associate Producer: Faith Wilding
Writer: Samuel Beckett
Recording and Production Engineer: Mike
Moran
Composer: Morton Feldman
Music: The Bowery Ensemble, conducted by
Nils Vigeland
Host: Henry Strozier
Cast: David Warrilow, Alvin Epstein
Commentary: Morton Feldman, Everett
Frost, Linda Ben-Zvi, Maurice Beja
Format: Audiocassette (60:00)
1 tape: drama (40:00); documentary and
commentary (20:00)

### Program 4
### Cascando (1963)
In this play, an Opener "opens" and
"closes" two characters; Voice des-
perately promises to tell a story he
can finish; and Music equally
struggles to create a finished compo-
sition.

Production Organizations: Voices
International, New York, NY, and WDR,
Cologne, Germany
Year Produced: 1989
Director/Producer: Everett C. Frost
Documentary Producer: Charles Potter
Associate Producer: Faith Wilding
Recording and Production Engineers: Mike
Moran, Tony May, Stephen Erickson
Host: Henry Strozier
Cast: Fred Neumann, Alvin Epstein
Commentary: Alvin Epstein, William Kraft,
Thomas Bishop, Porter Abbot
Composer: William Kraft
Music: Speculum Musicae, conducted by
William Kraft
Format: Audiocassette (60:00)
1 tape: drama (18:00); documentary (12:00);
discussion by Beckett scholars (30:00)

### Program 5
### Rough for Radio II (1976)
An animator, assisted by a stenogra-
pher and the whip-wielding mute
character Dick, has the task of elicit-
ing from Fox some unknown testimony of unknown significance.

Production Organization: Voices
International, New York, NY
Year Produced: 1989
Director/Producer: Everett C. Frost
Documentary & Sound Effects Producer:
Charles Potter
Associate Producer: Faith Wilding
Recording Engineer: Mike Moran
Production Engineer: Stephen Erickson
Host: Henry Strozier
Cast: W. Dennis Hunt, Amanda Plummer,
Barry McGovern, Charles Potter
Commentary: Barry McGovern, Everett
Frost, Rosette Lamont
Format: Audiocassette (60:00)
1 tape: drama (24:00); documentary (6:00);
discussion by Beckett scholars (30:00)

Series Originator: Martha Fehsenfeld
Project Director for The Beckett Festival of
Radio Plays: Everett C. Frost
Project Director for All That Fall: Louise
Cleveland
Series Award: Gabriel Award
Series Format: Audiocassette (360:00)
Five programs on six tapes: All That Fall, 2
(60:00); Programs 2–5 (60:00 each)
Distributor: Pacifica Program Service/Radio
Archive

## THE CAFETERIA
### Drama
The Cafeteria is an adaptation of a
story by Isaac Bashevis Singer
(1904–1991), which portrays the
experience of two refugees in the
United States, a European-born
writer and a young Holocaust survivor. (see also Isaac in America)

Production Organizations: Amram Nowak
Associates, Inc., and Isaac in America
Foundation, New York, NY
Year Produced: 1983 (first broadcast on
*American Playhouse*)
Executive Producer/Director: Amram
Nowak
Associate Producer: Kirk Simon
Adaptation: Ernest Kinoy
Cinematography: Jerry Pantzer
Editor: Jason Rosenfield
Cast: Zohra Lampert, Bob Dishy, Morris
Carnovsky
Awards/Festivals: CINE Golden Eagle;
American Film Festival, Honorable
Mention; San Francisco Film Festival; San
Francisco Jewish Film Festival; John D. and
Catherine T. MacArthur Foundation, a
MacArthur Video Classics Library selection
Format: Video (58:00)
Distributor: Direct Cinema Limited

## CARL SANDBURG: ECHOES
## AND SILENCES
### Documentary and Drama
Through a mix of dramatic
vignettes, archival material, and
poetry readings, this film explores
the life of Carl Sandburg (1878–
1967), American poet, folk singer,
novelist, journalist, social activist,
and biographer of Lincoln.

Production Organization: WNET/13, New York, NY
Year Produced: 1982
Executive Producer: Jac Venza
Producer/Director: Perry Miller Adato
Writer: Paul Shyre
Music: Scott Kuney
Cast: John Cullum, Frances Conroy, Michael Higgins
Award: Directors Guild of America, Pinnacle Award for Television Documentary; Matrix Award for Broadcasting; Women in Communication, Achievement in Television Documentary
Format: 16mm, Video (120:00)
Distributor: Not currently available

## CLASSIC THEATRE: THE HUMANITIES IN DRAMA AND CLASSIC THEATRE PREVIEWS
### Dramatic and Documentary Series

Classic Theatre: The Humanities in Drama is a BBC-produced series of thirteen great English and European plays from the Renaissance to the twentieth century. All the dramas are accompanied by half-hour documentaries which, taken together, form a series called Classic Theatre Previews. The Endowment supported the selection, acquisition, and broadcast of the BBC plays and production of the accompanying documentaries.

### Program 1
### The Tragedy of Macbeth (1606), by William Shakespeare

Set in Scotland, this play is a classic study of ambition, murder, and remorse.

Producer: Cedric Messina
Director: John Gorrie
Cast: Eric Porter, Janet Suzman, John Alderton, Michael Goodliffe, John Thaw, John Woodvine
Classic Theatre Preview with Shakespeare scholar S. Schoenbaum of Northwestern University.

### Program 2
### Edward the Second (1593), by Christopher Marlowe

King Edward, a confused, weak, and foolish man ruled by personal passions, is ennobled in a horrifying death.

Producer: Mark Shivas
Director: Tony Robertson
Cast: Ian McKellen, Timothy West, Diane Fletcher, James Laurenson
Classic Theatre Preview with Clifford Leech of the University of Connecticut at Storrs.

### Program 3
### The Duchess of Malfi (c. 1614), by John Webster

Obsessed by his love for the Duchess, her brother Ferdinand imprisons her and subjects her to mental torture after she marries her steward.

Producer: Cedric Messina
Director: James MacTaggart
Cast: Eileen Atkins, Michael Bryant, Charles Kay, T.P. McKenna, Gary Bond
Classic Theatre Preview with Michael Goldman of Queens College.

### Program 4
### Paradise Restored

Based on the life and work of the English poet and author John Milton (1608–1674), this dramatization portrays some of the personal triumphs and defeats that lie behind *Paradise Lost*, his epic poem on the fall of man.

Director/Writer: Don Taylor
Cast: John Neville, Polly James, Anne Stallybrass
Classic Theatre Preview with Judith A. Kates of Harvard University.

### Program 5
### She Stoops to Conquer (1773), by Oliver Goldsmith

When Young Marlow, a bashful young man who feels at ease only with serving girls, mistakes Mr. Hardcastle's house for an inn, Miss Hardcastle takes advantage of the situation by posing as a barmaid.

Producer: Cedric Messina
Director: Michael Elliott
Cast: Sir Ralph Richardson, Tom Courtenay, Thora Hird, Juliet Mills, Elaine Taylor
Classic Theatre Preview with William Appleton of Columbia University.

### Program 6
### Candide (1759), by Voltaire

This is a dramatic adaptation of the philosophical novel which satirizes the optimistic creed of Leibnitz: "All is for the best in this best of all possible worlds," through the story of young Candide, and his series of misadventures.

Producer: Cedric Messina
Director/Adaptation/Translation: James MacTaggart
Cast: Frank Finlay, Ian Ogilvy
Classic Theatre Preview with Georges May of Yale University.

### Program 7
### The Rivals (1775), by Richard Brinsley Sheridan

This comedy of double identity features the legendary Mrs. Malaprop.

Producer: Cedric Messina
Director: Basil Coleman
Cast: John Alderton, Jeremy Brett, Andrew Cruikshank, Beryl Reid, Jenny Linden, T.P. McKenna
Classic Theatre Preview with William Appleton of Columbia University.

**40**

*Program 8*

**The Wild Duck (1884), by Henrik Ibsen**

A guilt-ridden loner and idealist sets out to rehabilitate an impoverished but basically compatible family, destroying the props of illusion that sustain their common existence.

Producer: Cedric Messina
Director: Alan Bridges
Translation: Rolf Fjelde
Cast: Denholm Elliott, Derek Godfrey, Mark Digham, Rosemary Leach, John Robinson, Jenny Agutter
Classic Theatre Preview with Rolf Fjelde of Pratt Institute and the Juilliard School of Music.

*Program 9*

**Hedda Gabler (1890), by Henrik Ibsen**

Married to a pedantic scholar for whom she has no affection and living in a small, slow, backward Norwegian town of the 1860s, Hedda devises schemes for subtly asserting power over the people who come into her life.

Producer: Cedric Messina
Director: Waris Hussein
Translation: Michael Meyer
Cast: Janet Suzman, Ian McKellen, Tom Bell, Jane Asher, Dorothy Reynolds
Classic Theatre Preview with Eva Le Gallienne, actress and translator of Ibsen as well as cofounder of the American Repertory Theater.

*Program 10*

**Trelawny of the "Wells" (1898), by Arthur Wing Pinero**

In this play about the social acceptability of the stage, the actress heroine breaks her engagement to a young aristocrat to return to the theater. Undaunted, he follows and becomes an actor.

Producer: Cedric Messina
Director: Herbert Wise
Cast: John Alderton, Moira Taylor, Roland Culver, Elaine Taylor, Lally Bowers, Graham Crowden, Ian Ogilvy, Rachel Kempson, Elizabeth Seal
Classic Theatre Preview with Jane W. Stedman of Roosevelt University.

*Program 11*

**The Three Sisters (1901), by Anton Chekhov**

Through the experience of three sisters and their suitors, this play explores the need for illusion as a means of coping with a profoundly dispiriting reality.

Producer: Gerald Savory
Director: Cedric Messina
Translator: Elisaveta Fen
Cast: Janet Suzman, Eileen Atkins, Michele Dotrice, Anthony Hopkins, Michael Bryant, Joss Ackland, Sarah Badel, Ronald Hines, Richard Pearson
Classic Theatre Preview with Victor Erlich of Yale University.

*Program 12*

**The Playboy of the Western World (1907), by John Millington Synge**

A playboy claims to have killed his tyrannical father and is lionized by the villagers for his boldness until his father arrives to reclaim his errant son.

Producer: Cedric Messina
Director: Alan Gibson
Cast: John Hurt, Sinead Cusack, Pauline Delany, Joe Lynch, Donal McCann
Classic Theatre Preview with Ann Saddlemyer of the University of Toronto.

*Program 13*

**Mrs. Warren's Profession (1893), by George Bernard Shaw**

To the horror of her daughter, Mrs. Warren runs a chain of brothels in the capitals of Europe because it offers good hours, good money, and a chance for advancement otherwise unavailable to women.

Producer: Cedric Messina
Director: Herbert Wise
Cast: Coral Browne, Penelope Wilton, James Grout, Derek Godfrey, Robert Powell, Richard Pearson
Classic Theatre Preview with Dan H. Laurence, literary adviser to the estate of George Bernard Shaw.

*For Classic Theatre Previews and American Presentation of the Programs:*
Production Organization: WGBH, Boston, MA
Year Classic Theatre Acquired & Previews Produced: 1975
Project Director: Michael Rice
Series Producer: Joan Sullivan
Associate Producer: Monia Joblin
Director: David Atwood
Researcher: Elizabeth Deane
Music Composed/Conducted by: Joseph Payne
Videography: Bill Charrette, Dick Holden, F.X. Lane, Larry LeCain, Greg MacDonald, Lee Smith, Skip Warehan, Bob Wilson
Format: Video
Dramas: Programs 1,11 (150:00); Programs 2,3,5,7–10,12,13 (120:00); Programs 4,6 (90:00)
Documentary Previews: 13 (28:00) programs
Distributor: Films, Inc./PMI (plays only available)

# CREELEY

*Documentary*

Shot over a three-year period, this film looks at the life and work of American poet Robert Creeley (b.1926).

Production Organization: Documentary
Research, Inc., Buffalo, NY
Year Produced: 1988
Producers/Directors/Writers/Editors: Diane
Christian, Bruce Jackson
Cinematography: Bruce Jackson
Interviews: Alan Ginsberg, Ed Dorn, Diane
Di Prima, Philip Whalen, Stan Brakhage,
and others
Format: 16mm, Video (59:00)
Distributor: Documentary Research, Inc.

## DEAD SOULS

*Dramatic Radio Series*

This nine-part dramatization of the
novel by Nikolai Gogol (1809–1852)
follows the comic life of a Russian
man and his preposterous scheme to
enrich himself.

Production Organization: Globe Radio
Repertory, Seattle, WA
Year Produced: 1987
Producers/Writers: Jean Sherrard, John
Siscoe
Director: Jean Sherrard
Cast: John Gilbert, Ted D'Arms, Marjorie
Nelson, John Aylward, Mark Drusch
Commentary: Donald Farger, Harvard
University; Willis Konick, University of
Washington
Format: Audiocassette
9 (30:00) programs
Distributor: University of Washington Press

## DON QUIXOTE DE LA MANCHA

*Dramatic Radio Series*

This thirteen-part adaptation of the
novel by Miguel de Cervantes
(1547–1616) tells the story of an
impoverished country gentleman
who is convinced by reading tales of
chivalry that he should become a
knight-errant.

Production Organization: Globe Radio
Repertory, Seattle, WA
Year Produced: 1985
Producers/Writers: Jean Sherrard, John
Siscoe
Director: Jean Sherrard
Cast: Ted D'Arms, John Aylward, Glenn
Mazen, Marjorie Nelson, John Gilbert
Print Material: Study guide (24 pages) by
Professors George Shipley, University of
Washington; and Carrol Johnson,
University of California, Los Angeles
Format: Video
13 (30:00) programs
Distributor: University of Washington Press

## THE EDITH WHARTON SERIES

*Dramatic Series*

This three-part series presents the
life and work of Edith Wharton
(1862–1937), whose long and prolific
career included novels, short stories,
novellas, poetry, travel books, and
memoirs.

### *Program 1*
**The House of Mirth**

dramatizes Wharton's novel about
Lily Bart, a charming but penniless
member of turn-of-the-century New
York society who is intent on marry-
ing a rich and socially prominent
man.

Executive Producer: Jack Willis
Coproducers: Daniel A. Bohr, Dorothy
Cullman
Director: Adrian Hall
Adaptation: Adrian Hall, Richard Cumming
Cinematography: Paul Goldsmith, Hart
Perry
Editor: Charlotte Zwerin
Cast: Geraldine Chaplin, William Atherton

### *Program 2*
**Summer**

is the story of seventeen-year-old
Charity Royall's early disillusion-
ment with life followed by her
accomodation to reality.

Executive Producer: Jack Willis
Coproducers: Daniel A. Bohr, Dorothy
Cullman
Director/Editor: Deszo Magyar
Adaptation: Charles Gaines
Cinematography: Michael Fash
Cast: Diane Lane, Michael Ontkean, John
Cullum

### *Program 3*
**Looking Back**

is a dramatic retrospective of Edith
Wharton's life.

Executive Producer: Jack Willis
Coproducers: Dorothy Cullman, Sam Paul
Director: Kirk Browning
Writer: Steve Lawson
Cinematography: Francis Kenny
Cast: Kathleen Widdoes, John Cullum,
Richard Woods, John McMartin, Stephen
Collins

Production Organization: Cinelit, Inc.,
Santa Monica, CA
Year Produced: 1982 (first broadcast on
*Great Performances*)
Series Executive Producer: Jack Willis
Format: Video
Programs 1,2 (90:00), Program 3 (60:00)
Distributor: Cinelit

## EUGENE O'NEILL: A GLORY OF GHOSTS

*Drama and Documentary*

Eugene O'Neill: A Glory of Ghosts is
a two-part exploration of the life
and work of Eugene Gladstone
O'Neill (1888–1953) that blends segments of his plays with archival
footage, photographs, and interviews.

42

Production Organization: WNET/13, New York, NY
Year Produced: 1985
Executive Producers: Susan Lacy, Jac Venza
Producers: Perry Miller Adato, Megan Callaway
Director: Perry Miller Adato
Writer: Paul Shyre
Cinematography: Robert Baldwin
Editor: Jason Rosenfield
Cast: Jeffrey DeMunn as the voice of O'Neill, Zoe Caldwell, Colleen Dewhurst, Frances Conroy, Frank Converse, Paul Coombe, Blythe Danner, Joel Fabiani, Bette Henritze, Tom Hulce, Tony Lobianco, James Naughton, Jason Robards, Mario Van Peebles
Awards/Festivals: Directors Guild of America, Top Prize in Television Documentary/Actuality Category; International Film and Television Festival of New York, Silver Award
Format: 16mm, Video (150:00)
Part 1 (60:00), Part 2 (90:00)
Distributor: Not currently available

## EUGENE O'NEILL: JOURNEY INTO GENIUS

### Drama

Eugene O'Neill: Journey Into Genius dramatizes the early years of O'Neill's life, from his expulsion from Princeton at the age of eighteen to his first triumph as a dramatist in his early thirties.

Production Organizations: Lumiere Productions, Inc., New York, NY, and Connecticut Public Television
Year Produced: 1987 (first broadcast on *American Playhouse*)
Producer/Director: Calvin Skaggs
Adaptation: Lanie Robertson
Cinematography: Frank Prinzi
Editor: Sonia Polansky
Coproducer: Terry Benes
Associate Producer: Stephanie Keys
Cast: Matthew Modine, Dylan Baker, Kate Burton, Jeffrey DeMunn, Chris Cooper, Jane Kaczmarek
Format: Video (55:00)
Distributor: Caridi Entertainment

## FACES, MIRRORS, MASKS: TWENTIETH-CENTURY LATIN AMERICAN FICTION

### Radio Series (Documentary and Drama)

This series depicts the world and imagination of thirteen of Latin America's most esteemed twentieth-century authors.

### Program 1

**Gabriel García Márquez: The Solitude of Latin America**
features dramatic readings as well as interviews recorded in the author's home town of Aracataca, Colombia.

Producers: Keith Talbot, Lois Fishman

### Program 2

**Jorge Luis Borges: The Laughter of the Universe**
looks at the author's Argentine childhood and the influence of his father's library.

Producer: Robert Montiegel

### Program 3

**José María Argüedas: The Death of a Dancer**
examines Arguedas's divided allegiance between the Peru of the Quechua-speaking Indians and the Peru of the Spaniards.

Producers: Jay Allison, Katie Davis

### Program 4

**Guillermo Cabrera Infante: Memories of an Invented City**
reveals the author's musical and cinematic influences and how these put him at odds with the leaders of the Cuban revolution, who were more interested in social realism.

Producers: The Kitchen Sisters (Nikki Silva and Davia Nelson)

### Program 5

**Miguel Angel Asturias: The President and Other Myths**
considers the late Guatemalan writer's uneasy political relationship with his country's dictators.

Producers: Tom López, Marcelo Montealegre

### Program 6

**Jorge Amado: The Ballad of Bahia**
features Amado and his close friend, singer Harry Belafonte, discussing the writer's personal attachment to the people of Bahia, who are the subjects of his work.

Producers: Robert Malesky, Alfredo Cruz

### Program 7

**Carlos Fuentes: Beneath the Mask**
considers the Mexican diplomat/writer's work and the role of the novelist as historian.

Producers: Robert Malesky, Alfredo Cruz

### Program 8

**Luis Rafael Sánchez: Life as a Phenomenal Thing**
uncovers this Puerto Rican writer's celebration of the popular culture and forms of speech that flourish in San Juan.

Producers: Ignacio Acosta, Julio Marzan

### Program 9

**Clarice Lispector: The Poetry of Silence**
features actress Colleen Dewhurst's portrayal of the writer who revolutionized Brazilian fiction by combining a unique poetic style and a deeply introspective philosophy.

Producer: Frieda Werden

*Program 10*

**Juan Carlos Onetti: The Atmosphere of a Brief Life**

reviews the work of the writer, often called the "Faulkner of Uruguay," whose imaginary town of Santa María is inhabited by sinister and decadent characters.

Producers: Larry Massett, Jose McMurray

*Program 11*

**Alejo Carpentier: The Marvel of the Real**

features the late Cuban novelist's vision of the Americas as a land where Indian, African, and European mythologies merge.

Producers: Tom López, Elizabeth Pérez-Luna

*Program 12*

**Juan Rulfo: A Kind of Silence**

introduces the shy, mysterious author whose only two books changed Mexican writing.

Producers: Keith Talbot, Lois Fishman

*Program 13*

**Elena Poniatowska: The Voice of the Powerless**

shows how the popular Mexican author and journalist chronicles the heretofore ignored lives of her country's oppressed.

Producer: Freida Werden

Production Organization: National Public Radio, Washington, DC
Year Produced: 1984
Project Director: Frank Tavares
Executive Producer: Jo Ellyn Rackleff
Series Producer: Frieda Werden
Cast: Héctor Elizondo (Programs 3, 12); Colleen Dewhurst (9); Richard Bauer (10); Edward James Olmos, Meredith Monk, Charles Ludlam, Lupe Ontiveros (12); and others

Format: Audiocassette
13 (30:00) programs
Potentially offensive language in programs 1,4,13
Distributor: Not currently available

# FEAR AND THE MUSE: THE STORY OF ANNA AKHMATOVA
## *Documentary*

This program chronicles the life and times of one of the U.S.S.R.'s most celebrated cultural figures, the poet Anna Akhmatova (1899–1966), who served as the poetic "conscience of Russia" during the years of Stalinist repression.

Production Organization: New York Center for Visual History, New York, NY
Year Produced: 1990
Executive Producer/Director/Writer: Jill Janows
Coproducer: Molly Ornati
Cinematography: Richard P. Rogers
Editor: Jon Neuburger
Narrator: Christopher Reeve
Cast: Claire Bloom as the voice of Anna Akhmatova
Format: Video (58:00)
Distributor: New York Center for Visual History

# GO TELL IT ON THE MOUNTAIN
## *Drama*

Based on a semi-autobiographical novel by James Baldwin (1924–1987), this drama tells the story of John Grimes, a young black teenager who struggles to rid himself of a past that has left his family emotionally crippled.

Production Organization: Learning in Focus, Inc., New York, NY
Year Produced: 1984
Executive Producer: Robert Geller
Producer: Calvin Skaggs
Associate Producers: Sue Jett, Tony Mark
Director: Stan Lathan
Adaptation: Gus Edwards, Leslie Lee
Cinematography: Hiro Narita
Editor: Jay Freund
Cast: Paul Winfield, Rosalind Cash, James Bond III, Olivia Cole
Awards/Festivals: American Film and Video Festival, Blue Ribbon; San Francisco International Film Festival, Golden Gate Award, Best Television Feature of the Year; FILMEX (Los Angeles); Telluride International Film Festival; CINE Golden Eagle; *New York Times*, Best American Television Film of the Year; *Time* magazine, one of "Ten Best of 1985"; John D. and Catherine T. MacArthur Foundation, a MacArthur Video Classics Library selection; Berlin Film Festival; New Delhi Film Festival; London Film Festival
Format: 16mm (97:00)
Distributor: Films, Inc./P.M.I.

# HARD TIMES
## *Drama*

An adaptation of the novel by Charles Dickens, this four-part series centers on two men caught up in a utilitarian philosophy of hard work and hard facts, with no time for imagination or human warmth.

Production Organizations: WNET/13, New York, NY, in coproduction with Granada Television/U.K.
Year Produced: 1977 (first broadcast on *Great Performances*)
Project Director for WNET: Robert B. Kotlowitz
Producer: Peter Eckesley
Producers for *Great Performances*: Ronald F. Maxwell, Jac Venza
Director: John Irvin
Adaptation: Arthur Hopcraft
Cinematography: Ray Goode, Andy Stephens
Editor: Anthony Ham
Cast: Patrick Allen, Timothy West, Alan Dobie, Jacqueline Tong, Michelle Dibnah, Rosalie Crutchley, Barbara Ewing, Ursula Howells, Richard Wren

44

Postscripts: Lord Asa Briggs, Worcester College, Oxford; and Professor George Ford, University of Rochester
Format: 16mm, Video
4 (60:00) programs
Distributor: Not currently available

## HERMAN MELVILLE: DAMNED IN PARADISE

*Documentary*

This film tracks the personal and intellectual experiences that influenced such works as *Moby-Dick* and *Billy Budd*.

Production Organization: The Film Company, Washington, DC
Year Produced: 1985
Executive Producer/Director: Robert D. Squier
Producers: Robert D. Squier, Karen Thomas
Writers: George Wolfe, Robert D. Squier, Patricia Ward, Carter Eskew
Narrator: John Huston
Cast: F. Murray Abraham as Herman Melville
Award: Chicago International Film Festival, Gold Plaque
Format: 16mm, Video (90:00)
Distributor: Pyramid Film and Video

## THE HOLLOW BOY

*Drama*

An adaptation of a short story by Hortense Calisher, The Hollow Boy tells of the friendship between two young men whose families live in apartments that face each other across a courtyard in New York City in 1936. (see also Love and Other Sorrows, Pigeon Feathers, and The Revolt of Mother)

Production Organization: Learning in Focus, Larchmont, NY
Year Produced: 1990 (first broadcast on *American Playhouse*)
Executive Producers: Robert Geller, Brian Benlifer
Producer: David Kappes
Writer: Jay Neugeboren
Cinematography Declan Quinn
Editor: Sandra Adair
Cast: Alexis Arquette, Marty Finkelstein, Jerry Stiller, Kathleen Widdoes
Format: 16mm, Video (54:46)
Distributor: Coronet/MTI Film and Video

## ISAAC IN AMERICA: A JOURNEY WITH ISSAC BASHEVIS SINGER

*Documentary and Drama*

This program explores aspects of the life and work of Nobel laureate Isaac Bashevis Singer (1904–1991), combining documentary footage with dramatized scenes from "A Day in Coney Island" which describe the author's first impressions of America. (see also The Cafeteria)

Production Organizations: Amram Nowak Associates, Inc.; and the Isaac in America Foundation, New York, NY
Year Produced: 1985 (first broadcast on *American Masters*)
Executive Producer: Manya Starr
Producer: Kirk Simon
Director: Amram Nowak
Cinematography: Jerry Pantzer with Greg Andracke, Brian Kellman, David Lerner, Kirk Simon, Burleigh Wartes
Editor: Riva Friefield
Story Narrated by: Judd Hirsch
Awards/Festivals: Academy Award nominee, Best Documentary Feature; American Film and Video Festival, Finalist; National Educational Film and Video Festival, Gold Apple; New York Film Festival; CINE Golden Eagle; San Francisco Film Festival, Golden Gate Award; Denver Film Festival; Sundance Film Festival; Moscow Jewish Film Festival; Berlin Film Festival; San Francisco Jewish Film Festival; Nyon

(Switzerland) Film Festival, Sestere d'Argent (Second Grand Prize); U.S.A. (Dallas) Film Festival
Format: 16mm, Video (58:00)
Distributor: Direct Cinema Limited

## JAMES BALDWIN: THE PRICE OF THE TICKET

*Documentary*

This film examines the life and work of the American writer and civil rights activist, James Baldwin (1924–1987).

Production Organizations: Nobody Knows Productions in association with Maysles Films, Inc., WNET/New York, and American Masters
Year Produced: 1989 (first broadcast on *American Masters*)
Executive Producers: Albert Maysles, Susan Lacy
Producers: Karen Thorsen, William Miles
Coproducer: Douglas K. Dempsey
Director: Karen Thorsen
Writers: Karen Thorsen, Douglas K. Dempsey
Associate Producers: Joy Birdsong, Joe Wood
Cinematography: David Lenzer
Editors: Steve Olswang, Sandra Guthrie
Awards: 17 awards including The Academy of Motion Pictures, Top Ten Documentary; The National Educational Film and Video Festival, Gold Apple; CINE Golden Eagle; Festival dei Popoli, Florence, Italy, Premio di Ricerca; Chicago International Film Festival, Silver Hugo; Nyon (Switzerland) Documentary Film Festival, Silver Sesterce; American Film and Video Festival, Red Ribbon; Black Filmmakers Hall of Fame Award; Atlanta Film Festival, Special Jury Award; Sydney (Australia) Film Festival, Audience Approval Award; Sinking Creek Film and Video Festival, Sinking Creek Award; North Carolina Film Festival, Documentary Award; International Film and Television Festival (New York), Finalist; Banff International Television Festival (Alberta, Canada), Finalist; Sundance Film Festival, Special Tribute; Sundance in Tokyo Film Festival, Special Tribute, one of the "Ten Best American Independent Films" from the past two years; Istanbul (Turkey) International Film Festival, Special Tribute
Festivals: Over 50 film festivals worldwide

including the Margaret Mead Film Festival; Virginia Festival of American Film; INPUT Conference; London International Film Festival, Cinema du Reel, Paris; International Filmfestspiele, Berlin, West Germany; Weekly Mail Film Festival, Johannesburg, South Africa; International Documentary Film Festival, Vienna, Prague, and Budapest
Format: Video (87:00)
Distributors: California Newsreel; NKP, c/o Maysles Films, Inc.

## JOSEPH BRODSKY: A MADDENING SPACE

*Documentary*

In this profile of the Nobel Prize-winning poet, the artist and others speak about his work, his life in the Soviet Union, and his experience as an exile.

Production Organization: New York Center for Visual History, New York, NY
Year Produced: 1988
Executive Producer/Director/Writer: Lawrence Pitkethly
Producer: Sasha Alpert
Cinematography: Yuri Neyman
Editor: Richard Smigielski
Narrator: Jason Robards
Format: Video (58:00)
Distributor: New York Center for Visual History

## KATHERINE ANNE PORTER: THE EYE OF MEMORY

*Documentary and Drama*

Featuring a full dramatization of her short story, "The Grave," and excerpts from "The Witness" and "The Circus," this program shows the central Texas milieu that shaped Porter's writing.

Production Organization: KERA-TV, Dallas, TX
Year Produced: 1986 (first broadcast on *American Masters*)
Executive Producer: Patricia P. Perini
Producer: Calvin Skaggs
Director: Ken Harrison
Writers: Jordan Pecile, Ken Harrison
Cinematography: Bert Guthrie
Editor: Jay Freund
Cast: Dina Chandel, Paul Winfield, Bill Irwin, Yankton Hatten
Commentary: Eudora Welty, Robert Penn Warren, Eleanor Clark, Peter Taylor, Joan Givner, Paul Porter
Format: Video (58:00)
Distributor: Films for the Humanities and Sciences

## LOVE AND OTHER SORROWS

*Drama*

This adaptation of Harold Brodkey's short story "First Love and Other Sorrows" looks at the effect of courtship on an American family in 1950. (see also The Hollow Boy, Pigeon Feathers, and The Revolt of Mother)

Production Organization: Learning in Focus, Inc., New York, NY
Year Produced: 1987 (first broadcast on *American Playhouse*)
Executive Producer: Robert Geller
Producer: Brian Benlifer
Director: Steven Gomer
Adaptation: Dick Goldberg
Cinematography: Edwin Lynch
Editor: Pam Wise
Cast: Elizabeth Franz, Stephen Mailer, Haviland Morris, Christopher Collet, Sheila Ball, Tim Ransom, Spencer Garrett
Award: Houston International Film Festival, Gold Award
Format: Video (56:09)
Distributor: Coronet/MTI Film and Video

## MADAME BOVARY

*Dramatic Radio Series*

Madame Bovary is a thirteen-part radio dramatization of the novel by Gustave Flaubert (1821–1880), a chronicle of the rise and fall of Emma Bovary, the Norman bourgeoise whose dreams of romantic love remain unfulfilled.

Production Organization: Globe Radio Repertory, Seattle, WA
Year Produced: 1988
Executive Producers: John P. Siscoe, Jean R. Sherrard
Director: Jean R. Sherrard
Writers: John P. Siscoe, Jean R. Sherrard
Sound Design/Editor: Jerry Thompson
Narrator: Glenn Mazen
Translation: Francis Steegmuller
Cast: Mary Ann Owen, Bill Terkuile, Ted D'Arms Frank Corrado, Dan Renner, John Aylward, John Gilbert, Karen Cody, Michael MacRae, Michael Santo, Marjorie Nelson
Commentary: Roger Shattuck, Boston University
Format: Audiocassette
13 (30:00) programs
Distributor: Globe Radio Repertory

## THE MAHABHARATA

*Dramatic Series*

Based on a Sanskrit poem written more than two thousand years ago, The Mahabharata is a three-part dramatization of a feud of royal succession fought in northern India during the first millenium B.C. One of India's two major epics, it combines military and spiritual conflicts to instruct on dharma, the moral order in the universe, and includes the Bhagavad Gita, a mystical dialogue between a warrior and the god Krishna. Peter Brook, who first brought the epic to the West in a nine-hour stage version, provides the introductions.

45

**46**

Production Organizations: Brooklyn
Academy of Music, Brooklyn, NY, in
association with Les Productions du 3eme
Etage, Le Centre National du Cinema, Paris,
France, Channel 4/U.K., and Reiner Moritz
Associates, Ltd.
Year Produced: 1988 (originally presented as
a six-hour miniseries on *Great
Performances*)
Executive Producers: Michael Birkett,
Michael Kustow, Harvey Lichtenstein
Producer: Michel Propper
Coproducers: Ed Myerson, Rachel Tabori,
Micheline Rozan
Director/Host: Peter Brook
Writers: Peter Brook, Jean-Claude Carriere,
Marie-Helene Estienne
Cinematography: William Lubtchansky
Editor: Nicolas Gaster
Music: Toshi Tsuchitori
Production Design: Chloe Obolinsky
Cast: Georges Corraface, Mamadou
Dioume, Urs Bihler, Ryszard Cieslak,
Sotigui Kouyate, Tuncel Kurtiz, Miriam
Goldschmidt, Jeffrey Kissoon, Robert
Langdon Lloyd, Vittorio Mezzogiorno,
Bruce Myers, Yoshi Oida, Helene Patarot,
Mallika Sarabhai, Andrzej Seweryn
Introductions: Peter Brook
Festival: Venice Film Festival
Print Material: 24-page booklet comes with
the video set
Format: Video (360:00)
3 (120:00) programs
Theatrical film (180:00) also available
Distributors: Parabola Video; RM
Associates, Inc. (international)

## MARK TWAIN: BENEATH THE LAUGHTER
### Drama

In this program, Samuel Clemens
(1835–1910), known as Mark
Twain, reviews his life as if he were
writing a story: the young Sam joins
and then deserts the Confederate
army, becomes a newspaper reporter, and learns to pilot a Mississippi riverboat.

Production Organization: Foundation for
American Letters and Media, Los Angeles,
CA
Year Produced: 1979
Producer: Marsha Jeffer
Director: Larry Yust
Writers: Gill Dennis, Larry Yust
Cinematography: Howard Wexler
Cast: Dan O'Herlihy, Lynn Seibel, Kay
Howell
Awards: CINE Golden Eagle; American Film
Festival, Honorable Mention
Format: 16mm, Video (58:00)
Distributor: Pyramid Film and Video

## THE MARK TWAIN SERIES
### Dramatic Series

The series presents dramatizations
of several works by Mark Twain.

### Program 1
**Life on the Mississippi**
grew out of Twain's experiences
when, as a young man, he fulfilled
his boyhood ambition to become a
river-boat pilot.

Year Produced: 1980 (first broadcast on
*Great Performances*)
Director: Peter H. Hunt
Adaptation: Philip Reisman, Jr.
Cinematography: Walter Lassally
Editor: Cynthia Schneider
Music: William Perry
Host: Kurt Vonnegut
Cast: Robert Lansing, David Knell, James
Keane, Donald Madden,
John Pankow, Jack Lawrence, Stanley Reyes,
Marcy Walker
Awards: CINE Golden Eagle; International
Film and TV Festival of New York, Silver
Medal; Prix d'Italia, Silver Award; American
Cinema Editors (ACE), Eddie Award; TV
Guide, Top Ten Films of the Year
Format: Video (120:00)

### Program 2
**The Private History of a Campaign That Failed**
concerns a group of fifteen boys
from Hannibal, Missouri, who face
the reality of war. Twain's later anti-
war essay, "The War Prayer," has
been dramatized as an epilogue to
the production.

Year Produced: 1981 (first broadcast on
*Great Performances*)
Producer/Director: Peter H. Hunt
Adaptation: Philip Reisman, Jr.
Director of Research: Laurie Zwicky
Cinematography: Walter Lassally
Editor: Herbert H. Dow
Music: William Perry
Cast: Pat Hingle, Edward Herrmann, Joe
Adams, Garry McCleery, Henry Crosby,
Kelly Peese
Awards: George Foster Peabody Award;
CINE Golden Eagle; TV Guide, Top Ten
Films of the Year
Format: 16mm, Video (90:00)

### Program 3
**The Mysterious Stranger**
is set in a medieval Austrian town
and involves the arrival of a super-
natural being, Number 44, at the
town's printing shop.

Year Produced: 1982 (first broadcast on
*Great Performances*)
Director: Peter H. Hunt
Adaptation: Julian Mitchell
Cinematography: Walter Lassally
Music: William Perry
Cast: Lance Kerwin, Chris Makepeace, Fred
Gwynne, Bernhard Wicki
Format: Video (90:00)
Awards: CINE Golden Eagle; Association of
Visual Communicators (formerly IFPA),
Silver Cindy Award; American Film Festival,
Special Screening

### Program 4
**The Tragedy of Pudd'nhead Wilson**
tells how Roxy, a light-skinned
young slave of the 1830s, fears separation from her newborn son and
switches him with her white master's
child.

Year Produced: 1983 (first broadcast on *American Playhouse*)
Producer: Jane Iredale
Director: Alan Bridges
Adaptation: Philip Reisman, Jr.
Cinematography: Walter Lassally
Music: William Perry
Cast: Ken Howard, Lise Hilboldt, Steven Weber, Tom Aldredge
Format: 35mm, Video (90:00)
Awards: CINE Golden Eagle; National Educational Film and Video Festival, Special Screening and Bronze Apple

*Program 5*
**Adventures of Huckleberry Finn**
traces Huck's development from a trusting follower of Tom Sawyer to an independent-minded individual who is willing to risk eternal damnation rather than betray the black man he has come to understand and love.

Year Produced: 1985 (first broadcast on *American Playhouse*)
Producer: Jane Iredale
Director: Peter H. Hunt
Adaptation: Guy Gallo
Cinematography: Walter Lassally
Editor: Jerrold L. Ludwig
Cast: Jim Dale, Frederic Forrest, Lillian Gish, Barnard Hughes, Richard Kiley, Butterfly McQueen, Geraldine Page, Sada Thompson, Samm-Art Williams, Patrick Day
Music: William Perry
Format: Video (240:00)
4 (60:00) programs
Award/Festival: American Film Institute, Special Screening

Series Production Organizations: The Great Amwell Company, New York, NY; Nebraskans for Public Television, Inc.; and TaurusFilm, Germany
Years Produced: 1980–1985
Series Executive Producer: William Perry
Series Producer: Marshall Jamison
Format: see individual listings
Distributors: MCA Home Video, Inc. (all programs); Films, Inc./PMI (Life on the Mississippi only) Charles Fries Distribution (syndicated television in U.S. and Canada); and TaurusFilm, Munich, and Consolidated Distribution, London (international)

## THE MYSTERY OF EDGAR ALLAN POE
### Documentary and Drama

This program examines the life and work of Edgar Allan Poe (1809–1849), mixing dramatization of his stories with new footage, still photographs, and interviews.

Production Organization: Film Odyssey, Inc., Washington, DC
Year Produced: 1991
Producer: Karen Thomas
Director of Dramatic Sequences: Joyce Chopra
Writers: Karen Thomas, Daniel Blake Smith
Cinematography: James Glennon, Dyanna Taylor, Erich Roland, Foster Wiley
Editor of Dramatic Sequences: Joe Gutowski
Cast: Treat Williams, John Heard, René Auberjonois
Interviews: Joyce Carol Oates, Ira Levin, Philip Glass, and others
Format: Video (58:00)
Distributor: PBS Video

## NABOKOV ON KAFKA
### Drama

Adapted from Vladimir Nabokov's lectures on literature, which were delivered to undergraduates at Wellesley and Cornell between 1940 and 1948, this program features his account of Franz Kafka's *The Metamorphosis*.

Production Organization: Metropolitian Pittsburgh Public Broadcasting, Inc. (WQED), Pittsburgh, PA
Year Produced: 1986
Executive Administrator: Danforth Fales
Producer/Writer: James Fleming
Directors: Gilbert Cates, Paul Bogart
Cast: Christopher Plummer
Format: Video (28:00)
Distributor: Monterey Movie Company (home video)

## THE O/AURAL TRADITION: BEOWULF
### Radio Drama and Documentary

These two dramatic radio programs are based on the medieval epic poem, *Beowulf*, with readings from both the original Old English text and the modern translation by Burton Raffel. Each program includes short segments featuring interviews with scholars about the poem and related issues.

*Part 1*
**Beowulf and the Grendel Kind**
recounts the hero Beowulf's early battles with the monster Grendel and its mother.

*Part 2*
**Beowulf and the Dragon**
relates the later adventures of the old Beowulf and his final battle against a dragon, with flashbacks to his youthful exploits.

Producer/Director: Charles B. Potter
Year Produced: 1978
Adaptation: Robert P. Creed
Music: Mary Remnant
Technical Director: David Rapkin
Narrator: Earl Hammond
Performers: Robert P.Creed, readings; Mary Remnant, music
Commentaries: John M. Foley, Emory University, Atlanta, GA; Donald K. Fry, SUNY, Stony Brook, NY; Mary Remnant, Royal College of Music, London, England; Bruce A. Rosenberg, Brown University, Providence, RI
Award: CPB Award, Best Public Radio Local Program and Best Drama
Format: Audiocassette
2 (59:00) programs
Distributor: contact Charles B. Potter

## THE ODYSSEY OF HOMER

48

*Radio Series (Drama and Documentary)*

This eight-part series dramatizes Homer's epic about the Greek hero Odysseus (Ulysses), king of Ithaca, who is lost at sea and given up for dead after the Trojan War. For ten years he struggles to return home, as his wife, Penelope, wards off aggressive suitors and his son, Telemachus, searches for him. Each program dramatizes a portion of the work and contains a documentary segment analyzing an aspect of ancient Greek civilization.

### Program 1
**The Suitors of Penelope**
Odysseus' palace has been overrun by arrogant young nobles seeking Penelope's hand and humiliating Telemachus. Athena, Odysseus's patron, appeals to Telemachus to search for his father.

Richard Posner of the University of Chicago discusses law and government in Homeric times.

### Program 2
**The Voyage of Telemachus**
In his journey, Telemachus meets Nestor, aged counselor of the Greeks at Troy, and Menelaus, king of Sparta, who reports on the possible whereabouts of Odysseus.

Charles Bye, visiting professor at the University of Athens, explores ancient Greek concepts of host, guest, and gifts.

### Program 3
**Free at Last**
Odysseus has been shipwrecked and held prisoner since leaving Troy by the nymph Calypso. The gods persuade Calypso to release Odysseus, who then travels to the enchanted island of the Phaeacians.

Arthur Adkins and Wendy O'Flaherty of the University of Chicago and Gregory Nagy of Harvard University discuss how the ancient Greeks envisioned their gods and how they sought to gain their favor.

### Program 4
**The Great Wanderings**
The Phaeacians implore Odysseus to tell them about his trials.

Wendy O'Flaherty of the University of Chicago examines the women, both earthly and divine, whom Odysseus meets in his wanderings.

### Program 5
**Monsters of the Sea**
Continuing his saga, Odysseus describes his interviews in the Land of the Dead and his subsequent adventures.

Arthur Adkins of the University of Chicago explores Homeric notions of happiness and fulfillment.

### Program 6
**The Swineherd's Hut**
After describing the destruction of his crew and his own escape to Calypso's island, Odysseus returns to Ithaca, learns of the designs against his family, and with Telemachus plots the downfall of the suitors.

Arthur Adkins of the University of Chicago examines the hierarchical structure of ancient Greek society and the relationship between noble freemen and slaves.

### Program 7
**A Beggar's Homecoming**
Disguised as a beggar, Odysseus returns to his palace where he is abused by the suitors and made to fight a much younger man.

Eric Hamp of the University of Chicago discusses Homeric concepts of morality.

### Program 8
**The Contest of the Bow**
When none of the suitors has the strength to bend the bow, Odysseus seizes it, kills over 100 men, and at last reveals his identity to Penelope.

Albert B. Lord of Harvard University discusses elements of oral epic poetry and Homeric style.

Production Organization: National Radio Theatre of Chicago, Chicago, IL
Year Produced: 1981
Producer/Director/Writer: Yuri Rasovsky
Documentary Producer/Writer: Kerry Frumkin
Music: Eric Salzman
Cast: Irene Worth, Barry Morse, Shepperd Strudwick, John Glover
Host/Narrator: Ed Asner
Format: Audiocassette
8 (60:00) programs
Distributor: National Radio Theatre of Chicago

## O. Henry's Jimmy Valentine

### Drama

In 1899, William Sydney Porter, who wrote under the name of O. Henry, was sentenced to serve five years in the Ohio State Penitentiary for embezzling bank funds. This is a dramatization of his short story inspired by that experience.

Production Organization: Family Communications and Learning Corporation of America, New York, NY
Year Produced: 1985
Executive Producers: Fred Rogers, Frank Doelger
Producer: Robert McDonald
Director: Paul Saltzman
Adaptation: Paul Lally
Cast: Victor Ertmanis, Marc Strange, Gary Reinecke, Chris Wiggins, Gerard Parkes, Wendy Lyon
Awards/Festivals: Birmingham International Film Festival; Columbus (OH) International Film Festival; National Educational Film Festival, Selected Films for Young Adults (American Library Association)
Print Material: Teacher's Guide available
Format: 16mm, Video (two versions, 55:00 and 30:00)
Distributor: Coronet/MTI Film and Video

## Pigeon Feathers

### Drama

Adapted from the short story by John Updike, this film follows the way a thoughtful teenager's realization of his own mortality causes him to question what he has been taught about God and the immortality of the soul. (see also The Hollow Boy, Love and Other Sorrows, and The Revolt of Mother)

Production Organization: Learning in Focus, Inc., Larchmont, NY
Year Produced: 1987 (first broadcast on American Playhouse)
Executive Producer: Robert Geller
Producer: Brian Benlifer
Director: Sharron Miller
Adaptation: Jan Hartman
Cinematography: Hiro Narita
Editor: Rachel Igel
Cast: Christopher Collet, Lenka Peterson, Jeffrey DeMunn, Caroline McWilliams
Awards: CINE Golden Eagle; American Film and Video Festival, Finalist
Format: Video (38:30)
Distributors: Coronet/MTI Film and Video; Monterey Movie Company (home video)

## Poets in Person

### Radio Series (Interviews/Discussion/Readings)

This thirteen-part series presents and interprets the poetry of twelve contemporary American poets, from well-known authors to younger talents. Each program focuses on one poet and typically features readings of five or more poems.

### Program 1

This introduction to Poets in Person traces the evolution and varieties of poetry since the 1950s, examining the trend toward finding poetry in ordinary American speech and personal experience.

### Program 2

Allen Ginsberg discusses the Beat writers, the counter-culture of the 1960s, and the continuing influence of earlier poets.

### Program 3

Karl Shapiro explains why he first attacked T.S. Eliot, Ezra Pound, and the academic establishment, what he loves about Nebraska, and how he became known as "the bourgeois poet."

### Program 4

Maxine Kumin reviews her friendship with Anne Sexton, her roles as mother, grandmother, and writer, life on a horse farm, and her transformation from a "light versifier" to a serious poet.

### Program 5

W.S. Merwin considers the origin of images, surrealism, alienation, the assault on the environment, and the search for faith in the modern world.

### Program 6

Gwendolyn Brooks recounts her first meeting with Langston Hughes, the use of experiences from her own life in her work, and her efforts to encourage children to write poetry.

### Program 7

James Merrill reflects on the subjects of love and loss, feeling and form in poetry, and how he came to write a 17,000-line modern epic with the help of a Ouija board.

### Program 8

Adrienne Rich discusses coming of age in the 1950s and the evolution of her own life and work through the liberation movements of the 1960s and 1970s.

### Program 9

John Ashbery talks about the "New York School" of poets and artists and the impact of movies, paintings, and popular culture on his work.

### Program 10

Sharon Olds discusses motherhood, metaphors, teaching, and making art out of real life in the New York metropolis.

**50**

*Program 11*

Charles Wright remembers growing up in Tennessee, discovering the power of language in fifth grade, and becoming a poet in the U.S. Army at age 23.

*Program 12*

Rita Dove describes her parents and grandparents, her adolescence in Akron, her early fascination with German poetry, and the influence of slave narratives on her own work.

*Program 13*

Gary Soto talks about baseball games, tragedy in a Chicano boyhood, the work and lives of migrant families, and his unexpected beginnings and popularity as a poet.

Production Organization: Modern Poetry Association, Chicago, IL
Year Produced: 1991
Producer/Writer/Host: Joseph Parisi
Interviewers (by program): Lewis Hyde (2); Joseph Parisi (3, 13); Alicia Ostriker (4, 10); James Richardson (5); Alice Fulton (6); J.D. McClatchey (7, 11); Diane Wood Middlebrook (8); David Bromwich (9); Helen Vendler (12)
Print Material: Companion booklet forthcoming
Format: Audiocassette
13 (29:00) programs
Distributor: Modern Poetry Association

## THE REVOLT OF MOTHER

*Drama*

In The Revolt of Mother, adapted from a story by Mary Wilkins Freeman, two young people witness the loving but determined struggle of their mother to stand up to their father on a matter involving the family farm. (see also The Hollow Boy, Love and Other Sorrows, and Pigeon Feathers)

Production Organization: Learning in

Focus, Inc., Larchmont, NY
Year Produced: 1986 (first broadcast on *American Playhouse*)
Executive Producer: Robert Geller
Producer: Brian Benlifer
Director: Victor Lobl
Adaptation: Cynthia Cherbak
Cinematography: Tom Houghton
Editor: Rachel Igel
Cast: Amy Madigan, Jay O. Sanders, Katherine Hiler, Benjamin Bernovy
Awards: Houston International Film Festival Blue, Silver Award; Christopher Award; American Film and Video Festival, Blue Ribbon; U.S.A. Film Festival (Dallas), Finalist
Format: 16mm, Video (46:30)
Distributor: Coronet/MTI Film and Video; Monterey Movie Company (home video)

## THE SCARLET LETTER

*Dramatic Series*

This is a four-part dramatization of Nathaniel Hawthorne's 1850 novel. (see also The Scarlet Letter Radio Series)

Production Organization: WGBH, Boston, MA
Year Produced: 1979
Executive Producer: Herbert Hirschman
Producer/Director: Rick Hauser
Adaptation: Allan Knee, Alvin Sapinsley
Music: John Morris
Cast: Meg Foster, John Heard, Kevin Conway
Format: Video
4 (60:00) programs
Distributor: PBS Video

## THE SCARLET LETTER RADIO SERIES

*Radio Series (Documentary and Drama)*

This radio series is a two-part companion to the television dramatization of Hawthorne's *The Scarlet Letter*. (see also The Scarlet Letter)

*Part I*

The Legacy of the Letter: *The Scarlet Letter* Commentaries examines the major themes of the novel through four half-hour documentary programs.

*Program 1*

**Capital A**

traces the changing legal and social views of adultery from colonial times to the present.

*Program 2*

**The Dark Dilemma**

discusses psychological, theological, and literary perspectives on sin, guilt, revenge, and remorse in Puritan and modern American society.

*Program 3*

**A is for Able**

analyzes the evolution of the personal and cultural values of freedom and independence in America.

*Program 4*

**The Legacy of the Letter**

examines the values and attitudes that remain today from Puritan society and Hawthorne's influence on later generations of writers and readers.

Coproducers: Barbara Sirota, Clifford Hahn
Writer/Editor: Diane K. Miller
Narrator: Richard Provost

*Part II*

Nathaniel Hawthorne's *The Scarlet Letter* is a series of eighteen half-hour dramatic readings of the novel.

Producer: George Morency
Associate Producer: Clifford Hahn
Director: Joann Green
Cast: Kevin Conway, Deborah Solomon, Christopher Curry, Frank Licato, Lisa McMillan, Jon Polito
Series Production Organization: WGBH-Radio, Boston, MA
Year Produced: 1979
Series Executive Producer: Barbara Sirota
Format: Audiocassette
4 (30:00) documentary commentaries; 18 (30:00) dramatic readings
Distributor: WGBH

## A SEA OF LANGUAGE

### Radio Documentary

A Sea of Language explores how language is created; how it controls and affects us; how it is used as a tool of power; and how men and women use language differently.

Production Organization: Western Public Radio, San Francisco, CA
Year Produced: 1980
Producer: Barbara Boyer Walter
Technical Producer: Zane Blaney
Project Coordinator: Susan Horwitz
Reporter/Editor: Shelley Fern, Leo Lee
Format: Audiocassette (59:00)
Distributor: Pacifica Program Service/Radio Archive

## SEIZE THE DAY

### Drama

This dramatization of Saul Bellow's *Seize the Day* (1956) follows a brief period in the life of Tommy Wilhelm, a bumbling, clownish salesman facing financial and personal ruin.

Production Organization: Learning in Focus, Inc., New York, NY
Year Produced: 1986 (first broadcast on *Great Performances*)
Executive Producer: Robert Geller
Producer: Chiz Schultz
Associate Producer: Brian Benlifer
Adaptation: Ronald Ribman
Director: Fielder Cook
Cast: Robin Williams, Joseph Wiseman, Jerry Stiller, Glenne Headly, Katherine Borowitz, Tony Roberts
Award/Festivals: CINE Golden Eagle: Berlin Film Festival; Telluride Film Festival; Jerusalem Film Festival; *Time* magazine, one of "Ten Best of 1987"; *New York Post*, one of "30 Best Movies Ever Made for Television"; *Los Angeles Times*, one of "30 Best Movies Ever Made for Television"
Format: 16mm, Video, Laserdisc (94:00)
Distributor: HBO Video

## THE SHAKESPEARE HOUR

### Dramatic and Documentary Series

This series is a reformatting of five of the BBC/Time-Life Shakespeare plays into one-hour segments. Host Walter Matthau provides introductory and concluding remarks for each hour and narrates the short documentaries accompanying four of the dramas.

### Program 1
**A Midsummer Night's Dream**
with Peter McEnery as Oberon and Helen Mirren as Titania. Directed by Elijah Moshinsky. [2 (60:00) programs]

### Program 2
**Twelfth Night**
with Felicity Kendal as Viola, Sinead Cusack as Olivia, and Alec McOwen as Malvolio. Directed by John Gorrie. [3 (60:00) programs]

In Praise of Folly is a five-minute documentary that follows the first segment of Twelfth Night. It offers a brief history of the fool in literature, art, and society.

All the World's a Stage is an eight-minute documentary that follows the final segment of Twelfth Night. It explores Shakespeare's use of drama as both metaphor and theatrical device.

### Program 3
**All's Well That Ends Well**
with Ian Charleson as Bertram and Angela Down as Helena. Directed by Elijah Moshinsky. [3 (60:00) programs]

The Woman's Part is a five-minute documentary that follows the final segment of All's Well That Ends Well. It surveys Shakespeare's resourceful and witty comic heroines in the context of their real-life counterparts in England.

### Program 4
**Measure for Measure**
with Kate Nelligan as Isabella and Tim Piggott-Smith as Angelo. Directed by Desmond Davis. [3 (60:00) programs]

The Darkening of Comedy is a four-minute documentary that follows the final segment of Measure for Measure. It explores Shakespeare's mix of comedy and tragedy and the roots of this combination in medieval English drama.

### Program 5
**King Lear**
with Michael Hordern as Lear and Frank Middlemass as the Fool. Directed by Jonathan Miller. [4 (60:00) programs]

Poetic Illusion is a four-minute documentary that follows the third segment of King Lear. It discusses the play's famous Dover Cliff scene, exploring its use of Renaissance visual perspective to create a metaphor for the "tragic fall" that "cures" despair.

The Promised End is a sixteen-minute documentary that follows the final segment of King Lear. It discusses the significance of the characteristically ambiguous ending of each of the five plays.

*For Documentaries:*
Production Organization: WNET/13, New York, NY
Year Produced: 1985
Executive Producer: Donald Johnson
Producers: Harvey Bellin, Tom Kieffer
Director: Tony Marshall
Writer: Kenneth Cavander
Host/Narrator: Walter Matthau
Print Material: *The Shakespeare Hour* by Edward Quinn available, call Penguin Books, 212-366-2000; Teacher and Viewer Guides no longer available
Format: Video (15 hours)
1,2,3 and 4 one-hour programs, see individual listings
Distributor: Ambrose Video (plays only available)

# SoundPlay/*Hörspiel*

## *Radio Series (Drama and Documentary)*

SoundPlay/Hörspiel is an anthology of important works from the tradition of radio drama (*hörspiel*) in Germany and Austria. The Endowment supported acquisition of some programs, production of new versions of others, and all the introductory and documentary segments. Breakfast in Miami was supported by other funders.

*Program 1*
### The Flight of Lindbergh: A Radio Cantata (1929) by Bertolt Brecht and Kurt Weill

The cantata salutes Charles Lindbergh's historic 1927 transatlantic flight.

The accompanying documentary examines the beginnings of radio drama in Germany.

Production Organization: Voices International, New York, NY
Year Produced: 1991
Producers: Everett Frost, Faith Wilding
Documentary Producer: Everett Frost
Writer: Bertolt Brecht
Translation: Lys Symonette
Music: Kurt Weill
Recording Production Engineers: Stephen Erickson, Edward Haber, Gene Curtis
Music Performed by: the Stamford Master Singers, conducted by Steven Gross
Soloists: Jeffrey Lentz, Charles Kaye, Edward Pleasant
Host: Alvin Epstein
Format: Audiocassette (59:00)

*Program 2*
### The Outsider (1947) by Wolfgang Borchert

The first radio play produced in Germany after World War II, The Outsider tells the story of a soldier captured at Stalingrad who returns to post-war Germany from a Siberian concentration camp.

The documentary recreates the "sound" of German radio during the war and post-war era through a montage of archival recordings including the voices of Hitler, Goering, and an American Army colonel who helped set up German radio after the war.

Production Organizations: Voices International, New York, NY; WGBH, Boston; and Deutsche Welle, Cologne, Germany
Year Produced: 1985 (Production by permission of Rowohlt Verlag Publishers, New York, NY)
Production Coordinator/Documentary Producer: Everett Frost
Director: Georges Wagner Jourdain
Writer: Wolfgang Borchert
Translation: Michael Benedikt
Recording Engineer: Melanie Berzon
Production Engineer: Volker Herder
Narrator: Robert J. Lurtsema
Cast: Jeremiah Kissel, Jeremy Geidt, Judy Braha
Host: Alvin Epstein
Format: Audiocassette (89:00)

*Program 3*
### Dreams (1951) by Günter Eich

This play consists of five related dreams, each occurring on a different continent.

The documentary includes interviews with Eich, who discusses his experiences as a anti-Nazi writer and later as a prisoner, and selections from tape recordings of listeners' angry phone calls after the initial German broadcast.

Production Organization: Voices International, New York, NY
Year Produced: 1990 (Production by permission of Suhrkamp Verlag Publishers, Frankfurt)
Director/Producer: Everett Frost
Associate Producer: Faith Wilding
Writer: Günter Eich
Translation: Anselm Hollo
Commentary Writer: Karl Karst
Production Engineer: Stephen Erickson
Cast: Ruth Maleczech, Frederick Neumann, Bill Raymond, Avery Hart, Terry O'Reilly
Host: Alvin Epstein
Format: Audiocassette (89:00)

## Program 4
### The Other and I (1952) by Günter Eich

An American woman driving along the north Italian coast is drawn into another life and past, from which she cannot return.

The documentary includes comments by the author.

Production Organization: Bay Area Radio Drama, San Francisco, CA
Year Produced: 1984 (Production by permission of Suhrkamp Verlag, Publishers, Frankfurt)
Director/Producer: Erik Bauersfeld
Writer: Günter Eich
Translation: Robert Goss
Engineer: Danny Kopelson
Cast: Winifred Mann
Host: Erik Bauersfeld
Format: Audiocassette (89:00)

## Program 5
### The Good God of Manhattan (1958) by Ingeborg Bachmann

The title character is on trial for plotting the murder of two lovers and for having killed one of them.

The documentary features a discussion of the playwright.

Production Organization: Voices International, New York, NY
Year Produced: 1990 (Production by permission of R. Piper & Co, Verlag Publishers, Munich)
Producer: Faith Wilding
Director: Carey Perloff
Writer: Ingeborg Bachmann
Translation: Faith Wilding
Music: Elizabeth Swados
Production Engineer: Stephen Erickson
Cast: Elizabeth McGovern, Patrick O'Connell, Bill Raymond, Bob Gunton
Host: Alvin Epstein
Format: Audiocassette (89:00)

## Program 6
### Experimental Radio Drama Program I

This three-part program includes works by four poets that illustrate the ongoing interest of German radio drama in linguistic forms. The documentary segments include discussion of these works.

### Excerpt from the Ursonate (1932) by Kurt Schwitters

A pre-war experimental work for radio, the Ursonate reduces language to the simplest syllabic sounds, anticipating the avant garde movement in acoustic radio drama known as *Neues Hörspiel*.

Year Performed/Recorded: 1932
Realization: Kurt Schwitters

### Ophelia and the Words (1969) by Gerhard Rühm

Rühm took as his text all the words spoken by Ophelia in Shakespeare's *Hamlet*.

Production Organizations: Bay Area Radio Drama, Berkeley, CA, and Westdeutsche Rundfunk (WDR), Cologne, Germany
Year Produced: 1987
Text: Gerhard Rühm, from Shakespeare
Director/Dramaturg: Klaus Schöning
Engineer: Danny Kopelson
Cast: Sigrid Worschmidt

### Five Man Humanity (1968) by Ernst Jandl and Friederike Mayröcker

In Mother Goose-style language, the story describes five men who are born, raised, educated, conscripted, imprisoned, tried, executed, and born again.

Production Organizations: Bay Area Radio Drama, Berkeley, CA, and Westdeutsche Rundfunk (WDR), Cologne, Germany

Year Produced: 1984
Producer: Erik Bauersfeld
Directors: Robert Goss, Klaus Mehrländer
Writers: Ernst Jandl, Friederike Mayröcker
Translation: Robert Goss
Recording Engineer: Danny Kopelson
Cast: Sigrid Worschmidt, Leo Downey
For *Experimental Radio Drama Program 1*
Production Organization: Bay Area Radio Drama, Berkeley, CA
Producer: Erik Bauersfeld
Associate Producer: Maria Gilardin
Technical Production: Jim McKee (Earwax Studio)
Host: Erik Bauersfeld
Format: Audiocassette (59:00)

## Program 7
### Monologue: Terry Jo (1968) by Max Bense and Ludwig Harig

This play is based on a French newspaper account of the true story of an American family murdered during a vacation cruise in the Caribbean.

The documentary examines the distinction between how language is used in art and journalism, with *Monologue: Terry Jo* as a study of each.

Production Organizations: Bay Area Radio Drama, San Francisco, CA, and Westdeutsche Rundfunk (WDR), Cologne, Germany
Year Produced: 1984
Producer: Erik Bauersfeld
Director: Klaus Schöning
Writers: Max Bense, Ludwig Harig
Translation: Robert Goss
Engineer: Danny Kopelson
Cast: Sigrid Worschmidt
Host: Erik Bauersfeld
Format: Audiocassette: (59:00)

**54**

*Program 8*
**Gertrude (1978) by Wolfgang
Schiffer and Charles Dürr**
This drama tells the true story of
Gertrude, an incurable schizo-
phrenic and avid radio listener, who
sent a series of letters to radio station WDR in Cologne, where two
producers took an interest in her
and began to document her
struggles to find a new place in society. The drama is an example of
non-fiction recordings transposed
into radio art.

The documentary includes com-
ments by the real Gertrude and by
German co-author Wolfgang
Schiffer.

Production Organization: Bay Area Radio
Drama, San Francisco, CA
Year Produced: 1984
Producer: Erik Bauersfeld
Director: Oscar Eustis
Consulting Director: Wolfgang Schiffer
Writers: Wolfgang Schiffer, Charles Dürr
Translation: Robert Goss
Music: Maggi Payne
Engineer: Danny Kopelson
Technical Assistance: Karin Brocco
Cast: Abigail Booream
Host: Erik Bauersfeld
Format: Audiocassette (59:00)

*Program 9*
**Experimental Radio Drama
Program II**
This program illustrates two further
directions of German acoustic radio
drama, *Neues Hörspiel.*

**Radio (1983) by Ferdinand Kriwet**
The author analyzes the language of
media connected to particular pro-
fessions or activities, and the listener
is taken from America to Spain to
Latin America to Germany to Russia
to hear similarly worded newscasts,
entirely intelligible to anyone any-
where.

Production Organizations: Westdeutsche
Rundfunk (WDR), Cologne, Germany;
Radio France, Paris; and Sveriges Riksradio,
The Netherlands
Year Produced: 1985
Realization: Ferdinand Kriwet

**Wind and Sea (1970) by Peter
Handke**
In this brief work, Handke explores
the possibility of telling a story and
evoking emotions through the or-
chestration of sound.

Production Organization: Westdeutsche
Rundfunk (WDR),
Cologne, Germany
Year Produced: 1971
Director/Writer: Peter Handke
Documentary segments include discussion
of the works and Ferdinand Kriwet's
demonstration of his radio collage methods.

For *Experimental Radio Drama Program II*
Production Organization: Bay Area Radio
Drama, Berkeley, CA
Year Produced: 1991
Producer: Erik Bauersfeld
Associate Producer: Maria Gilardin
Technical Production: Jim McKee (Earwax
Studio)
Host: Erik Bauersfeld
Format: Audiocassette (59:00)

*Program 10*
**Radio Play (No. 1) (1968) by Peter
Handke**
In this surreal drama, a young man
is interrogated by five questioners
and a chief interrogator; it is never
clear what, if anything, the interro-
gators are trying to find out, whether
the Questioned knows anything or
not, or whether he is "innocent" or
"guilty."

The documentary includes an interview with Handke, who discusses
Group 47, the influential post-war
gathering of German writers concerned about repairing the damage
done to German language and literature and to the careers of writers
during the Third Reich.

Production Organization: Voices
International, New York, NY
Year Produced: 1988
Producer/Director: Klaus Schöning
Associate Producer: David Leveille
Writer: Peter Handke
Translation: Robert Goss
Adaptation for American Radio: Faith
Wilding
Recording Engineer: Marilyn Ries
Cast: Bill McElhiney, Frederick Neumann
Host: Alvin Epstein
Format: Audiocassette (59:00)

*Program 11*
**Houses (1969) by Jürgen Becker**
This drama explores the varied and
often contradictory feelings people
have about the suburban houses and
apartments in which they live.

The documentary includes a discussion of the use of ordinary people
rather than actors in the drama and
a comparison of the German and
English productions of the play and
what each reveals about the two
societies.

Production Organizations: Bay Area Radio
Drama, San Francisco, CA, and
Westdeutsche Rundfunk (WDR), Cologne,
Germany
Year Produced: 1991
Producer/Director/Dramaturg: Erik
Bauersfeld
Writer: Jürgen Becker
Translation: Robert Goss
Sound Design/Music & Technical
Production: Jim McKee (Earwax Studio)
Assistant Producer: Maria Gilardin
Host: Erik Bauersfeld
Format: Audiocassette (59:00)

*Program 12*
**Centropolis (1975) by Walter Adler**
This drama presents an imagined future in which the state, Centropolis, has solved all problems and is bio-engineering a triumph over death itself.

The documentary features a discussion of the play's effectiveness and its popularity in Germany.

Production Organization: Bay Area Radio Drama, San Francisco, CA
Year Produced: 1990
Producer/Director/Dramaturg: Erik Bauersfeld
Writer: Walter Adler
Translation: Robert Goss
Music/Sound Design/Technical Production: Jim McKee (Earwax Studio)
Cast: Fredi Olster, Will Marchetti
Host: Erik Bauersfeld
Format: Audiocassette (59:00)

*Program 13*
**The Tribune (1980) by Mauricio Kagel**
The play presents a Head of State rehearsing a long speech he will give to his assembled people, while the taped reactions of an absent but well-schooled crowd are played through loudspeakers.

The documentary includes comments by Kagel.

Production Organization: Voices International, New York, NY
Year Produced: 1990
Producer/Director/Dramaturg: Everett Frost
Associate Producer: Faith Wilding
Writer: Mauricio Kagel
Translator: Anselm Hollo
Music: Mauricio Kagel (courtesy S. Peters Verlag Publishers & WDR)
Production Engineer: Stephen Erickson
Cast: Bill Raymond
Host: Alvin Epstein
Format: Audiocassette (59:00)

*Program 14*
**Breakfast in Miami (1978 and 1989) by Reinhard Lettau**
In this satiric play, six deposed dictators living in retirement in Miami gather for a series of discussions about their experiences as heads of state.

Production Organization: Voices International, New York, NY
Year Produced: 1990
Producer/Director/Dramaturg: Everett Frost
Writer: Reinhard Lettau
Translation: Reinhard Lettau, Julie Prandl
Recording and Production Engineer: Stephen Erickson
Cast: Norberto Kerner, Jeremy Dempsey, Christian Bruckner, William Duff-Griffen, Miguel Perez, Hewitt Brooks
Host: Alvin Epstein
Format: Audiocassette (59:00)

*Program 15*
**Moscow Time (1988) by Helmut Kopetzky**
Based on extensive field recordings, this program looks at the Russian people during the beginnings of glasnost.

The program features a short introductory discussion by Kopetzky.

Production Organizations: Voices International, New York, NY, and Hessicher Rundfunk, Frankfurt, Germany
Years Produced: 1989–1990
Realization/Translation: Helmut Kopetzky, Faith Wilding
Music: Dmitri Shostakovitch
English Narrator: David McBride
Host: Alvin Epstein
Format: Audiocassette (59:00)

*Program 16*
**Roaratorio: An Irish Circus on Finnegans Wake (1979) by John Cage**
Created for German radio broadcast, the drama contains 2,293 sound effects, all mentioned in James Joyce's experimental novel, *Finnegans Wake.*

Production Organizations: WDR, Cologne, Germany; SDR, Stuttgart Germany; and KRO, Hilversum, The Netherlands
Year Produced: 1979
Realization: John Cage, John David Fullemann
Producer/Editor: Klaus Schöning
Text Arrangement/Adaptation: John Cage
Cast: John Cage (Voice), Joe Heaney (Singer)
Host: Alvin Epstein
Format: Audiocassette (59:00)

For the *SoundPlay/Hörspiel* series
Production Organizations: Voices International, New York, NY, in cooperation with Bay Area Radio Drama (BARD), Berkeley, CA
Years Produced: 1984–1991
Project Director: Everett Frost
Codirector: Faith Wilding
Associate Producer: Molly Bernstein
Technical Producer: Stephen Erickson
BARD Project Director: Erik Bauersfeld
BARD Associate Producer: Maria Gilardin
BARD Technical Producer: Jim McKee (Earwax Studio)
Documentary Interviews (by program): Bertolt Brecht, Kurt Weill, Dr. Reinhold Grimm, Dr. Kim Kowalke, Steven Gross (1); Hans Quest, Gotz Naleppa, Dr. Georges Wagner Jourdain (2); Günter Eich, Fritz Schroder-Jahn, Klaus Schöning, Dr. Karl Karst (3); Günter Eich, Klaus Schöning, Erik Bauersfeld, Dr. Frederic Tubach (4); Dr. Karen Achberger, Carey Perloff (5); Gerhard Rühm, Ernst Jandl, Friederike Mayröcker, Klaus Schöning (6); Klaus Schöning (7); Gertrude, Wolfgang Schiffer, Oscar Eustis (8); Erik Bauersfeld, Klaus Schöning, Ferdinand Kriwet (9); Peter Handke (10); Dr. Frederic Tubach, Erik Bauersfeld (11); Walter Adler, Dr. Frederick Tubach (12); Mauricio Kagel (13); Helmut Kopetzky (15)
Print Material: English translations of most of the plays appear in the anthology *German Radio Plays,* eds. Everett Frost and Margaret Herzfeld-Sander [Volume 86 of the German Library series], published by the Continuum Publishing Company, 370 Lexington Avenue, New York, NY 10017
Format: Audiocassette
Programs 2–5 (89:00); Programs 1,6–16 (59:00)

Distributor: The Pacifica Program Service/
Radio Archive
[Note: Program 4 (89:00) and Programs
1,9,10,13,16 (59:00) are not currently
available]

## THE STATE OF THE LANGUAGE: SO TO SPEAK

*Documentary*

The program examines some of the
challenges encountered by various
people directly involved in the translation process, from translators of
novels and plays to State Department interpreters and the foreign
language producer of *Sesame Street*.

Production Organizations: The English-
Speaking Union and Power/Rector
Productions, San Francisco, CA
Year Produced: 1983
Executive Producers: Jules Power, Richard
R. Rector
Producer: Lynn O'Donnell
Cinematography: Tom Tucker, Jim
McCutcheon
Editor: Michael Chandler
Host: Edward Herrmann
Print Material: Companion book *The State
of the Language*, eds. Christopher Ricks and
Leonard Michaels (University of California
Press, 1990)
Format: Video (27:00)
Distributor: The English-Speaking Union

## STAUS: GROWING OLD IN AMERICA

*Drama*

Set in the steel and mining region
just south of Pittsburgh, this drama,
based on a short story by Mary Ann
Rishel, centers on an aging widower
who is encouraged by his sisters to
start his life again.

Production Organization: The Labor
Theater/Realizations, Inc., New York, NY
Year Produced: 1983
Executive Producer: C.R. Portz
Associate Producer: Bette Craig
Director: Bob Walsh
Adaptation: Nancy Musser, Peter Almond
Music: Martin Burman
Cinematography: Jim Crispi
Cast: Theodore Bikel, Hope Cameron,
Charlotte Jones, Rebecca Schuller
Format: Video (40:00)
Distributor: Realizations, Inc.

## TELL ME A STORY

*Radio Series (Interviews/Discussion/
Readings)*

This multi-part, multi-year series is
devoted to contemporary short stories read in their entirety by the authors themselves. Then, through
conversation and commentary, the
writers explore their own back-
grounds, their art, and the relationship of their stories to other fiction
of our era and past ages.

*Program 1*
**Wright Morris, "Victrola."**

*Program 2*
**Lucia Berlin, "Maggie May."**

*Program 3*
**William Maxwell, "Love" and "The
Woman Who Never Drew Breath
Except to Complain."**

*Program 4*
**Kay Boyle, "Winter Night."**

*Program 5*
**Tim O'Brien, "How to Tell a True
War Story."**

*Program 6*
**Linda Svendsen, "Heartbeat."**

*Program 7*
**Richard Ford, "Optimists."**

*Program 8*
**Jayne Anne Phillips, "Heavenly
Animal."**

*Program 9*
**D.R. MacDonald, "Sailing."**

*Program 10*
**Stephanie Vaughn, "Able, Baker,
Charlie, Dog."**

*Program 11*
**Kaye Gibbons, "The Proof."**

*Program 12*
**Eudora Welty, "A Visit of Charity."**

*Program 13*
**Ellen Gilchrist, "Victory over
Japan."**

*Program 14*
**John L'Heureux, "The Anatomy of
Bliss."**

*Program 15*
**Toni Cade Bambara, "My Man
Bovanne."**

*Program 16*
**William Trevor, "Teresa's
Wedding."**

*Program 17*
**Ron Hansen, "Wickedness."**

*Program 18*
**Cynthia Ozick, "A Drugstore in
Winter."**

*Program 19*
**Robert Coover, "The Gingerbread
House."**

*Program 20*
**Don Carpenter, "Road Show."**

*Program 21*
**James Alan McPherson, "Why I Like Country Music."**

*Program 22*
**Joy Williams, "The Blue Men."**

*Program 23*
**Peter Taylor, "Three Heroines."**

*Program 24*
**Ann Beattie, "Desire."**

*Program 25*
**John Updike, "The Persistence of Desire."**

*Program 26*
**Roald Dahl, "The Great Switcheroo."**

*Program 27*
**Louise Erdrich, "A Wedge of Shade."**

*Program 28*
**Leo Litwak, "The Therapist."**

*Program 29*
**Jamaica Kincaid, "Gwen."**

*Program 30*
**Ethan Canin, "Star Food."**

*Program 31*
**Molly Giles, "Heart and Soul."**

*Program 32*
**J.F. Powers, "The Old Bird: A Love Story."**

*Program 33*
**Hannah Green, "Mr. Nabokov."**

*Program 34*
**John Edgar Wideman, "Presents."**

*Program 35*
**Lee Smith, "Between the Lines."**

*Program 36*
**John Barth, "Night Sea Journey."**

*Program 37*
**Paul Bowles, "A Distant Episode."**

*Program 38*
**Amy Tan, "Half and Half."**

*Program 39*
**Tobias Wolff, "The Other Miller."**

*Program 40*
**Peter Matthiessen, "Horse Latitudes."**

*Program 41*
**Gloria Naylor, "Eve's Song."**

*Program 42*
**Charles D'Ambrosio, "The Point."**

*Program 43*
**Deborah Eisenberg, "Days."**

*Program 44*
**Charles Baxter, "Horace and Margaret's Fifty-Second."**

*Program 45*
**Joyce Carol Oates, "Four Miniature Narratives."**

*Program 46*
**Jim Shepard, "Reach for the Sky" and "Messiah."**

*Program 47*
**Denise Chávez, "The Last of the Menu Girls."**

*Program 48*
**E.L. Doctorow, "Willi."**

*Program 49*
**Harriet Doerr, "The Red Taxi."**

*Program 50*
**Charles Simmons, "Wrinkles."**

*Program 51*
**Gail Godwin, "A Sorrowful Woman."**

*Program 52*
**Wallace Stegner, "In the Twilight."**

Production Organization: Tell Me a Story, San Francisco, CA
Years Produced: Programs 1–13, 1988; Programs 14–26, 1989; Programs 27–39, 1990; Programs 40–52, 1991
Producers: Marjorie Leet (Programs 1–26); Marjorie Leet and David Litwin (Programs 27–52)
Technical Directors: Vance Frost (Programs 1–14,17,19,25); David Litwin (Programs 15–16,18,20–24,26–52)
Writer/Interviewer Marjorie Leet
Host: Herbert Gold
Format: Audiocassette
Programs 1–6,8–20,22–24,27–52 (30:00); Programs 7,21 (45:00); Program 25 (two versions, 30:00 and 45:00); Program 26 (60:00)
Distributor: Tell Me a Story, attn: Marjorie Leet

## TO BE YOUNG, GIFTED, AND BLACK
*Drama*

To Be Young, Gifted, and Black is a portrait of playwright Lorraine Hansberry (1930–1965), drawn largely from her unpublished letters, poems, diaries, and scenes from her plays.

**58**

Production Organization: WNET
Educational Broadcasting Corporation, New
York, NY
Year Produced: 1972
Producer: Robert Fresco
Director: Michael Schultz
Adaptation: Robert Fresco
Cast: Ruby Dee, Al Freeman, Jr., Claudia
McNeil, Roy Scheider, Blythe Danner,
Barbara Barrie, Lauren Jones
Award: American Film Festival, Blue Ribbon
Format: 16mm, Video (90:00)
Distributor: Indiana University, Audio-
Visual Center

## TO RENDER A LIFE: *LET US NOW PRAISE FAMOUS MEN* AND THE DOCUMENTARY VISION

*Documentary*

To Render a Life explores the legacy
and themes of *Let Us Now Praise
Famous Men* (1941), the classic work
of American documentary literature
by writer James Agee and photographer Walker Evans. Along with
scholarly reflection, the film records
the daily life of a contemporary poor
rural family in southern Virginia
whose circumstances parallel those
of the cotton tenant farmers that
Agee and Evans portrayed fifty
years ago.

Production Organization: James Agee Film
Project, Johnson City, TN
Year Produced: 1991
Producers: Ross Spears, Silvia Kersusan
Director: Ross Spears
Writers: Silvia Kersusan, Ross Spears
Cinematography: Ross Spears, Neil Means,
Anthony Forma
Editors: Grahame Weinbren, Ross Spears
Composers: Kenton Coe, Edgar Meyer
Music: Performed by the Edgar Meyer
Group

Narrator: Ross Spears
Interviews: Robert Coles, Jonathan Kozol,
Ted Rosengarten, Wilma Dykeman, Rev.
Will Campbell, Fred Wiseman, Jonathan
Yardley, Alex Harris, Ruth Behar, William
Allard, James Hubbard, and others
Format: Video (88:00)
Distributor: James Agee Film Project

## VOICES AND VISIONS

*Documentary Series*

Voices and Visions presents the
achievements of thirteen American
poets over the last 150 years, using
archival materials, location cinematography, drama, dance, animation
sequences, and interviews. In addition, each program includes a select
group of poems, presented by the
author or actors.

### Program 1
### Elizabeth Bishop: One Art (1911–1979)

illustrates the writer's wandering
spirit, from a childhood in Nova
Scotia to travels in Brazil, and the
central themes of her work: geography, landscape, and the quest for
consciousness and identity through
travel.

Year Produced: 1987
Director/Producer/Writer: Jill Janows
Co-Producer: Ellen Weissbrod
Cinematography: Richard Dallet
Editor: Arnold Glassman
Animation: Anita Thacher
Cast: Blythe Danner as the voice of Elizabeth
Bishop
Interviews: Octavio Paz, Mary McCarthy,
Mark Strand, James Merrill, Howard Moss,
Frank Bidart, and others
Format: 16mm, Video (56:30)

### Program 2
### Hart Crane (1899–1932)

traces the poet's boyhood in Ohio,
his complex relationship with his
parents, and the sources of his ambition and inspiration.

Year Produced: 1986
Producer: Lois Cunniff
Director: Lawrence Pitkethly
Writers: Derek Walcott, Margot Feldman
Cinematography: Jonathan David
Editor: Jessica Bendiner
Narrator: Jose Ferrer
Cast: Dan Ziskie as the voice of Hart Crane
Interviews: Derek Walcott, Richard Howard,
Malcolm and Peggy Cowley, and others
Format: 16mm, Video (56:00)

### Program 3
### Emily Dickinson (1830–1868)

explores the reclusive poet's accom-
plishments, education, and interests,
dispels the belief that she was
unworldly and naive, and considers
why her poems were not appreciated
during her lifetime.

Year Produced: 1987
Producer: Jill Janows
Director: Veronica Young
Writer: Judith Thurman
Cinematographer: Jeri Sopanen
Editor: Lisa Jackson
Cast: Jane Alexander as the voice of Emily
Dickinson
Interviews: Richard Sewell, Joyce Carol
Oates, Adrienne Rich, Anthony Hecht, and
others
Format: 16mm, Video (56:00)

### Program 4
### T.S. Eliot (1888–1965)

considers the work of a writer many
regard as the most influential
American poet of his century against
the backdrop of a life beset by enor-
mous unhappiness and a troubled
search for spiritual solace.

Year Produced: 1987
Producers: Sasha Alpert, Lawrence Pitkethly
Director/Writer: Lawrence Pitkethly
Cinematographer: Nic Knowland
Editor: Jessica Bendiner
Music: Performed by The Endellion Quartet
Interviews: Frank Kermode, Peter Ackroyd,
Joseph Ciari, Stephen Spender, and others
Format: 16mm, Video (56:00)

## Program 5
### Robert Frost (1874–1963)

examines the poet's lengthy career, from his move to England at the age of 40 where his work was first published and celebrated, to his return to New England and the poetic speech with which he is most associated.

Year Produced: 1985
Producer: Robert Chapman
Associate Producer: Michael Hendricks
Director/Editor: Peter Hammer
Research Supervisor: Minda Novek
Writer: Margot Feldman
Cinematography: Tom Hurwitz, Jonathan David, Robert Fulton, Peter Hoving
Composer: Michael Bacon
Narrator: Laurence Luckinbill
Cast: Jason Robards III, Joan Allen, Frank Maraden
Interviews: Seamus Heaney, Joseph Brodsky, Richard Wilbur, William Pritchard, Richard Poirier, Alfred Edwards, and others
Format: 16mm, Video (56:30)

## Program 6
### Langston Hughes: The Dream Keeper (1902–1967)

explains how Hughes wrote about the problems, cares, and dignity of African-Americans, as well as the way his poetry derives from African American musical sources and the vocabulary and dialect patterns of black urban speech.

Year Produced: 1986
Producer: Robert Chapman
Director: St. Clair Bourne
Writer: Leslie Lee
Cinematography: Arthur Albert, Don Lenzer
Editor: Sam Pollard
Composer: Stanley Cowell
Poetry Narrated by: Novella Nelson, Roscoe Orman
Interviews: James Baldwin, Amiri Baraka, Gwendolyn Brooks, Arnold Rampersad, George Houston Bass, Faith Berry, Raoul Abdul, Rowena Jelliffe, Louise Patterson, and others
Format: Video (56:00)

## Program 7
### Robert Lowell: A Mania for Phrases (1917–1977)

examines the life of a writer who descended from old Yankee stock and who incorporated the torments of his own psyche into his art, amplifying them to reflect the turmoil he saw in American society.

Year Produced: 1987
Producer: Robert Chapman
Coproducer: David Schmerler
Director/Editor: Peter Hammer
Cowriters: Lawrence Pitkethly, Peter Hammer
Cinematography: Robert Levi
Composer: Michael Bacon
Interviews: Derek Walcott, Frank Bidart, Anthony Hecht, John Thompson, Robert Hass, Robert Giroux, Elizabeth Hardwick, and others
Format: 16mm, Video (56:00)

## Program 8
### Marianne Moore: In Her Own Image (1887–1972)

treats the life and work of this inventive and idiosyncratic poet, including her belief in a principled life and her close observation of nature.

Year Produced: 1987
Producers: David Schmerler, Robert Chapman
Director: Jeffrey Schon
Writer: Vickie Karp
Cinematography: Mark Trottenberg, with Brian O'Connell, Jonathan David, Timothy Housel, Mead Hunt, Nic Knowland, Robert Levi
Editor: Joelle Schon
Animation: Veronika Soul
Composer: Richard Einhorn
Narrator: Peter Maloney
Cast: Laurie Heineman as the voice of Marianne Moore
Interviews: Charles Tomlinson, Clive Driver, Grace Schulman, Richard Howard, Patricia Willis, and others
Format: 16mm, Video (56:30)

## Program 9
### Sylvia Plath (1932–1963)

examines the work of a poet whose achievement has been obscured by the drama of her suicide at age thirty.

Year Produced: 1987
Director/Producer: Lawrence Pitkethly
Coproducer: Sasha Alpert
Writer: Susan Yankowitz
Cinematography: Nic Knowland, Bob Chappell
Editor: Jessica Bendiner
Interviews: Aurelia Plath, Wilbury Crockett, Clarissa Roche, Dido Merwin, Margaret Shook, A. Alvarez, Sandra M. Gilbert, and others
Format: 16mm, Video (56:30)

## Program 10
### Ezra Pound: American Odyssey (1885–1972)

considers the life and work of this poet, musician, editor, and essayist, who was one of the leading and most erudite forces behind modernism.

Year Produced: 1983
Producer/Director/Writer: Lawrence Pitkethly
Cinematography: Jonathan David
Animation Camera: Gary Becker, Mead Hunt
Graphics and Animation: Jeffrey Schon
Editor: Variety Moszynski
Consulting Editor: Peter Hammer
Narrator: Paul Hecht
Interviews: Olga Rudge, Mary de Rachewiltz, James Laughlin, Basil Bunting, Alfred Kazin, Hugh Kenner, and others
Format: 16mm, Video (two versions, 56:30 and 87:00)

**60**

*Program 11*
**Wallace Stevens: Man Made Out of Words (1879–1955)**
contrasts the writer's separate but connected identities: his sedate public career as an insurance lawyer in Hartford, Connecticut, and his exotic and adventurous inner life as a poet.

Year Produced: 1987
Producer: Jill Janows
Director: Richard P. Rogers
Writer: Robert Seidman
Cinematography: Richard P. Rogers, Nancy Schreiber
Editor: Corey Shaff
Composer: Martin Bresnick
Interviews: Mark Strand, James Merrill, Harold Bloom, Joan Richardson, Helen Vendler, A. Walton Litz, and others
Format: 16mm, Video (56:30)

*Program 12*
**Walt Whitman (1819–1892)**
spans the writer's career as a typesetter, journalist, and Civil War nurse and considers why he is credited with revolutionizing American letters and inaugurating modern poetry.

Year Produced: 1983
Coordinating Producer: Lois Cuniff
Director: Jack Smithie
Cinematography: Lloyd Freidus, Robert Fulton, with Jonathan David, Robert Hanna, Pamela Katz
Editors: Peter Hammer, Mark Rappaport
Narrator: Peter MacNichol
Cast: Louis Turenne as the voice of Whitman
Interviews: Justin Kaplan, Harold Bloom, Allen Ginsberg, Galway Kinnell, Donald Hall, and others
Format: 16mm, Video (56:00)

*Program 13*
**William Carlos Williams (1883–1963)**
examines the writer's bold experiments in verse and the relationship between his art and his life as a family doctor in New Jersey.

Year Produced: 1986
Producer/Writer: Jill Janows
Director: Richard P. Rogers
Cinematography: Richard P. Rogers, Gerry Cotts, Lisa Rinzler
Editor: Corey Shaff
Animation/GRAPHIC Design: George Griffin, Maureen Selwood
Composer: Martin Bresnick
Interviews: Hugh Kenner, Majorie Perloff, Allen Ginsberg, Robert Coles, Dickran Tashjiam, James Laughlin, Dr. William Eric Williams, and others
Format: 16mm, Video (56:00)

Series Production Organization: The New York Center for Visual History, New York, NY
Years Produced: 1982–1987
Series Executive Producer: Lawrence Pitkethly
Senior Producers: Robert Chapman, Jill Janows
Print Materials: *Voices & Visions: The Poet in America*, edited by Helen Vendler (essays), *Modern American Poets: Their Voices and Visions*, edited by Robert DiYanni (text/anthology), Viewer's Guide, Joseph Parisi
Format: 16mm, Video (56:00)
Distributors: Intellimation (for Annenberg/CPB Project); Adult Learning Service, PBS (telecourse)

# WILLA CATHER: A LOOK OF REMEMBRANCE
## *Dramatic Radio Series*
This series presents the life and legacy of the Nebraska novelist (l876–1947) and an examination of the principal themes of her work.

*Program l*
**The Land**
traces Cather's early years and her friendship with journalist Elizabeth Sergeant.

*Program 2*
**The Cave**
explores Cather's ideas on art and womanhood as she becomes increasingly reclusive.

*Program 3*
**The Rock**
examines Cather's notions of what the artist should be.

Production Organization: National Public Radio, Washington, DC
Year Produced: 1983
Producers: Joe N. Gwathmey, Jo Ellyn Rackleff, Frieda Werden
Directors: Jo Ellyn Rackleff, Joan Micklin Silver
Writer: Jo Ellyn Rackleff
Cast: Colleen Dewhurst, Dianne Wiest
Award: The National Commission on Working Women, Women at Work Broadcast Awards Competition, Honorable Mention
Format: Audiocassette
3 (30:00) programs
Distributor: Not currently available

# WILLIAM FAULKNER: A LIFE ON PAPER
## *Documentary*
A profile of the life of William Faulkner (1897–1962), this film blends interviews with people who knew him, excerpts from his books, and scenes in Oxford, Mississippi.

Production Organization: Mississippi Authority for Educational Television, Jackson, MS
Year Produced: 1979
Producer: Walter Lowe
Director: Robert Squier
Writer: A. I. Bezzerides
Narration/Reading: Raymond Burr, Arthur Ed Foreman
Interviews: Jill Faulkner Summers, Malcolm Cowley, Tennesse Williams, Robert Penn Warren, Lauren Bacall, Anita Loos, Howard Hawks, Marc Connelly, Joseph Blotner, Carvel Collins, Albert Erskine, and others
Awards: Dupont-Columbia Award; CINE Golden Eagle; Chicago International Film Festival, Gold Plaque; CPB, Local Program Award; Houston International Film Festival, Silver Award; New York International Film and Television Festival, Gold Plaque
Format: Video (120:00)
Distributor: Mississippi Authority for Educational Television

## THE WORLD OF F. SCOTT FITZGERALD

### Radio Series (Documentary and Drama)

Each program in this series combines the dramatization of a short story by F. Scott Fitzgerald (1896–1940) with a documentary examining his life and times.

### Program 1
**The Death of Heroism**
documents the naive heroism of Fitzgerald and his Ivy League classmates at the outset of World War I, and includes the short story "Emotional Bankruptcy."

### Program 2
**The Spoiled Priest**
examines the conflict between rigid Catholic attitudes and romantic glamorous visions in Fitzgerald's own life and as he wrote about them in "Absolution."

### Program 3
**He Called It "The Jazz Age"**
portrays the gaiety and irreverence of the 1920s, especially as depicted in "The Offshore Pirates."

### Program 4
**The Golden Boom**
considers the "Jazz Age" and Fitzgerald's bittersweet American success story, "Winter Dreams."

### Program 5
**Lost and Lucky**
follows F. Scott Fitzgerald and his wife Zelda to Europe in the 1920s with the short story "One Trip Abroad."

### Program 6
**The End of an Era**
combines a look at the stockmarket crash and Zelda Fitzgerald's breakdown with the short story "Family in the Wind."

### Program 7
**The Most Forgotten Writer in America**
satirizes Fitzgerald's deepening financial troubles in "Financing Finnegan," the story of a famous but financially irresponsible writer.

### Program 8
**The Last of the Novelists**
treats Fitzgerald's film writing career and includes the story "The Lost Decade," a fictional account of his search for success in Hollywood.

Production Organizations: National Public Radio, Washington, DC (documentary segments); National Radio Theatre of Chicago (dramatic readings)
Year Produced: 1979
Producers: Jo Ellyn Rackleff, documentaries; Yuri Rasovsky, dramatic readings
Associate Producers: Robert Haslach, documentaries; Michelle M. Faith, dramatic readings
Readings: Richard Thomas, Studs Terkel, Barbara Rush, Hugh O'Brian, Jerry Orbach
Music: Hans Wurman
Interviews: Scottie Fitzgerald Smith, Malcolm Cowley, Marc Connelly, Ginevra King Pirie, Morley Callaghan, Irving Howe, Warren Susman, Budd Schulberg, and others
Format: Audiocassette
8 (60:00) programs
Distributor: Not currently available

## WORLD REP

### Dramatic Radio Series

World Rep presents plays of Western literature, following their chronological order to show the development of drama from Aeschylus to Chekhov in tandem with other social, political, and philosophical developments in Western history and thought.

### Program 1
**Prometheus Bound, by Aeschylus, and Medea, by Euripides (5th century B.C.).**

### Program 2
**The Frogs, by Aristophanes (c. 5th century B.C.) and The Pot of Gold, by Plautus (3rd century B.C.).**

### Program 3
**Abraham and Isaac and Everyman, two anonymous medieval liturgical dramas. Dr. Faustus, by Christopher Marlowe (c. 1588).**

62

*Program 4*
**The Tempest, by William
Shakespeare (c. 1611).**

*Program 5*
**Phaedra, by Jean Racine (1677).**

*Program 6*
**The Imaginary Invalid, by Jean-
Baptiste Poquelin Molière (1673).**

*Program 7*
**The Beaux' Stratagem, by George
Farquhar (1707).**

*Program 8*
**Danton's Death, by Georg Büchner
(1835).**

*Program 9*
**The Lady of the Camellias, by
Alexandre Dumas (1852).**

*Program 10*
**An Enemy of the People, by Henrik
Ibsen (1882).**

*Program 11*
**Uncle Vanya, by Anton Chekhov
(1899).**

*Program 12*
**Arms and the Man, by George
Bernard Shaw (1894).**

Production Organization: National Radio
Theatre, Chicago, IL
Year Produced: 1986
Producer/Director/Adaptations: Yuri
Rasovsky
Cast: F. Murray Abraham, Rene
Auberjenois, Len Cariou, Rosemary Harris,
Barry Morris, Nancy Marchand, Lois
Nettleton, Sam Waterston, Fritz
Weaver
Format: Audiocassette
12 (120:00) programs
Distributor: National Radio Theatre

*World
Culture &
History*

## ABODE OF ILLUSION

*Documentary*

The film considers differences between Chinese and Western aesthetics through an examination of the work of Chang Ta-Ch'ien (1899–1983), one of China's foremost modern painters.

Production Organization: Long Bow Group, New York, NY
Year Produced: 1992
Producers: Carma Hinton, Richard Gordon, Kathy Kline, Carl Nagin
Directors: Carma Hinton, Richard Gordon
Writer: Carma Hinton
Cinematography: Richard Gordon
Editor: David Carnochan
Format: 16mm, Video (60:00)
Distributor: Long Bow Group, Inc.

## ALL UNDER HEAVEN: LIFE IN A CHINESE VILLAGE

*Documentary*

All under Heaven examines the effect of political change, particularly collectivization and decollectivization, on Long Bow, a village about 400 miles southwest of Beijing, China.

Production Organization: Long Bow Village Film Group, Philadelphia, PA
Year Produced: 1985
Producers: Richard Gordon, Carma Hinton, Kathy Kline, Dan Sipe
Associate Producers: Tim Callahan, David Carnochan
Directors: Carma Hinton, Richard Gordon
Writers: Carma Hinton, with Laurie Block, John Crowley
Editor: David Carnochan
Cinematography: Richard Gordon
Sound Recordist: Yand Ifang
Awards/Festivals: Earthwatch Film Award; Margaret Mead Film Festival; Hawaii International Film Festival; San Francisco International Film Festival
Format: 16mm, Video (58:00)
Distributor: New Day Films

## BIQUEFARRE

*Drama*

This film is a sequel to director Georges Rouquier's landmark feature *Farrebique,* a portrait of rural French society in the Aveyron district of southern France.

Production Organizations: Midas S.A., Paris; Mallia Films, Gentilly, France; and Community Animation, Inc., Ithaca, NY
Year Produced: 1983
Coproducers: Marie-Françoise Mascaro, Bertrand Van Effenterre, William Gilcher
Director: Georges Rouquier
Editor: Genevieve Louveau
Cinematography: André Villard, Pierre-Laurent Chenieux
Award: Venice International Film Festival, Special Jury Prize
Format: 35mm, 16mm (90:00)
Distributors: New Yorker Films (U.S.); Les Films René Malo (Canada)

## BOSWELL FOR THE DEFENCE

*Drama*

This film explores the issues of quality of life and justice in eighteenth-century Scotland through the story of James Reid, a butcher accused of stealing nineteen sheep and sentenced to hang. It focuses on Reid's defense by Scottish lawyer and writer James Boswell.

Production Organizations: Yale University Films, New Haven, CT, and BBC, Scotland
Year Produced: 1983
Executive Producer: Howard Sayre Weaver
Producer: Roderick Graham
Editor: Robert Bathgate
Writer: Mark Harris
Cinematography: Stuart Wyld
Cast: David McKail, Alec Heggie, Isobel Black, Andrew Keir
Award: Television and Radio Club of Scotland, Best Single Drama on Television
Format: Video (90:00)
Distributor: Films for the Humanities and Sciences

## BOSWELL IN LONDON

*Drama*

Adapted from James Boswell's *London Journal,* this two-part dramatization portrays Boswell's attempts to seek acceptance in London society, his historic meeting and developing friendship with Samuel Johnson, and his departure for Holland to study law.

Production Organizations: Yale University Films, New Haven, CT and BBC, Scotland
Year Produced: 1984
Executive Producer: William Peters
Producer/Director: Roderick Graham
Writer: Mark Harris
Editor: Brian Ashcroft
Cinematography: Stuart Wyld
Cast: Ian Sharp, Annette Lynton, Tony Steedman
Format: Video (112:00)
Part 1 (60:00), Part 2 (52:00)
Distributor: Films for the Humanities and Sciences

## CASTLE

*Documentary*

Based on a book by David Macaulay, this film explains the architectural design, social organization, and military significance of a thirteenth-century Welsh castle through a blend of animated dramatic sequences and live action. (see also Cathedral and Pyramid)

Production Organization: Unicorn Projects, Inc., Washington, DC
Year Produced: 1983
Executive Producer: Ray Hubbard
Coproducers: Larry Klein, Mark Olshaker
Writer: Mark Olshaker
Director of Animation: Jack Stokes
Animation: The Animation Partnership in association with TV Cartoons, Ltd.
Hosts: David Macaulay, Sarah Bullen
Voices: Ronald Baddily, Brian Blessed, Ellis Jones, Freddie Jones, Roy Purcell, Marie Sutherland

65

66

Awards: American Film and Video Festival, Red Ribbon; CINE Golden Eagle
Format: 16mm, Video (two versions, 57:20 and 30:00)
Distributors: PBS Video (video); Unicorn Projects, Inc. (16mm)

## CATHEDRAL

*Documentary*

Drawn from the book by architect/ illustrator David Macaulay, Cathedral combines animated dramatic episodes with location sequences to tell the story of the planning, construction, and dedication of a fictional cathedral in medieval France. (see also Castle and Pyramid)

Production Organization: Unicorn Projects, Inc., Washington, DC
Year Produced: 1985
Executive Producer: Ray Hubbard
Producers/Writers: Larry Klein, Mark Olshaker
Animation: The Animation Partnership
Animation Created & Directed by: Tony White
Hosts: David Macaulay, Caroline Berg
Voices: Derek Jacobi, Brian Blessed, Geoffrey Matthews, Paul Bacon, Sean Barrett, Paul Bacon, Peter Pacey, Ellis Jones
Awards: American Film and Video Festival, Blue Ribbon; International Film and Television Festival of New York, Finalist; Chicago International Film Festival, Certificate of Merit; CINE Golden Eagle
Format: Video (two versions, 58:00 and 29:00)
Distributors: PBS Video (video); Unicorn Projects, Inc. (16mm)

## CHINA'S COSMOPOLITAN AGE: THE TANG

*Documentary*

This program examines the legacy of the Tang dynasty (A.D. 618–907) in government, art, religion, and philosophy, and its far-reaching contribution to the humanistic traditions of China, Korea, and Japan.

Production Organization: The George Washington University, Washington, DC
Year Produced: 1991
Executive Producers: Joan Chung-wen Shih, Peter Montagnon
Directors: Joan Chung-wen Shih, Maddalena Fagandini
Cinematography: Andy Parkinson, Mike Fox, Christopher Li
Editors: Hamilton Hawksworth, Michael Danks, Penny Trams, Mike Ritter
Narrator: Theo Feng
Format: Video (58:00)
Distributor: Dr. Chung-wen Shih

## CHINA IN REVOLUTION, 1911–1949

*Documentary*

China in Revolution, 1911–1949 explores the establishment of the Chinese communist state, from the fall of the boy emperor, Pu Yi, to the birth of the People's Republic of China.

Production Organizations: Film News Now Foundation and Ambrica Productions, New York, NY
Year Produced: 1988
Executive Producer: Judith Vecchioni
Producers: Sue Williams, Kathryn Dietz
Director/Writer: Sue Williams
Codirector: Kathryn Dietz
Cinematography: Richard Gordon
Editor: Howard Sharp
Narrator: Will Lyman
Awards/Festivals: National Educational Film and Video Festival, Bronze Apple; American Film and Video Festival, Red Ribbon; International Chinese Film Festival, Montreal

Format: Video (135:00)
Part I: Battle for Survival, 1911–36 (58:00);
Part II: Fighting for the Future, 1936–49 (58:00)
Distributors: Coronet/MTI Film and Video (U.S.); Jane Balfour Films, London (international)

## COLUMBUS AND THE AGE OF DISCOVERY

*Documentary Series*

Columbus and the Age of Discovery is a seven-part series on Christopher Columbus, his era, and his legacy.

*Program 1*
**Columbus' World**
travels to China, the Spice Islands, Cairo, Genoa, Venice, and Istanbul to explore the world of the fifteenth century and set the stage for Columbus's great seagoing adventure.

Producer/Writer: Thomas Friedman
Director: Stephen Segaller

*Program 2*
**An Idea Takes Shape**
considers the advances in shipbuilding and navigation that made Columbus's voyages possible, examines his motivations, and chronicles his long and arduous search for patronage to fund his westward route to the Orient.

Producer/Writer: Thomas Friedman
Director: Stephen Segaller

## Program 3
**The Crossing**
recreates Columbus's first transatlantic route with working replicas of the Nina, the Pinta, and the Santa María as well as from excerpts from his logs and journal.

Producer/Director/Writer: Zvi Dor-Ner

## Program 4
**Worlds Found and Lost**
follows a modern-day crew as they sail the route of Columbus's first voyage, from his landfall at San Salvador, through the Bahamas to Cuba, Haiti, and the Dominican Republic, searching for the Caribbean that
Columbus saw, and the changes left in his wake.

Producer/Director/Writer: Zvi Dor-Ner

## Program 5
**The Sword and the Cross**
shows how the Americas evolved from the new blend of peoples, diseases, motives, and attitudes brought by Columbus and those who followed him. In addition, the impact of the conquistadors and the Catholic church on the indigenous population is explored.

Producer/Director/Writer: Graham Chedd

## Program 6
**The Columbian Exchange**
examines the interchange of horses, cattle, corn, potatoes, and sugar cane between the Old World and the New, and the lasting impact on the people of both worlds.

Producer/Director/Writer: Graham Chedd

## Program 7
**In Search of Columbus**
follows the path of the admiral's fourth and final voyage and explores perceptions of Columbus by different nations and cultures on the eve of the quincentenary.

Producer/Director/Writer: Graham Chedd

Series Production Organization: WGBH, Boston, MA
Years Produced: 1985–1991
Series Executive Producer: Zvi Dor-Ner
Original Music Composed by: Sheldon Mirowitz
Host: Mauricio Obregon
Narrator: Will Lyman
Print Material: Companion Volume: *Columbus and the Age of Discovery* by Zvi Dor-Ner with William Scheller; interactive videodisc; audio cassette; resource guides; teachers' guides; student newspaper (to be printed in 1992)
Format: Video
7 (58:00) programs
Distributor: Films for the Humanities and Sciences, Inc., The WBGH Collection

# CORPUS DUENDE: ECHOES OF THE SPANISH CIVIL WAR
*Radio Documentary*

Corpus Duende documents the Spanish Civil War and its international repercussions through the testimony of survivors as well as through period music, poetry, and news reports.

Production Organization: Metropolitan Pittsburgh Public Broadcasting, Inc. (WQED)
Year Produced: 1981
Executive Producer: Thomas B. Skinner
Producer/Director: Bill Howell
Story: Based on a script by Robert E. Lee
Narrator: Karl Hardman
Cast: Eli Wallach, Denise Hunt, Pip Theodor, Wilson Hutton, Hugh A. Rose
Format: Audiocassette (59:00)
Distributor: WQED-FM

# DE GAULLE AND FRANCE
*Documentary Series*

De Gaulle and France is a three-part series on the life, impact, and legacy of the French general and statesman Charles de Gaulle (1890–1970).

## Program 1
**A Vision of France**
traces the rise of de Gaulle with the establishment of his French government-in-exile in London and the restructuring of post-war Europe.

Producer/Writer/Director: Sue Williams
Editor: Sharon Sachs

## Program 2
**Return of the General**
examines de Gaulle's re-entry into politics during the Algerian crisis, his efforts at revising the French constitution, and his abandonment of the notion of a French empire.

Producer/Writer: Tom Weidlinger
Editor: Constance Ryder

## Program 3
**Challenging the World**
considers de Gaulle's policies and actions as he worked toward insuring France's place as a major international power during the 1960s.

Producer/Writer/Director: Christina von Braun
Editor: Claire Painchault

68

Production Organizations: WGBH
Educational Foundation, Boston, MA, and
LMK Images, Paris, France
Year Produced: 1991
Executive Producers: Judith Vecchione, Yves
Eudes
Producer/Writers: Sue Williams, Tom
Wiedlinger, Christina von Braun
Directors: Sue Williams, Christina von
Braun
Cinematography: Georges Diane, Alain
Thiollet, Michel Gau, Jean-Claude Barxell
Editors: Sharon Sachs, Constance Ryder,
Claire Painchault
Narrator: Gene Galusha
Format: Video
3 (60:00) programs
Distributors: WGBH Educational
Foundation (U.S.); Jane Balfour Films,
London (international)

## THE GLOBAL ASSEMBLY LINE

### Documentary

The Global Assembly Line explores
the impact of transnational expansion and relocation in the electronics
and garment industries through the
experience of women and men
working in these industries in developing countries and in North
America.

Production Organization: Educational
Television and Film Center, Washington,
DC
Year Produced: 1986
Coproducers: Lorraine Gray, Anne Bohlen,
Maria Patricia, Fernandez Kelly
Director/Writer: Lorraine Gray
Cinematographers: Sandi Sissel, Baird
Bryant, Lorraine Gray
Editors: Mary Lampson, Sarah Fishko
Awards: Emmy Award; National
Educational Film and Video Festival, Gold
Apple; Leipzig International Film Festival,
Special Jury Prize; American Film and Video
Festival, Blue Ribbon; Museum of Modern
Art, New Directors/New Films
Format: 16mm, Video (58:00)
Distributor: New Day Films

## HERITAGE: CIVILIZATION AND THE JEWS

### Documentary Series

Heritage is a nine-part documentary
series that chronicles the 3,000-year
history of the Jewish people.

### Program 1

**A People Is Born (c. 3500 B.C.E. to
sixth century B.C.E.)**
recounts the origins of the Jewish
people from their exodus out of
Egypt to their Babylonian exile.

Producer/Director: Eugene Marner
Story: Marc Siegel
Writer: John Sharnik

### Program 2

**The Power of the Word (sixth
century B.C.E. to second century
C.E.)**
examines how the Jewish people
formed an identity based on ideas as
opposed to territory during the
Babylonian exile.

Directors: Eugene Marner, Patricia Sides,
Julian Krainin, Howard Enders
Story: Marc Siegel
Writer: John Lord
Post-Production Producer: Len Morris
Associate Producers: Petra Lent, Rivalyn
Zweig

### Program 3

**The Shaping of Traditions (first to
ninth centuries)**
describes how different Jewish sects
dispersed throughout the Mediterra-
nean region and how this influenced
the emergence of Christianity and
Islam.

Producers: John G. Fox, Julian Krainin
Director: Julian Krainin
Writers: John G. Fox, Marc Siegel

### Program 4

**The Crucible of Europe (ninth to
fifteenth centuries)**
explores Jewish life and religion
throughout western Europe during
the Middle Ages.

Producer: Michael Joseloff
Director: Julian Krainin
Writers: John G. Fox, Marc Siegel, Michael
Joseloff, Howard Enders

### Program 5

**The Search for Deliverance (1492–
1789)**
describes the Jewish-European experience, from the expulsion of Jews
from Spain in 1492 to the French
Revolution.

Producer/Director: Eugene Marner
Writer: John G. Fox

### Program 6

**Roads from the Ghetto (1789–1917)**
traces the impact on the Jewish
experience of the Industrial and
French Revolutions.

Producer/Director: Eugene Marner
Writers: Eugene Marner, John G. Fox

### Program 7

**The Golden Land (1654–1932)**
examines the stages of Jewish immigration to America and the conver-
gence of the American ideal of
democracy with the ancient Jewish
heritage of freedom.

Producer/Directors: Marc Siegel, Morton
Silverstein
Writer: Marc Montfrey

*Program 8*
**Out of the Ashes (1917–45)**
describes the Nazi ideology, Jewish "shtetl" life, repression and persecution leading to "The Final Solution," and Jewish resistance.

Producer/Director: Alan Rosenthal
Writer: Brian Winston

*Program 9*
**Into the Future (1945 to the present)**
focuses on events leading up to the creation of Israel, its early history and relationship with Jews worldwide, and the long-range issues of identity and security.

Producer/Director: Alan Rosenthal
Writer: Aleck Jackson

Series Production Organization: WNET/13, New York, NY
Year Produced: 1984
Series Executive Producers: Arnold Labaton, Marc Siegel
Series Producer: John G. Fox
Senior Editorial Consultant: Marc Siegel
Host: Abba Eban
Awards: Emmy Award; Christopher Award; American Film Festival, Red Ribbon
Format: Video
9 (60:00) programs
Distributor: Films, Inc./PMI

# HOMES APART: KOREA

*Documentary*

This film looks at the division of Korea through the eyes of the producer/narrator and a Korean-American who is reunited with his sister in North Korea.

Production Organization: Third World Newsreel, New York, NY
Year Produced: 1991
Project Director: Orinne J.T. Takagi
Producer/Narrator: Christine Choy
Director: J.T. Takagi
Writer: David Henry Hwang
Cinematography: Christine Choy, Nick Doob
Editor: Maro Chermayeff
Print Material: Study guide available
Format: 16mm, Video (55:00)
Distributor: Third World Newsreel

# IMAGE BEFORE MY EYES

*Documentary*

Image before My Eyes recreates Jewish life in Poland from the late nineteenth century through the 1930s.

Production Organization: YIVO Institute for Jewish Research, New York, NY
Year Produced: 1980
Producers: Josh Waletzky, Susan Lazarus
Director/Editor: Josh Waletzky
Writer: Jerome Badanes
Award: Mannheim Film Festival, Gold Dukat Award
Format: 16mm (90:00)
Distributor: Almi Pictures, Inc.

# INDIA SPEAKS

*Documentary*

This program reveals India's cultural, linguistic, economic, and philosophical diversity through a look at the lives of several of its citizens.

Production Organization: Ganesha Productions, Los Angeles, CA
Year Produced: 1986
Producer/Director: Paula Haller
Cinematography: Rickie Gauld
Editor: Jan Roblee
Award: CINE Golden Eagle
Format: 16mm, Video (23:00)
Distributor: Coronet/MTI (for Disney Educational Productions)

# THE JEWS OF SHANGHAI

*Radio Documentary*

Through the testimony of survivors, this two-part program looks at the experience of the more than one hundred thousand European Jews who fled to Shanghai from Hitler's Third Reich.

Production Organization: National Public Radio, Washington, DC
Year Produced: 1990
Executive Producers: Bill Buzenberg, Ellen Weiss
Producer/Writers: Art Silverman, Susan Stamberg
Editor:: Brooke Gladstone
Narrator: Susan Stamberg
Format: Audiocassette
2 (23:00) programs
Distributor: National Public Radio

# KADDISH

*Documentary*

Kaddish is a film about growing up as the American-born child of a Holocaust survivor in the Orthodox Jewish community of Boro Park, New York.

Production Organization: Ways & Means Production, New York, NY
Year Produced: 1984
Producer/Director/Editor: Steve Brand
Narrator: Yossi Klein
Festivals: U.S. Film Festival; Global Village Film Festival; FILMEX (Los Angeles); Museum of Modern Art and Film Society of Lincoln Center, New Directors/New Films
Format: 16mm, Video (92:00)
Distributor: First Run/Icarus Films

70

## LODZ GHETTO

*Documentary*

This film focuses on Poland's Lodz Ghetto (1941–44), the longest surviving community of Jews trapped in Hitler's Europe, and is drawn entirely from the secret daily journals and photographs which these people left behind.

Production Organization: The Jewish Heritage Project, New York, NY
Year Produced: 1990
Executive Producer: Stephen Samuels
Producer: Alan Adelson
Directors: Kathryn Taverna, Alan Adelson
Script compiled by: Kathryn Taverna, Alan Adelson
Cinematography: Buddy Squires, Jozef Piwkowski
Editor: Kathryn Taverna
Music: Wendy Blackstone
Voices: Jerzy Kosinski, Nicholas Kepros, Barbara Rosenblat, David Warrilow, Gregory Gordon
Awards/Festivals: Federation of European Film Critics Award; Leipzig International Film Festival, Best Film; U.S. (Sundance) Film and Video Festival; Montreal International Film Festival; San Francisco International Film Festival; Festival dei Popoli, Florence, Italy; Berlin International Film Festival; London International Film Festival: Valladolid International Film Festival; Dallas International Film Festival; Yamagata (Japan) International Film Festival
Print Material: The film is based on *The Chronicle of the Lodz Ghetto*, commissioned by the Eldest of the Jews and written for the purpose of historical illumination
Format: 35mm, Video (103:00)
Distributor: The Jewish Heritage Project

## LOS CORRIDOS

*Radio Documentary*

This program explores the history and significance of the Mexican ballads or story songs known as *corridos* and how they pass on traditions, oral history, and cultural values.

Production Organization: Voces Unidas Bilingual Broadcasting Foundation, Salinas, CA
Year Produced: 1983
Program Director: C. Beatriz López-Flores
Producer: Chris Strachwitz
Format: Audiocassette (30:00)
Distributor: Not currently available

## MANOS A LA OBRA: THE STORY OF OPERATION BOOTSTRAP

*Documentary*

Manos a la obra (Put Your Hands to Work) traces the historical background of Operation Bootstrap and the economic development of Puerto Rico from the 1930s to the 1960s.

Production Organization: Centro de Estudios Puertorriqueños, Hunter College of the City University of New York
Year Produced: 1983
Executive Director: Jaime Barrios
Associate Producers/Directors: Pedro Angel Rivera, Susan Zeig
Cinematography: Susan Zeig, Alicia Weber
Narrator: Ilka Tania Payan
Awards/Festivals: American Film and Video Festival, Finalist; First LASA Invitational Film Festival; Independent Focus; *Choice,* Outstanding Nonprint Material (American Library Association)
Format: 16mm, Video (59:00)
Distributor: The Cinema Guild

## THE MYSTERY PLAY OF ELCHE

*Documentary and Drama*

As the only play performed continually since the Middle Ages, *The Mystery Play of Elche* has been declared a National Cultural Monument in Spain, re-enacted every year by the townspeople of Elche.

### Program 1

A documentary study of the town of Elche and its people precedes an edited presentation of the play sung in Valenciano.

### Program 2

An unedited version of the play, without interpretive material.

Production Organization: Folger Shakespeare Library, Washington, DC
Year Produced: 1979
Producer: O.B. Hardison, Jr.
Director: Gudie Lawaetz
Co-Director: Michael Dodds
Awards: Chicago International Film Festival, Certificate of Merit; Hemisfilm '80 Festival, Special Jury Prize
Format: 16mm, Video
Program 1 (120:00); Program 2 (180:00)
Distributor: Folger Shakespeare Library, Museum Shop

## THE PARCHING WINDS OF SOMALIA

*Documentary*

This film examines the history of the Islamic-African nation of Somalia.

Production Organization: Metropolitan Pittsburgh Public Broadcasting Inc. (WQED)
Year Produced: 1984
Executive Producer: David Roland
Producer: Charles Geshekter
Writers: Charles Geshekter, Mary Rawson
Editors: Gary Hines, Frank George
Cinematography: Andre Gunn
Narrator: Mary Rawson
Format: Video (27:48)
Distributor: Indiana University, Audio Visual Center

## PARTISANS OF VILNA

*Documentary*

Through archival footage and interviews with former partisans, this film explores Jewish resistance in Vilna during World War II.

Production Organization: Ciesla Foundation, Washington, DC
Year Produced: 1985
Producer: Aviva Kempner
Director/Editor: Josh Waletzky
Narrator: Roberta Wallach
Cinematography: Danny Shneuer
Awards/Festivals: Anthropos Film Festival, Los Angeles, First Prize Winnner; American Film and Video Festival, Honorable Mention; CINE Golden Eagle; Berlin Film Festival; FILMEX (Los Angeles); INPUT Conference; Toronto Film Festival; London Film Festival; Troia-Haifa Film Festival; London Jewish Film Festival; San Francisco Jewish Film Festival; Australian Jewish Film Festivals (Sydney and Melbourne)
Print Material: Viewer's guide and record, with or without booklet, available. Record booklet contains essays on the songs and lyrics in English and in transliterated Yiddish. For these materials contact: Aviva Kempner, Ciesla Foundation, 1707 Lanier Place, NW, Washington, DC 20009.
Telephone: 202-462-7528
Format: 35mm, 16mm, Video (133:00)
Distributor: Capitol Entertainment

## PASSAGES TO INDIA

*Documentary Radio Series*

Recorded in 1986–88, Passages to India presents ten "passages" or keys to understanding modern India.

### Program 1
**A Kaleidoscope of Cultures**
examines India's diverse language, race, religion, geography, and climate.

### Program 2
**The Presence of the Past**
discusses Indian notions of time and how Mahatma Gandhi consciously blended past and present for political ends.

### Program 3
**Puja: Darsan Dena, Darsan Lena**
looks at Hinduism as worship in the daily lives of Indians.

### Program 4
**Biryani and Plum Pudding**
focuses on Muslim and British influences and the manner in which they have been adapted.

### Program 5
**Vedas, Ragas, and Storytellers**
looks at the oral tradition in classical, folk, and popular cultures and the role of Indian cinema.

### Program 6
**In Search of Filmwallahs**
considers film as a dominant cultural form in today's India.

### Program 7
**Praneschacharya's Dilemma**
examines how traditional notions of right action or *dharma* intersect with modernization to create new tensions between individual and community roles.

### Program 8
**Sita Speak!**
looks at the tension between the all-powerful women of Hindu mythology and traditionally submissive feminine roles in Hindu society; it also explores a new self-assertiveness among many Indian women.

### Program 9
**Swadeshi: The Quest for Self-Reliance**
chronicles India's policy of economic self-reliance and political non-alignment as an outgrowth of broader Indian culture.

### Program 10
**Ram Rajya: In Search of Indian Democracy**
examines the state of Indian democracy in light of strains from communalism, caste warfare, and pervasive corruption.

*Additional Audio Tapes* developed for use in the classroom include a 30-minute portrait of Rabindranath Tagore, a 15-minute feature on the Durga Puja festival in Calcutta, and a 20-minute discussion with Indian teenagers on their goals and values.

72

*Educational Materials:* An integrated audio/ print curriculum for grades 9–12 and for college use includes: the ten programs, additional audio materials, and a 375-page curriculum compiled by Marilyn Turkovich of the Associated Colleges of the Midwest (Chicago), with the assistance of teachers in Missouri, New York, and Massachusetts. The curriculum includes photographs, maps, drawings, and separate transparencies. For information contact Independent Broadcasting Associates, Inc., or the Education Department, The Asia Society, 725 Park Avenue, New York, NY 10021, 212-288-6400.

Production Organization: Independent Broadcasting Associates, Inc., Littleton, MA
Year Produced: 1989 (excerpts broadcast on NPR's "All Things Considered" and "Morning Edition")
Executive Producers: Julian Crandall Hollick, Martine Crandall Hollick
Associate Producers (INDIA): Rana Behal, Raja Chatterjee, Rajasekharan
Engineers: Dean Cappello, Simon Negri
Editors: Dean Cappello, Julian Crandall Hollick
Host/Narrator: Julian Crandall Hollick
Actors: Arati Rao, Harsh Nayyar, Arjun Sajnani, Pradip Krishen, Dipika Roy, Sanjay Hazarika
Awards: For series: Ohio State Award; A Kaleidoscope of Cultures: Gabriel Award; Association of Visual Communicators, Gold Cindy, Best Educational Program; Puja: Darson Dena, Darson Lena: Bronze Cindy; Sita Speak!: Silver Cindy; Special Achievement Cindy Award for Music; New York Radio Festival, Finalist
Format: Audiocassette
10 (60:00) programs
Distributor: Independent Broadcasting Associates, Inc.

# THE PRINCE
## Documentary

The Prince focuses on the evolution of a distinct social type—the princes and rulers who governed Europe from the fifteenth to the seventeenth centuries. (see also The Warrior)

Production Organization: The Medici Foundation, Princeton, NJ
Year Produced: 1988
Executive Producer/Director: William C. Jersey
Writers: Lee Bobker, Mark Page, Theodore K. Rabb
Cinematography: William C. Jersey
Editor: Jeffrey Friedman
Host/Narrator: Peter Donat
Format: Video (88:00)
Distributor: contact Professor Theodore Rabb, Department of History, Princeton University

# PYRAMID
## Documentary

Based on the book by architect/illustrator David Macaulay, this film combines animation with location photography to tell the story of the planning, construction, and cultural significance of the Great Pyramid at Giza. (see also Castle and Cathedral)

Production Organization: Unicorn Projects, Inc., Washington, DC
Year Produced: 1988
Executive Producer: Ray Hubbard
Producers: Larry Klein, Mark Olshaker
Director: Larry Klein
Writer: Mark Olshaker
Cinematography: Ron Van Nostrand
Editors: Michael Ritter, Elsie Hull
Animation: The Animation Partnership
Directors of Animation: Tony White, Richard Burdett
Host/Narrator: David Macaulay
Voices: Derek Jacobi, John Hurt, Brian Blessed, Tim Pigott-Smith, Sian Phillips, Sarah Bullen, Geoffrey Matthews, Timothy Spall, Peter Pacey, Ysanne Churchman
Awards: National Educational Film and

Video Festival, Gold Apple; CINE Golden Eagle
Print Material: Teacher and Student Guides available
Format: Video (58:00)
Distributors: PBS Video (video); Unicorn Projects, Inc. (16mm)

# A QUESTION OF PLACE
## Documentary Radio Series

A Question of Place introduces twelve seminal figures in modern intellectual history and explores some of their ideas regarding human nature and the place of men and women in the larger order.

## Program 1
### Sigmund Freud (1856–1939)
explores Freud's life and work and dramatically recreates his classic case study "Dora."

Producer/Director: John Madden, Tom Voegeli
Writer: Elsa First
Narrator: Fritz Weaver
Cast: Tom Voegeli, Dianne Wiest

## Program 2
### James Joyce (1882–1941)
features excerpts from *Ulysses* and other works, performed by the Radio Telefis Eireann Repertory Company.

Producers: National Public Radio and Radio Telefis Eireann, Dublin
Performances: RTE Repertory Company

*Program 3*
**Robert Frost (1874–1963)**
explores the different voices of
Frost's poetry through dramatizations, readings, and the writer's
comments to fellow poet John
Ciardi.

Producer: Robert Montiegel
Performers: Robert Frost, Russell Horton,
Leslie Cass, Terrence Currier, John Wylie

*Program 4*
**Igor Stravinsky (1882–1971)**
combines dramatizations of events
from the composer's life with excerpts from his works and analysis of
his place in music.

Director: Daniel Freudenberger
Writers: Mary Lou Finnegan, Carol Malmi
Performers: Theodore Bikel, Carole Shelley,
Russell Horton, Donald Madden, Joe
Mahar, John Tillinger

*Program 5*
**Bertrand Russell (1872–1970)**
includes excerpts from Russell's
writings, letters, and memoirs.

Producer: Mary Lou Finnegan
Performers: John Houseman, Tammy
Grimes

*Program 6*
**Noam Chomsky (b. 1928)**
looks at transformational grammar,
Chomsky's revolutionary contribution to the field of linguistics.

Producer: Mary Lou Finnegan

*Program 7*
**Simone de Beauvoir (1908–1986)**
considers the concerns and legacies
of this feminist existentialist philosopher.

Producer: Mary Lou Finnegan
Performers: Viveca Lindfors, Kristoffer
Lindfors, Tammy Grimes, Ti Grace
Atkinson, Elaine Marks

*Program 8*
**William Faulkner (1897–1962)**
includes the recollections of friends,
Faulkner's famous Nobel Prize
acceptance speech, and dramatized
excerpts from his work with Tennessee Williams playing Faulkner.

Producer: Robert Montiegel
Performer: Tennessee Williams

*Program 9*
**Claude Levi-Strauss (b. 1908)**
looks at how the anthropologist
became the father of structuralism
and how his approach has been
applied to a range of academic fields.

Producer: Robert Montiegel

*Program 10*
**W.E.B. DuBois (1868–1963)**
presents DuBois's life through
excerpts from his writings performed by members of the Negro
Ensemble Company.

Producer: Mary Lou Finnegan
Director: Douglas Turner Ward
Performers: Graham Brown, Frances Foster,
and other members of the Negro Ensemble
Company

*Program 11*
**Bertolt Brecht (1898–1956)**
describes the playwright's life
through reminiscences of friends
and collaborators and includes dramatized excerpts from his plays.

Producer/Director: John Madden
Writer: Richard Gilman
Performers: Alvin Epstein, Tammy Grimes

*Program 12*
**Michel Foucault (1898–1956)**
examines the controversies surrounding Foucault's challenge to
traditional concepts of civilization
and humankind.

Producer: Robert Malesky
Writer: Jonathan Arac

Production Organization: National Public
Radio, Washington, DC
Year Produced: 1980
Series Executive Producers: Mary Lou
Finnegan, Robert Montiegel
Format: Audiocassette
12 (60:00) programs
Distributor: Not currently available

# THE RESTLESS CONSCIENCE
*Documentary*
The Restless Conscience explores the
motivating principles and activities
of a small group of individuals
within wartime Germany who com-
prised the anti-Nazi underground.

Production Organizations: Hava Kohav
Theatre Foundation, Inc., Riverside, NY,
and New York Foundation for the Arts,
New York, NY
Year Produced: 1991
Executive Producer/Director/Writer: Hava
Kohav Beller
Cinematography: Volker Rodde, Martin
Schaer, Gabor Bagyoni, and others
Editors: Tonicka Janek, Juliette Weber,
David Rogow
Narrator: John Dildine
Award: Academy Award nomination, Best
Documentary Feature
Format: 16mm, Video (113:00)
Distributors: contact Hava Kohav Beller
(U.S.); Jane Balfour Films, Ltd.
(international)

74

## RETURN FROM SILENCE: CHINA'S REVOLUTIONARY WRITERS

### Documentary

This film profiles five leading Chinese writers whose work has had a great impact on the development of modern China: the poet Ai Qing; the dramatist Cao Yu; and writers Mao Dun, Ba Jin, and Ding Ling.

Production Organization: The George Washington University, Washington, DC
Year Produced: 1982
Producer/Director/Writer: Joan Chung-wen Shih
Editor: Martha Conboy
Cinematography: Robert Sullivan
Narrator: Joan Chung-wen Shih
Print Material: Bilingual transcript available (103 pages with thirty photographs)
Format: 16mm, Video (58:00)
Distributor: contact Dr. Chung-wen Shih

## ROUTES OF EXILE: A MOROCCAN JEWISH ODYSSEY

### Documentary

Routes of Exile examines the 2000 year history of the Moroccan Jews.

Production Organization: Cultural Research and Communication, Inc., Emeryville, CA
Year Produced: 1982
Producer/Director: Eugene Rosow
Coproducers: Howard Dratch, Vivian Kleiman
Writers: Eugene Rosow, Linda Post
Editors: Eugene Rosow, Anne Stein
Narrator: Paul Frees
Festivals: FILMEX (Los Angeles); American Film Festival; Toronto Film Festival; Edinburgh Film Festival; Mill Valley (CA) Film Festival
Format: 16mm, Video (90:00)
Distributor: First Run/Icarus Films

## SHOULDER TO SHOULDER

### Dramatic Series

Shoulder to Shoulder follows the lives of three members of the Pankhurst family and those of other pioneers of women's suffrage in England at the end of the nineteeth century. Originally aired on Masterpiece Theatre, the Endowment provided funds to acquire the series for re-broadcast and to support the production of introductory material by actress Jane Alexander.

### Program 1
**The Pankhurst Family**
Emmeline Pankhurst, who shares her deceased husband's passion for social reform, emerges as the force behind the new Manchester-based organization, the Women's Social and Political Union and, with daughters Christabel and Sylvia, mobilizes other women in efforts to change British attitudes and laws.

### Program 2
**Annie Kenney**
By age 13, Annie Kenney was working full-time in the Lancaster mills. When the women's movement moves to London, Kenney becomes a suffrage organizer after a chance meeting with Christabel Pankhurst. Her efforts bring the working class into the women's movement.

### Program 3
**Lady Constance Lytton**
A member of the aristocracy, Lady Constance Lytton becomes convinced of the need for confrontational tactics in the struggle for suffrage. She also strikes out against the class system.

### Program 4
**Christabel Pankhurst**
Emmeline Pankhurst's oldest daughter, Christabel, emerges as a youthful militant leader. This program explores her opinions and ideology.

### Program 5
**Outrage On Derby Day**
June 4, 1913, Emily Wilding Davidson throws herself under the hoofs of the King's horse at the Derby. Her death makes her the first of many martyrs for women's rights. This episode also tells the story of the critical break that develops between sisters Sylvia and Christabel Pankhurst.

### Program 6
**Sylvia Pankhurst**
Women in England win the vote as a direct result of suffragette support for World War I, but for some, like Sylvia Pankhurst, it is a shallow victory. Sylvia, a pacifist who has broken with her mother and sister because she opposes England's entry into the war, becomes a strong supporter of the Russian Revolution, writes a book on Russia, completes a biography of her mother, and campaigns for the greater freedom and independence of all people.

*Premiere Presentation*
Production Organizations: BBC Television, England, in association with Warner Brothers Television, New York, NY
Year Produced: 1974 (first American broadcast on *Masterpiece Theatre,* 1975)
Producers: Midge McKenzie, Georgia Brown, Verity Lambert
Writers: Ken Taylor, Douglas Livingstone, Hugh Whittemore, Alan Plater
Directors: Waris Hussein, Moira Armstrong
Cast: Sian Phillips, Angela Down, Patricia Quinn, Michael Gough, Georgia Brown, Judy Parfitt, Sheila Grant, Pat Beckett, Liz Ashley, Jenny Till, Martin Matthews, Antonia Pemberton
Award: British Television Critics, Best Dramatic Series
*Encore Presentation*
Production Organizations: WETA, Washington, DC, in association with The Institute for Research in History, New York, NY
Year Produced: 1988
Producer/Director/Writer: Midge McKenzie
Coordinating Producer: Barbara Abrash
Editor: Stephen Prockter
Host: Jane Alexander
Print Material: *Shoulder to Shoulder* by Midge McKenzie (Alfred A. Knopf, 1975 and Vintage Paperback, 1988)
Format: Video
6 (57:50) programs
Distributor: PBS Video

## SO FAR FROM INDIA

*Documentary*

This film examines the cultural transitions experienced by an Indian immigrant in New York.

Production Organization: Film News Now Foundation, New York, NY
Year Produced: 1982
Producer/Director: Mira Nair
Cinematography: Alex Griswold
Editor: Ann Schaetzel
Awards/Festivals: CINE Golden Eagle; American Anthropology Association; International Conference in Visual Communication; FILMEX (Los Angeles); New York Film Festival; American Film Festival; Cinema du Reel; Margaret Mead Film Festival
Format: 16mm, Video (52:00)
Distributor: Filmakers Library

## SONG OF SURVIVAL

*Documentary*

Song of Survival traces the experiences of 600 women and children who were incarcerated for three and a half years in a Japanese prison camp in South Sumatra during World War II. Nine survivors describe their captivity and recreate the "vocal orchestra" they formed there, singing orchestral and piano music from notes written from memory.

Production Organizations: Veriation Films, Palo Alto, CA, and Film Arts Foundation, San Francisco, CA
Year Produced: 1985
Producers: Stephen Longstreth, David Espar, Robert Moore, Helen Colijn
Director: Stephen Longstreth
Writers: David Espar, Stephen Longstreth
Cinematography/Editor: David Espar
Award: American Film Festival, Finalist
Print Material: Viewer's Guide available
Format: 16mm, Video (57:00)
Distributors: The Altschul Group, Janson Associates

## SORCERESS

*Drama*

This film examines thirteenth-century French village life and beliefs through the story of the ascetic friar Etienne de Bourbon who condemns a compassionate herbalist to death for heresy.

Production Organization: Lara Classics, Inc., Cambridge, MA
Year Produced: 1987
Executive Producers: Vincent Malle, Martine Marignac
Producers: Pamela Berger, Georges Reinhart, Annie Leibovici
Director: Suzanne Schiffman
Cowriters: Pamela Berger, Suzanne Schiffman
Editor: Martine Barraque
Cinematography: Patrick Blossier

Art Direction: Bernard Vezat
Music: Michel Portal
Cast: Tcheky Karyo, Christine Boisson, Jean Carmet, Raoul Billery, Catherine Frot, Feodor Atkine, María de Medeiros
Awards/Festivals: Nominated for a César (French Academy Award), Best First Time Director (for Suzanne Schiffman); Toronto International Film Festival; Boston Film Festival
Format: 35mm, Video (90:00)
In French (with English subtitles) or in English
Distributors: Lara Classics (35mm); Mystic Fire Video (home video)

## TELEVISION'S VIETNAM: IMPACT OF THE MEDIA/THE REAL STORY

*Documentary*

A response to the thirteen-part PBS series *Vietnam: A Television History,* this program features a critique of the original series and an examination of the role of the media in creating perceptions that influenced the course of the war. A two-hour version includes an introduction and a panel discussion focusing on the major issues raised in the critique.

Production Organization: Accuracy In Media, Inc., Washington, DC
Year Produced: 1985
Producer/Director/Writer: Peter C. Rollins
Editor: Bill Crane
Host/Narrator: Charlton Heston
Moderator/Panel Discussion: Arthur Miller
Format: Video (two versions, 58:30 and 112:00)
Distributors: SVS, Inc. (58:30 only); Penn State Audio-Visual Services (112:00 only, ask for "Inside Story: Vietnam—a Public Inquiry")

76

# VIETNAM: A TELEVISION HISTORY

*Documentary Series*

With the history of French colonial Indochina as background, Vietnam: A Television History chronicles three decades of conflict in Southeast Asia.

## Program 1
### Roots of a War

covers a rebellion against the Chinese in the first century A.D., the development of the Vietnamese revolutionary movement during the Second World War, and Indochina's return to French rule after the war.

## Program 2
### The First Vietnam War (1946–1954)

considers how, after eight years of fighting, the French lost their empire in Indochina.

## Program 3
### America's Mandarin (1954–1963)

chronicles President Eisenhower's decision to support Ngo Dinh Diem as the leader of a separate, anti-Communist state in South Vietnam; it also considers President Kennedy's choice, nine years later, not to interfere in a plot to overthrow Diem.

## Program 4
### LBJ Goes to War (1964–1965)

examines how, as a result of events in the Gulf of Tonkin in August 1964, the United States increased the number of American troops.

## Program 5
### America Takes Charge (1965–1967)

tells the story of some of those sent as part of the military build-up.

## Program 6
### America's Enemy (1954–1967)

presents the escalating conflict in Vietnam from the different perspectives of Communist leaders in Hanoi, Vietcong guerillas, North Vietnamese soldiers and civilians, and Americans held as prisoners of war.

## Program 7
### Tet, 1968

examines the Communist offensive and its political consequences for President Johnson.

## Program 8
### Vietnamizing the War (1968–1973)

explores the impact of American withdrawal on American soldiers, Vietnamese civilians, the economy of Vietnam, and the conduct of the war.

## Program 9
### No Neutral Ground: Cambodia and Laos

traces American activities in the two countries from 1961 when President Kennedy sent in special forces to aid guerilla troops against Communist forces.

## Program 10
### Peace Is at Hand (1968–1973)

analyzes the course of the complex peace talks in Paris, from their inception in mid-1969 to the final cease-fire agreement nearly five years later.

## Program 11
### Homefront USA

traces the eroding public support for the war.

## Program 12
### The End of the Tunnel (1973–1975)

considers the fall of Saigon and the capitulation of South Vietnam.

## Program 13
### Legacies

examines the results of the war in Asia and the United States, particularly its effects on Vietnam and on American foreign policy.

Production Organizations: WGBH Educational Foundation, Boston, MA; Central Independent Television/UK; and Antenne 2/France
Year Produced: 1983
Executive Producer: Richard Ellison
Producers: Elizabeth Deane, Austin Hoyt, Martin A. Smith, Judith Vecchione, Bruce Palling, Andrew Pearson
Director of Media Research: Lawrence Lichty
Chief Correspondent: Stanley Karnow
Music: Mickey Hart
Awards: For Series: Alfred I. Dupont/Columbia University Broadcast Journalism Award; 6 National Emmy awards; George Foster Peabody Award; International Film Festival of Nyon, Certificate of Merit; George Polk Award, Documentary Television Award; Organization of American Historians, Erik Barnouw Award; New England Historical Society, Certificate of Merit; San Francisco International Film Festival, Golden Gate Award for Network Documentary, Television Special Program Category; America Takes Charge: Global Village Film and Video Documentary Festival, Best Program Made for Television; Roots of a War: American Film Festival, Red Ribbon; Tet 1968 American Film Festival, Honorable Mention
Print Materials: Anthology, Textbook, and Instructor's Guide available.
Study Guide and Anthology—Steven Cohen, *Vietnam: Anthology and Guide to a*

*Television History.* (New York: Alfred A. Knopf), 1983. Nearly 150 documents, along with photographs, maps, chronologies, and historical summaries. Desk copies of the study guide are available through McGraw-Hill, 1-800-338-3987.

Textbook—Stanley Karnow, *Vietnam.* (New York: Viking Press) 1983. In the first full history of the war, chief correspondent for the television series Karnow combines scholarship with information from thirty years of reporting on the French and American wars in Indochina. Personal, desk, and examination copies of the textbook are available from Penguin USA, 1-800-331-4624.

*Instructor's Guide to Vietnam,* 1983. Interdisciplinary material and instructional suggestions for using the series as a television course or in existing courses in history, political science, or philosophy. Colleges, universities, and other organizations can license the use of Vietnam from the PBS Adult Learning Service as a credit or non-credit television course and receive one copy of the guide and the right to tape the programs off-air and to use them with enrolled telecourse students for the term of the license.

Format: Video
13 (60:00) programs
Distributors: Films, Inc./P.M.I.; Sony Video (home video); Adult Learning Service, PBS (telecourse)

# THE WARRIOR
## Documentary

Focusing on the changing role of the warrior, a distinct social figure common in the Renaissance, this film traces important themes and ideas of the period through drama, architecture, literature, philosophy, and art. (see also The Prince)

Production Organization: The Medici Foundation, Princeton, NJ
Year Produced: 1985
Executive Producers: William C. Jersey, Ian Martin
Producers: Paul Kafno, Alan Horrox
Director: Paul Kafno
Writers: Paul Kafno, Theodore Rabb
Editor: Michael Chandler
Cinematography: Ray Siemens
Narrator/Host: Theodore Rabb
Format: Video (58:00)
Distributor: Professor Theodore Rabb, Department of History, Princeton University

# WESTWARD TO CHINA
## Documentary

Through eye witness accounts, Westward to China examines the experiences of the diverse groups of Americans who lived and worked in China during the turbulent Nanking Decade, 1927–37: missionaries, entrepreneurs, soldiers, journalists, doctors, and diplomats.

Production Organizations: Film Arts Foundation and James Culp Productions, San Francisco, CA
Year Produced: 1990
Producer/Director: James Culp
Writers: James Culp, Yasha Aginsky, Erica Marcus
Cinematography: James Culp, Richard Gordon, Len McClure
Editor: Yasha Aginsky
Host: Harrison Salisbury
Narrator: Peter Thomas
Cast: Ed Asner as the voice of Edgar Snow
Festival: Hawaii Film Festival
Format: Video (57:40)
Distributor: The Film History Foundation

# THE WORLD OF ISLAM
## Documentary Radio Series

Recorded on location in fifteen Muslim countries, The World of Islam is a thirteen-part series of radio documentaries exploring Islam as a faith, culture, and political ideology.

## Program 1
**Islam: A Complete Way of Life** introduces the basic elements of Islam.

## Program 2
**The Five Pillars of Islam** features individuals from several countries and walks of life discussing what it means personally to be a Muslim.

## Program 3
**Muhammed and His Heirs** examines the character and influence of Muhammed and the origins of the factional split between Sunni and Shiite Muslims through the observations of Muslim scholars.

## Program 4
**The Rise and Fall of the Caliphate** describes the ascent and decline of one of the world's most powerful empires.

## Program 5
**The Magnificent Heritage: The Golden Age of Islamic Civilization** presents Muslim historians and others describing the Islamic Golden Age (800 to 1500 A.D.) and its achievements in art and science—algebra, Arabic numerals, abstract design.

## Program 6
**Decay or Rebirth? The Plight of Islamic Art Today** features Muslim artists from several countries discussing the pressures on them to conform to Western styles and tastes and their efforts to revive Islamic art forms.

78

*Program 7*

**Islam and the West**

presents Muslims from several countries discussing the often strained relationships with Christians and offering opinions on how to improve them.

*Program 8*

**Resurgent Islam Today**

examines Islam's political and cultural revival and its implications for the West from the perspective of Muslim leaders and activists.

*Program 9*

**Voices of the Resurgence**

traces the efforts of members of Muslim revivalist groups as they attempt to make Islam relevant to the twenty-first century.

*Program 10*

**Islam in America: The Immigrant Experience**

presents Muslim immigrants to the United States speaking of both the problems and advantages of making new lives in this country.

*Program 11*

**Black Islam**

chronicles the growth of Islam among African Americans and considers the two rival African-American Muslim groups, Nation of Islam and the American Muslim Mission.

*Program 12*

**Women and Family in Muslim Societies**

considers the views of Muslim women and men about the teachings of Islam concerning women and the influence of traditional patriarchal values on their lives.

*Program 13*

**Whither Islam: The Future of Islam**

explores the relevance of Islamic values and institutions for the twenty-first century.

Production Organization: Independent Broadcasting Associates, Inc., Littleton, MA
Year Produced: 1983
Executive Producer/Director/Writer/ Narrator: Julian Crandall Hollick
Host: Peter Jennings
Awards: Corporation for Public Broadcasting, Best Public Affairs Documentary; National Conference of Christians and Jews, Inc., Fellowship Award; National Mass Media Brotherhood Award
Format: Audiocassettes
13 (29:00) programs
Distributors: Independent Broadcasting Associates, Inc.

*History*
*Theory &*
*Criticism*
*of the Arts*

# AMERICAN CINEMA

*Documentary Series*

This series is designed to examine central concepts and themes in American feature films from 1927 to the present.

By mid-1991, two programs had been completed. Eight more are planned, one each on the following subjects: classic Hollywood style; the influence of technology; the studio system; the American comedy; the combat film; film in the age of television; women and film; and realism and Hollywood in the sixties.

*Program 1*
**Film Noir: Night for Night**
examines the origins of the *film noir* tradition and introduces the stylistic elements of the genre.

Year Produced: 1990
Executive Producer: Lawrence Pitkethly
Producer: Sasha Alpert
Director: Jeffrey Schon
Writer: Mark Horowitz
Cinematography: Jim Chressanthis
Editor: Joelle Schon
Interviews: Andre de Toth, Joseph Lewis, Abraham Polonsky, Edward Dmytryk, Martin Goldsmith, Albert Bezzerides, Martin Scorcese, Paul Schrader, Kathryn Bigelow, Janey Place, Paul Arthur, and others
Print Material: Study Guide by Edward Sikov; Faculty Guide by Edward Sikov and John Belton; Textbook by John Belton; and Trade book by Jeanine Basinger (available 1992)

*Program 2*
**The Western**
examines images of the West and the portrayal of Western expansion in American cinema.

Year Produced: 1991
Executive Producer: Lawrence Pitkethly
Producers: Lesley Karsten, Sasha Alpert
Director/Writer: Sasha Alpert
Cinematography: Gregory Andracke
Editor: Kate Hirson
Interviews: Rudy Wurlitzer, John Ford, Howard Hawks, Anthony Mann, Sergio Leone, John Wayne, James Colburn, Clint Eastwood, Richard Slotkin, Thomas Schatz, and others
Print Material: Study Guide by Edward Sikov; Faculty Guide by Edward Sikov and John Belton; Textbook by John Belton; and Trade book by Jeanine Basinger (available 1992)
Production Organizations: The New York Center for Visual History, New York, NY, in coproduction with BBC, London, England

Format: Video
2 (55:30) programs
Distributor: The New York Center for Visual History

# THE ARTIST WAS A WOMAN

*Documentary*

The Artist Was a Woman examines the lives and works of women artists who lived between 1550 and 1950 and surveys the contributions women have made to artistic movements.

Production Organization: Women Artists, Westport, CT
Year Produced: 1980
Producers: Suzanne Bauman, Mary Bell
Director: Suzanne Bauman
Narrator: Jane Alexander
Format: Video (58:00)
Distributor: Filmakers Library

# ARTISTS AT WORK: A FILM ON THE NEW DEAL ART PROJECTS

*Documentary*

Artists at Work is a portrait of the WPA's Federal Art Project and other New Deal programs that supported artists during the 1930s.

Production Organizations: New Deal Films, Inc., and The Film Fund, New York, NY
Year Produced: 1981
Producer/Director: Mary Lance
Writer: Peter Lance
Cinematography: Ted Churchill, Charles Gustafson, Judy Irola, James Szalapski, Jerry Pantzer, Kip Durrin
Animation Photography: Lawrence Quartararo, Anthony Quartararo
Supervising Editor: Lawrence Solomon
Editor: Charles Marcus
Narrator: Morgan Freeman
Awards: American Film and Video Festival, Blue Ribbon; CINE Golden Eagle; Chicago International Film Festival, Silver Plaque; San Francisco Film Festival, Honorable Mention
Format: 16mm, Video (35:00)
Distributor: Direct Cinema Limited

# CITIES FOR PEOPLE

*Documentary*

Cities for People considers the space and the quality of life left in a city after the buildings are built. It was filmed in San Antonio, Savannah, San Francisco, Atlanta, Boston, and New York, as well as in historic and modern locations in Italy.

Production Organization: KPBS-TV, San Diego, CA
Year Produced: 1972
Producers/Directors/Writers: Amanda Pope, John Louis Field
Executive Producer: Paul Marshall
Music: John Lewis
Narrator: Cloris Leachman
Awards: San Francisco International Film Festival, Golden Gate Award; Broadcast Media Award; Ohio State Award
Format: 16mm, Video (49:00)
Distributor: University of California, Extension Media Center

# DIEGO RIVERA: I PAINT WHAT I SEE

*Documentary*

This film examines the life and work of Mexican artist Diego Rivera (1886–1957).

82

Production Organizations: New Deal Fims
Inc., Brooklyn, and
New York Foundation for the Arts, New
York, NY
Year Produced: 1989
Executive Producer: Patricia McFate
Producers: Mary Lance, Eric Breitbart
Director: Mary Lance
Writer: Eric Breitbart
Cinematography: Eric Breitbart, Nancy
Schreiber, Emiko Omori, Miguel Ehrenberg
Editor: Sara Fishko
Narrator: John Hutton
Voices: Julio Medina, Rosana de Soto, Joe
Barett, Philip Bosco, Steve Culp, Margaret
Hall, Ron Parady, Larry Robinson, Ted
Sorel, Donald Symington
Awards/Festivals: CINE Golden Eagle;
Biennial of Films on Art, Paris, Special Jury
Prize, Best Biographical Film; National
Educational Film and Video Festival, Bronze
Apple; Chicago International Film Festival,
Gold Plaque; Cork (Ireland) Film Festival,
Certificate of Merit; Festival dei Popoli,
Florence, Italy; American Film and Video
Festival; International Festival of Films on
Art, Montreal; The Documentary Festival of
New York; Leipzig (Germany) International
Film Festival; Melbourne (Australia) Film
Festival
Format: Video (58:00)
Distributor: Direct Cinema Limited

## DUKE ELLINGTON: REMINISCING IN TEMPO

### Documentary

This film considers Duke Ellington's
musical development and quest for
national prominence in the context
of America's changing racial attitudes and perceptions.

Production Organization: New York
Foundation for the Arts,
New York, NY
Year Produced: 1991 (premiere on *American
Experience*)
Executive Producer/Director: Robert S. Levi
Producers: David Schmerler, Andrew
Reichsman
Consulting Producers: Jaqueline Schearer,
Edward Gray
Writers: Robert S. Levi, Geoffrey C. Ward
Cinematography: Larry Banks, Neil
Reichline, Brian Clery

Editors: Ken Levis, Ken Eluto
Host/Narrator: Paul Winfield
Audio Material: Companion album, *Duke
Ellington: Reminiscing in Tempo* (Columbia
Legacy-Sony Music, available in record
stores)
Format: 16mm, Video (90:00)
Distributor: Robert S. Levi

## HIGH LONESOME: THE STORY OF BLUEGRASS MUSIC

### Documentary

This film traces the history and cultural origins of bluegrass music from
the 19th century to the present, with
special emphasis on the contributions and musical legacy of Bill
Monroe.

Production Organizations: Northside Films,
Brooklyn, NY in collaboration with
Hampshire College, MA
Year Produced: 1991
Producers: Rachel Liebling, Andrew Serwer
Director/Writer: Rachel Liebling
Senior Consultant: Jerome Liebling
Cinematography: Buddy Squires, Allen
Moore
Editor: Toby Shimin
Host/Narrator: Mac Wiseman
Musicians Include: Bill Monroe, Mac
Wiseman, Ralph Stanley, Jimmy Martin,
The Osborne Brothers, The Seldom Scene,
Alison Krauss, the Nashville Bluegrass Band,
Jim and Jesse McReynolds, and others.
Awards: Atlanta Film Festival, Best Feature
Documentary; American Film Festival, Red
Ribbon; CINE Golden Eagle; Houston
International Film Festival, Silver Award for
Feature Documentary
Format: Video (95:00)
Distributor: Northside Films

## ISENHEIM

### Drama

This film examines the Isenheim al-
tarpiece, completed about 1515, and
the period in which it was produced.

Production Organization: Imago Mundi,
Inc., Fraser, MI
Year Produced: 1985
Producer/Director/Writer: Giovanna
Costantini
Editor: Gabriella Christiani
Cinematography: Massimo DiVenanzo
Format: Video (28:00)
Distributor: Joanna Costantini

## JACK LEVINE: FEAST OF PURE REASON

### Documentary

This film looks at the complexities of
this social realist painter and his
work.

Production Organizations: David
Sutherland Productions and The Artists
Foundation, Boston, MA
Year Produced: 1986
Producer/Director: David Sutherland
Writers: David Sutherland, Nancy
Sutherland, Tess Cederholm
Cinematography: Joe Seamans
Editor: Mavis Lyons Smull
Host/Narrator: Jack Levine
Awards/Festivals: Chicago International
Film Festival, Gold Plaque, Documentary
Feature; CINE Golden Eagle; American Film
and Video Festival, Blue Ribbon; National
Educational Film and Video Festival, Silver
Apple; Columbus (OH) International Film
and Video Festival, Chris Bronze Plaque;
Atlanta Film Festival, Honorable Mention;
Leipzig (Germany) International
Documentary Film Festival, Finalist;
*Booklist,* Nonprint Editor's Choice
(American Library Association); *Village
Voice,* Nat Hentoff's pick as Outstanding
Television Show of 1989; INPUT
Conference; Whitney Museum Film
Festival, Curator's Choice; Global Village
Film Festival; Sinking Creek Film Festival,
Cash Award
Format: 16mm, Video (59:00)
Distributor: Home Vision, Films Inc./PMI

## LOUIE BLUIE

*Documentary*

This film explores African-American contributions to country music through a detailed study of the life and musical career of fiddle player Howard Armstrong.

Production Organization: Superior Pictures and Film Arts Foundation, San Francisco, CA
Year Produced: 1985
Coproducers: Terry Zwigoff, Frank Simeone
Director: Terry Zwigoff
Editor: Victoria Lewis
Cinematography: David Myer, John Knoop, Chris Li
Festivals: FILMEX (Los Angeles); San Francisco Film Festival
Format: 16mm, Video (58:00)
Film contains adult material
Distributor: Corinth Films

## MUSIC IN THE TWELFTH CENTURY

*Documentary*

Music in the Twelfth Century traces the development of music in both the sacred and secular life of twelfth-century Europe, with members of The Folger Consort performing in authentic costume in France.

Production Organization: Millenium Ensemble, Inc., Washington, DC
Year Produced: 1986
Executive Producers: Allan Miller, Anthony Ames, Christopher Kendall
Producer: Jeff Folmsbee
Director: Mark Mannucci
Writer: Isaiah Sheffer
Cinematography: Daniel Vogel
Editor: Armond Lebowitz
Host/Narrator: Fritz Weaver
Music: The Folger Consort
Format: Video (55:00)
Distributor: International Film Bureau

## OLD TRADITIONS, NEW SOUNDS

*Documentary Radio Series*

This series profiles different ethnic folk artists who, in addition to being masters of their native traditional music, have also incorporated newer, popular American sounds into their repertoire and performance style. Folk revivalist/songwriter Judy Collins hosts the series.

*Program 1*
Sid Beckerman of Brooklyn, New York, is a traditional Yiddish (klezmer) clarinetist who also plays American dance standards.

*Program 2*
Carmine Ferraro is a Southern Italian traditional singer, now of Westerly, Rhode Island, who also performs pop songs with an Italian-American band.

*Program 3*
Souren Baronian is an Armenian clarinetist of New York City who incorporates jazz elements into traditional styles of Middle Eastern music.

*Program 4*
Martin Mulhaire, now of Queens, New York, is an Irish button accordionist turned electric guitarist who is a member of an Irish-American show band.

*Program 5*
Syl Groeschl is a German-American musician from northeastern Wisconsin who specializes in both traditional polka band music and contemporary standard pieces.

*Program 6*
José Gutierrez of Los Angeles, California, is a traditional jarocho harpist from Veracruz, Mexico, whose repertoire includes a variety of popular Mexican music.

*Program 7*
Thuli Dumakude is a traditional South African (Zulu) singer who also performs contemporary songs.

*Program 8*
Sang Won Park is a Korean kayagum player who also experiments with avant-garde compositions.

*Program 9*
Simon Shaheen is a Palestinian violinist and oud player who merges his native Arab musical tradition with Western classical influences.

*Program 10*
Man Chhoeuy is a Cambodian traditional musician now living in Long Beach, California, who also plays keyboards in a Cambodian pop band. (Dith Pran of *The Killing Fields* hosts this program)

*Program 11*
Foday Musa Suso is a Mandingo kora player and *griot* (oral historian) from West Africa who merges his native traditional music with American rock, jazz, and punk. A Chicago resident, Suso frequently performs with Philip Glass and Herbie Hancock.

*Program 12*
Garry Robichaud is a master old-style French-Canadian fiddler who also performs in a country western band.

**84**

*Program 13*
Lora Chiorah-Dye, who lives in
Seattle, Washington, plays traditional Mbira music from Zimbabwe
and leads a nine-piece contemporary
marimba band.

Production Organization: World Music
Institute, New York, NY
Years Produced: 1988–91
Producer: Rebecca Miller
Technical Producer: Stephen Erickson
Editors: Becca Pulliam, Lou Giansante
Host: Judy Collins
Format: Audiocassette
13 (30:00) programs
The series is also available with an additional
half-hour per program of uninterrupted
performance by the artist
Distributors: World Music Institute, attn.:
Becky Miller; Murray Street Enterprise (for
radio broadcast inquiries)

## THE PAINTER'S WORLD: CHANGING CONSTANTS OF ART FROM THE RENAISSANCE TO THE PRESENT

*Documentary Series*

The six programs in The Painter's
World trace the development of
themes, conventions, conditions,
and institutions that have affected
the practice and appreciation of
Western painting from the Renaissance to the present.

*Program 1*
**The Artist and The Nude**
traces the representation of the human body and changing ideals of
beauty.

Producer/Director/Writer: Judith Wechsler
Year Produced: 1985
Script Consultants: Adam Gopnik, Jehane
Kuhn
Editor: Alexandra Anthony
Cinematography: Mark Koninckx, Nicola
Pecorini
Animation Camera: Edy Joyce

Narrator: Diane D'Aquilla
Award: CINE Golden Eagle
Format: 16mm, Video (28:00)

*Program 2*
**The Arrested Moment**
explores how movement and the
passage of time remain one of the
greatest tests of a painter's skill. It
features artist and photographer
David Hockney.

Producer/Director/Writer/Narrator: Judith
Wechsler
Year Produced: 1988
Script Consultant: Peter Cook
Editor: Alexandra Anthony
Cinematography: Steve Ascher, Jonathan
David, Robb Moss
Animation Camera: Ed Joyce, Ken Morse,
Ed Searles
Award: Cine Golden Eagle
Format: 16mm, Video (28:00)

*Program 3*
**Portraits**
shows how modern portraiture has
been affected by both changing conventions and the invention of photography.

Producer/Director/Narrator: Judith
Wechsler
Year Produced: 1988
Writers: Linda Nochlin, Judith Wechsler
Script Consultant: Peter Cook
Editor: Alexandra Anthony
Cinematography: Alistair Cameron, Robb
Moss, Michel Negroponte
Animation Camera: Ed Joyce, Ken Morse,
Ed Searles
Award: American Film and Video Festival,
Red Ribbon; CINE Golden Eagle
Format: 16mm, Video (28:00)

*Program 4*
**The Training of Painters**
explores the relationship between
prevailing techniques and styles in
art and corresponding art school
doctrine and curricula.

Executive Producer/Director/Writer/
Narrator: Judith Wechsler
Year Produced: 1987
Producers: Mike Dibb, Penny Forster
Editor: Jane Wood
Cinematography: Alistair Cameron
Animation Camera: Ken Morse
Award: American Film and Video Festival,
Finalist
Format: 16mm, Video (28:00)

*Program 5*
**Abstraction**
traces the development of abstract
art through the works of its major
innovators: Paul Cézanne, Pablo
Picasso, Georges Braque, Piet
Mondrian, Vassily Kandinsky, and
Jackson Pollock. It features painter
Frank Stella.

Producer/Director/Narrator: Judith
Wechsler
Year Produced: 1989
Writers: Henri Zerner, Judith Wechsler
Script Consultant: Peter Cook
Editor: Polly Moseley
Cinematography: Robb Moss, Michel
Negroponte
Animation Camera: Ken Morse
Format: 16mm, Video (28:00)

*Program 6*
**Painting and the Public: Patronage,
Museums, and the Art Market**
explores the history of art collecting
and the evolution of art museums as
popular public places.

Executive Producer/Director/Writer/
Narrator: Judith Wechsler
Year Produced: 1988
Producer: Linda Zuck
Scolarly Consultants: Francis Haskell,
Daniel Robbins
Script Consultant: Peter Cook
Editor: Polly Moseley
Cinematography: Mark Koninckx, Michel
Negroponte
Animation Camera: Ken Morse
Format: 16mm, Video (28:00)

Production Organizations: WGBH
Educational Foundation, Boston, MA;
Channel Four/London; and Judith
Wechsler, Inc., Brookline, MA
Years Produced: 1985–1989
Series Producer/Director: Judith Wechsler
Format: 16mm, Video
6 (28:00) programs
Distributor: Coronet/MTI Film and Video

## THE PERSISTENCE OF SURREALISM

*Documentary*

This film examines the origins,
nature, and persistence of the surre-
alist movement in painting and
other fields, from its nineteenth-
century roots through the impact of
World War I and the ideas of Dar-
win, Einstein, and Freud.

Production Organization: Malone-Gill
Projects, Inc., New York, NY
Year Produced: 1981
Producer/Director: Peter Newington
Executive Producer: Michael Gill
Associate Producer: Tim Hill
Writers: Jack J. Roth, Peter Newington,
George Melly
Narrator: George Melly
Award: CINE Golden Eagle
Format: 16mm (90:00)
Distributor: contact Jack J. Roth

## ROUTES OF RHYTHM WITH HARRY BELAFONTE

*Documentary*

Routes of Rhythm with Harry
Belafonte traces the five-hundred-
year odyssey of Afro-Cuban music
from its origins in Spain and Africa
(Program 1) through its blending
with Carribbean forms (Program 2)
to the sounds of modern artists in
the United States and around the
world (Program 3).

Production Organization: Cultural Research
and Communication, Inc., Santa Monica,
CA
Year Produced: 1990
Producers/Directors: Howard Dratch and
Eugene Rosow
Writers: Linda Post, Howard Dratch,
Eugene Rosow
Cinematography: Les Blank and others
Editor: Eugene Rosow
Host: Harry Belafonte
Performances by: Xavier Cugat, Desi Arnaz,
Carmen Miranda, Dizzy Gillespie, Pérez
Prado, Tito Puente, Celia Cruz, Fred Astaire,
Rita Hayworth, Gloria Estefan, Ruben
Blades, Conjunto Libre, King Sunny Ade,
Los Van Van, Irakere, Issac Oveido, and Son
de la Loma, among others
Audio Material: *Routes of Rhythm Volume l:
A Carnival of Cuban Music* and *Routes of
Rhythm Volume 2: Cuban Dance Party*
(Rounder Records, available in record
stores)
Format: Video
3 (58:00) programs
Distributor: The Cinema Guild

## SAY AMEN, SOMEBODY

*Documentary*

This film depicts gospel music as a
vital force in black culture through
the lives and work of some of its
pioneers.

Production Organization: Folk Traditions,
Inc., New York, NY
Year Produced: 1982
Executive Producer/Director: George
Nierenberg
Producer: Karen Nierenberg
Editor: Paul Barnes
Cinematography: Ed Lachman, Don Lenzer
Awards/Festivals: American Film and Video
Festival, Blue Ribbon; Ten Best of the Year
lists: *People Magazine, Chicago Sun Times,
Los Angeles Herald Examiner, Rolling Stone,
At the Movies, Entertainment Tonight*; New
York Film Festival; Telluride Film Festival;
Toronto Festival of Festivals; London Film
Festival
Format: 16mm, Video (103:00)
Distributor: Films, Inc./PMI

## THE STATIONS OF BACH

*Documentary*

Through his music and commentary
by contemporary Bach scholars, this
film presents the life and work of
German composer and musician
Johann Sebastian Bach (1685–1750).

Production Organizations: Timely
Productions and Music for Television, Inc.,
New York, NY
Year Produced: 1990
Executive Producer: Mordecai Bauman
Producers: Marc Bauman, Irma
Commanday Bauman
Director: Kirk Browning
Writer: Arthur Waldhorn
Cinematography: Don Lenzer
Sound: Peter Miller
Editor: Nicole Houwer
Host/Narrator: James Buswell
Format: Video (90:00)
Distributor: contact Mordecai Bauman

## THOMAS HART BENTON

*Documentary*

This is a cinematic portrait of
Thomas Hart Benton (1889–1975),
the Midwestern regionalist painter
who became one of America's most
popular and controversial artists.

Production Organizations: Florentine Films,
Walpole, NH, and WGBH Educational
Foundation, Boston, MA
Year Produced: 1988
Executive Producer/Director: Ken Burns
Producers: Ken Burns, Julie Dunfey
Writer: Geoffrey C. Ward
Cinematography: Ken Burns, Buddy Squires
Editor: Donna Marino
Narrator: Jason Robards
Awards/Festivals: CINE Golden Eagle;
American Film and Video Festival, Blue
Ribbon; National Educational Film and
Video Festival, Gold Apple; Baltimore Film
Competition, First Prize
Format: Video (86:00)
Distributor: Direct Cinema Limited

## VOULKOS AND COMPANY

*Documentary*

Voulkos and Company examines the process by which a large, cast bronze sculpture is brought to completion in the studio environment of contemporary sculptor Peter Volkos (b. 1924).

Production Organization: University Extension Film Production, University of California, Berkeley
Year Produced: 1971
Project Director: Clyde B. Smith
Format: 16mm (60:00)
Distributor: University of California, Extension Media Center

## W. EUGENE SMITH: PHOTOGRAPHY MADE DIFFICULT

*Documentary and Drama*

This film examines the life and work of American photojournalist W. Eugene Smith (1918–1978).

Production Organization: WQED, Pittsburgh, PA, and Wes Foree Productions, New York, NY
Year Produced: 1989 (premiere "American Masters")
Executive Producers: Susan Lacy, Greg Andorfer
Producers: Kirk Morris, Marthe Smith
Director: Gene Lasko
Writer: Jan Hartman
Cinematography: William Megalos
Editor: Susan Steinberg
Cast: Peter Riegert
Interviews: Aileen Smith, John Berger, Ben Maddow, William Johnson, Jim Hughes, Red Valens, Ed Thompson
Award: Director's Guild nomination, Best Television Documentary
Format: Video (90:00)
Distributor: WQED/Pittsburgh

## WAGNER'S RING CYCLE: FIVE PERSONAL VIEWS

*Documentary Series*

This series explores aspects of Richard Wagner (1813–1883) and the four operas of *The Ring*. NEH supported four lectures to accompany the first television presentation of the complete Ring Cycle, the Bayreuth Festival's centennial production staged by Patrice Chéreau and conducted by Pierre Boulez.

### Program 1

**The Music of The Ring**

A musical analysis of *The Ring* is provided by Edward Downes, musicologist and former host of the Metropolitan Opera Saturday afternoon radio quiz.

### Program 2

**The Centennial Ring from Weimar to Paris**

Noted Wagner biographer Robert Gutman discusses how the idea of *The Ring* developed into a monumental epic on which Wagner worked for nearly a quarter of a century.

### Program 3

**The Impossibility of Innocence**

Historian Peter Gay discusses the complex and controversial personality of the composer, including his notorious anti-Semitism and how this can color audience responses to Wagner's music.

### Program 4

**Theater of The Ring**

The program features interviews with leading Wagnerian soprano Birgit Nilsson and Sir Peter Hall, director of England's National Theatre.

Production Organization: Educational Broadcasting Corporation/WNET, New York, NY
Year Produced: 1983
Director: Peter Weinberg
Host: Robert Jacobson
Format: Video
4 (60:00) programs
Distributor: Films for the Humanities and Sciences (operas only available)

## WILD WOMEN DON'T HAVE THE BLUES

*Documentary*

Wild Women Don't Have the Blues examines the talent and artistic legacy of a generation of women blues performers, recounting the stories of Ma Rainey, Bessie Smith, Ida Cox, Alberta Hunter, and Marie Smith.

Production Organization: Calliope Film Resources, Arlington, MA
Year Produced: 1989
Producers: Christine Dall, Carol Doyle Van Valkenburgh
Director/Writer: Christine Dall
Cinematography: Steven Ascher
Editor: Jeanne Jordan
Narrator: Vinie Borrows
Awards/Festivals: American Film and Video Festival, Red Ribbon; New England Film Festival, Jury Award; Sydney International Film Festival; Mannheim International Film Festival; CINE Golden Eagle; American Library Association, Selected Films for Young Adults
Format: 16mm, Video (60:00)
Distributor: California Newsreel

# Archaeology & Anthropology

## THE LIVING MAYA

*Documentary Series*

Filmed in a small Yucatán village over the course of a year, this four-part series explores the ancient agricultural and religious customs that ground contemporary Maya communal and family life in traditional values, even as modern Mexico comes to the village.

Production Organization: The Anthropology Project, Santa Monica, CA
Year Produced: 1982
Producer/Director/Writer/Host: Hubert Smith
Editor: David Lebrun
Cinematography: Peter Smokler
Awards: CINE Golden Eagle; Margaret Mead Film Festival, Honoree; Choice, Outstanding Nonprint Media Award (American Library Association)
Format: Video
4 (58:00) programs, in English, Spanish, and Maya, with English subtitles
Distributor: University of California, Extension Media Center

## LUCY IN DISGUISE

*Documentary*

Lucy in Disguise discusses the collaborative efforts of experts from many disciplines to place the discovery of a 2.8 million-year-old partial skeleton in a paleohistorical perspective.

Production Organization: Ohio University in cooperation with the Cleveland Museum of Natural History
Year Produced: 1981
Executive Producer/Codirector: David Prince
Writer/Codirector/Writer: David Smeltzer
Assistant Director: Ann Smeltzer
Editor: Andy Marko
Narrator: Dave Kanzeg
Format: 16mm, Video (two versions, 58:00 and 29:00)
Distributor: Smeltzer Films

## THE MYSTERY OF THE LOST RED PAINT PEOPLE

*Documentary*

The Mystery of the Lost Red Paint People sheds light on an early Indian culture of northeastern North America as it follows scientists to various sites in America and Europe in their search for links between seafaring cultures across great distances.

Production Organization: Northeast Archaeology Project, New York, NY
Year Produced: 1987 (first broadcast on NOVA)
Producer/Director: T.W. Timreck
Writer: William N. Goetzmann
Cinematographer: Peter Stein
Awards: CINE Golden Eagle; American Film and Video Festival, Red Ribbon; National Educational Film and Video Festival, Bronze Apple; Booklist, Editor's Choice (American Library Association)
Format: Video (56:00)
Distributor: Bullfrog Films, Inc.

## ODYSSEY I

*Documentary Series*

This series follows the work of anthropologists and archaeologists as they attempt to understand the complexities and similarities of human societies at different times and in different places.

### Program 1
**Seeking the First Americans**
follows archaeologists from Alaska to Texas as they search for clues to the identity of the earliest inhabitants of North America.

Producer/Director: Graham Chedd

### Program 2
**Franz Boas (1852–1942)**
tells the story of the German physicist who shaped the methods of American anthropology, bringing discipline and order to a field that had previously dealt in subjective "race classification."

Producer/Director: T.W. Timreck

### Program 3
**The Incas**
examines the sixteenth-century Inca Empire through the work of three archaeologists.

Producers: Anna Benson-Gyles, Marian White

### Program 4
**Other People's Garbage**
explores the work of historical archaeologists across the United States: the excavation of slave quarters in Georgia; an investigation of a nineteenth-century multi-ethnic community near northern California coal mines; and an urban archaeology project in the Boston area.

Producers: Ann Peck, Claire Andrade-Watkins

### Program 5
**The Chaco Legacy**
explores the puzzling technological achievements of the inhabitants of the Chaco Canyon in New Mexico and speculates on their demise.

Producer/Director/Writer: Graham Chedd

*Program 6*

**N!ai, The Story of a !Kung Woman**
focuses on changes in the life of the
!Kung of Namibia through the
reflections of one woman over a
twenty-eight year period.

Producers: John Marshall, Sue Marshall
Cabezas
Directors: John Marshall, Adrienne Miesmer

*Program 7*

**Ongka's Big Moka**
explores the lavish ceremonial pre-
sentations of gifts, called moka, in
the New Guinea highlands through
the preparations of one man.

Producer/Director: Charlie Naim
Producer (Odyssey version): Melanie
Wallace, Sanford Low

*Program 8*

**Maasai Women**
looks at the women of the Maasai
tribe—from childhood through
marriage and old age—in the East
African Rift Valley.

Producer: Christopher Curling
Producers (Odyssey version): Melanie
Wallace, Sanford Low

*Program 9*

**The Sakuddei**
considers how government development programs in tribal Indonesia
may disrupt traditional ways of life
among the Sakuddei.

Producer/Director: John Sheppard
Producer (Odyssey version): Sanford Low

*Program 10*

**Shipwreck: La Trinidad Valencera**
examines the wreck of La Trinidad
Valencera, the fourth largest ship in
the Spanish Armada, which was dis-
covered in thirty feet of water off the
coast of Ireland.

Producer: Ray Sutcliffe
Producer (Odyssey version): Terry Kay
Rockefeller, Sue Simpson

*Program 11*

**Key to the Land of Silence**
illumines the history of the Rosetta
stone and its contribution to an understanding of life in ancient Egypt.

Director: Anna Benson-Gyles
Producers: (Odyssey version): Ashton Peery,
Terry Kay Rockefeller, Vivian Ducat

*Program 12*

**Cree Hunters of Mistassini**
looks at the Cree Indians of Canada
who trek northward every winter to
hunt and trap game.

Directors: Tony Lanzelo, Boyce Richardson

Series Production: Public Broadcasting
Associates, Inc., Boston, MA
Year Produced: 1980
Series Executive Producer: Michael
Ambrosino
Print Materials: Educator's Guide available
with the programs distributed by
Documentary Educational Resources
Formats: 16mm, Video
12 (58:00) programs
Distributors: PBS Video (Programs 1–5);
Documentary Educational Resources
(16mm only: Programs 1–5,12; 16mm and
video: Program 6); Films, Inc./P.M.I.
(Program 8); Not currently available
(Programs 7, 9–11)

# ODYSSEY II
*Documentary Series*
The second Odyssey series continues
to explore the diversity of past and
present cultures.

*Program 1*

**The Ancient Mariners**
considers excavation from three
shipwrecks, with special emphasis
on techniques of modern underwa-
ter archaeology, the attempted re-
constructions of ships and cargo,
and theories about ancient shipbuilding processes.

Producer: Sanford Low
Director: Werner Bundschuh

*Program 2*

**On the Cowboy Trail**
explores the lives of contemporary
cowboys in southeastern Montana.

Producers: Randy Strothman, Margot
Liberty
Artistic Director/Writer: Barry Head

*Program 3*

**Lucy and the First Family**
traces anthropologist Donald
Johanson's discovery of "Lucy," the
oldest skeleton of any human ances-
tor, and at least thirteen of her con-
temporaries in Ethiopia.

Producer: Milton B. Hoffman
Producer (Odyssey Version): Vivian Ducat

### Program 4
**The Kirghiz of Afghanistan**
relates the story of the Kirghiz nomads, who relocated in Pakistan after being forced out of their home territory in Afghanistan.

Producers/Directors: Charlie Nairn, M. Nazif Shahrani
Producers/Writers (Odyssey Version): Robert Burns, Melanie Wallace

### Program 5
**Bath Waters**
follows a group of archaeologists as they excavate the famous two thousand year-old Roman baths in Bath, England, to learn more about the Romans and their influence in Great Britain.

Producer: Antonia Benedak
Producer/Writer (Odyssey Version): Marian White

### Program 6
**Little Injustices: Laura Nader Looks at the Law**
introduces anthropologist Laura Nader's fieldwork in a small Zapotec village in Mexico and her comparison of Mexican and American systems of settling disputes and consumer complaints.

Producers: Terry Kay Rockefeller, Laurie Manny, Ashton Peery

### Program 7
**Myths and the Moundbuilders**
reviews the evolution of theories on Indian-built mounds scattered throughout the eastern half of the United States.

Writer/Producer/Director: Graham Chedd

### Program 8
**The Three Worlds of Bali**
explores the pageantry, poetry, and song that permeate daily life on the Indonesian island of Bali.

Producer/Director: Ira R. Abrams

### Program 9
**Masters of Metal**
traces the way new dating techniques have allowed archaeologists to challenge the once widely accepted notion that Europeans learned how to work with metal from peoples in the Middle East.

Producer: Dominic Flessati
Producer/Writer (Odyssey Version): Kathleen Bernhardt

### Program 10
**Dadi's Family**
explores family relationships in a household in northern India in light of socio-economic change that threatens its cohesion.

Producers: James MacDonald, Michael Camerini
Director/Writer: Michael Camerini, Rina Gill

### Program 11
**Ben's Mill**
looks at one of the few water-powered, wood-working mills left in this country.

Producers: Michel Chalufour, John Karol

### Program 12
**Margaret Mead: Taking Note**
reveals Mead's personal history and intellectual contributions through interviews held shortly before her death, archival materials, and conversations with friends, family, and former students.

Producer/Director/Writer: Ann Peck

### Program 13
**Some Women of Marrakech**
explores the lives of a group of Islamic women in Morocco, who share their feelings about friendship, marriage, family, and religion.

Producer: Melissa Llewelyn-Davis
Producer (Odyssey Version): Melanie Wallace

### Program 14
**Maya Lords of the Jungle**
reviews a number of theories concerning the rise and fall of the great Maya civilization of Central America.

Producer/Director/Writer: John Angier

### Program 15
**We Are Mehinaku**
shows how a small Indian tribe of the Brazilian Amazon River Basin sustains its group harmony through rituals that play out the tensions between the sexes.

Producer/Director: Carlos Pasini
Producers (Odyssey Version): Melanie Wallace

92

Series Production: Public Broadcasting Associates, Inc., Boston, MA
Year Produced: 1981
Series Executive Producer: Michael Ambrosino
Awards: Academy Award nominee, Best Documentary Feature; Cinema du Reel, Grand Prize; The International Festival of Grand Reporting Films, First Prize; Alfred I. DuPont-Columbia University, Special Citation; International Film and TV Festival of New York, Gold Award, Documentaries; Bronze Award; CINE Golden Eagle; American Film Festival, Blue Ribbon, Red Ribbon; Chicago International Film Festival, Gold Plaque; Cindy Award; ANZAAS International Scientific Film Exhibition, Australia, Commendation
Print Material: Educator's Guide available with programs distributed by Documentary Educational Resources
Format: 16mm, Video
15 (58:00) programs
Distributors: PBS Video (Programs 1–2,6–8,10–12,14); Documentary Educational Resources (16mm only: Programs 1–2,6–8,10–12,14); Cleveland Museum of Natural History, Education Division (Program 3); University of Texas, Austin, Department of Anthropology (Program 13); Not currently available (Programs 4,5,9,15)

## PATTERNS OF THE PAST
### Documentary Radio Series

Patterns of the Past focuses on important archaeological discoveries. Fifty-two modules (2 minutes each) contain archaeological reports in the form of brief telegrams and newsbreaks from the field, while fifty-two other modules (7–11 minutes each) explore intellectual issues surrounding contemporary archaeology.

Production Organization: Western Public Radio, San Francisco, CA
Year Produced: 1985
Producer/Director: Leo C. Lee
Writer: Brian M. Fagan
Format: Audiocassette
104 programs (two- to eleven-minute modules)
Distributor: Western Public Radio

## PLEASING GOD
### Documentary Series

Filmed in the town of Vishnupur in West Bengal, Pleasing God is a three-part series about the devotional practices associated with three major deities of the Hindu pantheon, with special attention on festivals dedicated to these gods.

### Program 1
**Loving Krishna**

examines a local manifestation of the cult of Krishna and displays the continuing link between worship, arts and crafts, bazaar exchanges, and everyday life.

### Program 2
**Sons of Shiva**

depicts the four-day annual Gajan festival of Shiva, the Great Lord and God of destruction, along with the ritual practices of the devotees of this god.

### Program 3
**Serpent Mother**

relates the myth of the goddess, Manasha, and depicts the making of images for her worship.

Production Organization: Harvard University Film Study Center, Cambridge, MA
Year Produced: 1985
Producers/Writers: Robert Gardner, Akos Ostör, Allen Moore
Awards/Festivals: Loving Krishna: Baltimore Film Festival Prize; Sons of Shiva: CINE Golden Eagle; Serpent Mother: Sinking Creek Film Festival, Cash Award
Format: 16mm, Video
3 (30:00) programs
Distributor: Centre Productions, Inc.

## POPOL VUH: THE CREATION MYTH OF THE MAYA
### Documentary

Using images from Maya ceramics of the Classic Period, this animated film recounts the first part of the heroic adventures recorded in the Popol Vuh, a narrative account of the myths and legends of the Maya of southern Mexico and Central America.

Production Organization: Film Arts Foundation, San Francisco, CA
Year Produced: 1987
Producer/Director/Writer: Patricia Amlin
Animation: Patricia Amlin, Joanne Corso, Martha Gorzycki
Lipsynch Animation: Bud Luckey
Camera: Martha Gorzycki
Editors: Yasha Aginsky, Jennifer Chinlund, Louis Hough
Narrator: Tony Shearer (29:00 version), Larry George (59:00 version)
Voices: El Teatro Campesino, directed by Luis Valdez, and others
Awards/Festivals: National Educational Film and Video Festival, Bronze Apple; Latin American Studies Association, Award of Merit; CINE Golden Eagle; American Film and Video Festival, Finalist; Media and Methods Award; Native American Film Festival, Honoree; American Anthropological Association, Honoree
Print Material: Teacher's Guide for elementary and secondary schools available
Format: 16mm, Video (two versions, 29:00 and 59:00)
Distributor: University of California, Extension Media Center

## THE ROYAL ARCHIVES OF EBLA

*Documentary*

The film discusses the importance of 17,000 cuneiform tablets and fragments found in 1975 at the site of the ancient kingdom of Ebla in northwest Syria.

Production Organization: Milberg Productions, Inc., Norwalk, CT
Year Produced: 1980
Producer: Mildred Freed Alberg
Directors: Richard Ellison, Mildred Freed Alberg
Writers: Mildred Freed Alberg, Fred Warshofsky
Narrator: Arthur Kennedy
Awards: New York International Film and Television Festival, Gold Medal; Chicago International Film Festival, Certificate of Merit; San Francisco Film Festival, Honorable Mention
Format: 16mm, Video (58:32)
Distributor: Films Inc./PMI

## SEARCH FOR A CENTURY

*Documentary*

Search for a Century chronicles the archaeological discoveries at Martin's Hundred and Wolstenholme Towne, a seventeenth-century settlement on the banks of the James River in Virginia.

Production Organization: Colonial Williamsburg Foundation, Williamsburg, VA
Year Produced: 1980
Producer: Arthur L. Smith
Director/Editor: Gene Bjerke
Writer/Narrator: Ivor Noel Hume
Award: International Film and Television Festival of New York, Gold Medal
Print Material: Discussion Guide available
Format: 16mm, Video (58:30)
Distributor: Colonial Williamsburg Foundation

## SHAMANS OF THE BLIND COUNTRY

*Documentary*

Shamans of the Blind Country records the Great Inner Asian tradition of shamanism, as preserved in the secluded society of the Northern Magar tribe in central west Nepal.

Production Organization: The New York Center for Visual History, New York, NY
Year Produced: 1985
Producer: Wieland Schulz-Keil
Editorial Consultant: Fred Pressburger
Format: Video (58:00)
Distributor: Not currently available in U.S. For European distribution contact Freunde der Deutschen Kinemathek (Friends of the German Cinema), attn: Sylvia Anderson

## SONS OF THE MOON

*Documentary*

This film, told from the point of view of a Ngas bard, traces the moon's influence on the Ngas who live in Nigeria's Jos Plateau.

Production Organization: Institute for the Study of Human Issues, Philadelphia, PA
Year Produced: 1984
Producer: Michael Camerini
Associate Producer: Bankole Bello
Writer: Deirdre LaPin
Editor: Paul Marcus
Cinematography: Francis Speed
Print Material: Accompanying guide available
Format: 16mm, Video (29:00)
Distributor: University of California, Extension Media Center

## TREE OF IRON

*Documentary*

Set in Tanzania on the western shores of Lake Victoria, Tree of Iron explores the subject of African iron smelting, presenting evidence that early indigenous technologies were far more complex than previously believed.

Production Organizations: Foundation for African Prehistory and Archaeology, Gainesville, FL, and Audio-Visual Institute, Tanzania
Year Produced: 1988
Producers: Peter O'Neill, Peter Schmidt
Director/Writer: Frank Muhly
Cinematography: Peter O'Neill
Editors: Peter O'Neill, Winnie Lambrecht
Awards: National Film and Video Festival, Gold Apple; Society of Visual Anthropology, Award of Excellence; American Film and Video Festival, Red Ribbon
Format: 16mm, Video (57:50)
English and Swahili
Distributor: Foundation for African Prehistory

*Philosophy Religion & Ethics*

## BORN AGAIN: LIFE IN A FUNDAMENTALIST BAPTIST CHURCH

### Documentary

Focusing on one independent Baptist congregation outside Worcester, Massachusetts, this film examines how the church serves its members' needs and what it demands of them in everyday life.

Production Organization: Five Colleges, Inc., Amherst, MA
Year Produced: 1987
Producers/Directors: James Ault, Michael Camerini
Associate Director: Adrienne Miesmer
Editors: Adrienne Miesmer, Sarah Stein
Cinematography: Michael Camerini
Music: Paul Moravec
Awards/Festivals: American Film and Video Festival, Blue Ribbon; CINE Golden Eagle; Margaret Mead Film Festival
Format: 16mm (87:00), Video (two versions, 87:00 and 55:00)
Distributor: James Ault Films

## THE DEAN OF THIN AIR

### Drama

This drama tells the story of the eighteenth-century philosopher Bishop George Berkeley who developed the theory that the physical world exists only in our perception of it.

Production Organizations: WSBE, Providence, RI, in cooperation with Irish National Television (RTE)
Year Produced: 1984
Executive Producer: Peter Frid
Associate Producers: Frank Muhly, Jr., Christine Herbes
Director: Deirdre Friel
Writer: Frank Muhly, Jr.
Editor: Christine Dall
Cinematography: Brian Heller
Cast: Dan Von Bargen, Keith Jochim, Richard Kneeland, Melanie Jones
Format: 16mm, Video (60:00)
Distributor: WSBE-TV

## DYING

### Documentary

This film presents portraits of several terminally ill cancer patients through their comments and those of their families and friends.

Production Organization: WGBH, Boston, MA
Year Produced: 1975
Executive Producer: Michael Ambrosino
Producer/Director: Michael Roemer
Associate Producer/Cinematography: David Grubin
Awards: New York Film Festival, Blue Ribbon; Gabriel Award; American Cancer Society, Media Award; Virgin Island International Film Festival, Gold Medal; Columbus (OH) International Film and Video Festival, Chris Award; CINE Golden Eagle
Format: 16mm, Video (97:00)
Distributor: PBS Video

## HARD CHOICES

### Documentary Series

The series examines ethical questions and issues raised as a result of remarkable achievements in medicine, biology, and medical technology.

### Program 1
**Boy or Girl: Should the Choice Be Ours?**
looks at new experimental procedures that are moving toward the possibility of sex choice at the time of conception.

### Program 2
**Genetic Screening: The Ultimate Preventive Medicine**
examines the ethical dilemmas posed by the possibility of genetic screening in the prenatal stage.

### Program 3
**Human Experiments**
examines how experiments with human subjects affect society and individuals.

### Program 4
**Behavior Control**
considers the dilemma of distinguishing between helpful and harmful uses of behavior modification techniques.

### Program 5
**Death and Dying**
looks at the questions raised by new life-prolonging medical technology concerning the rights of dying people and the definition of death.

### Program 6
**Doctor, I Want…**
explores the attitudes and expectations of those seeking medical care and those providing it.

Production Organization: KCTS, Seattle, WA
Year Produced: 1980
Project Director: Sandra Clement Walker
Executive Producer: John Coney
Executive in Charge of Production: Ron Rubin
Series Producers: Graham Chedd, Steven Katten, Richard O. Moore
Series Host: Dr. Willard Gaylin, M.D., President of the Hastings Center, Institute of Society, Ethics, and Life Sciences
Format: Video
6 (60:00) programs
Distributor: PBS Video (only Program 5, Death and Dying, available)

98

## IN PURSUIT OF LIBERTY

*Documentary Series*

In Pursuit of Liberty examines four civil and personal liberties in the United States: privacy, work, thought, and the press. Hosted by Charles Frankel, the series views the evolution of these liberties, perceived threats to them, and the ways each may conflict with other freedoms.

*Program 1*
**The Private Life**
explores the right of privacy from Greek and Roman times through medieval France to present day New York City.

*Program 2*
**The Curse of Adam**
looks at the the Industrial Revolution, the labor movement, and the contradiction between economic imperatives and the growing demand for spontaneity and leisure.

*Program 3*
**The Trouble That Truth Makes**
considers the problematic aspects of freedom of thought as illustrated by examples of recent and past controversies.

*Program 4*
**The First Freedom**
discusses censorship, press centralization, the Fairness Doctrine in broadcasting, and other freedom of press issues.

Production Organization: WNET/13, New York, NY
Year Produced: 1977
Writer/Editor/Host: Charles Frankel
Executive Producer: Don Dixon
Coordinating Producer/Director: Jack Sameth
Director of Research: John Chambers
Format: Video
4 (60:00) programs
Distributor: Not currently available

## THE LAW, THE COURTS, AND THE PEOPLE: THE LAW AND SEXUAL FREEDOM

*Documentary*

This film explores the American judicial response to sexual freedom and homosexual conduct, including a history of the Supreme Court's development of the rights of privacy beginning with *Griswold v. Connecticut.*

Production Organization: Pacific Street Film Projects, Inc., Brooklyn, NY
Year Produced: 1982
Producers/Directors: Steven Fischler, Joel Sucher
Writer: Lora Myers
Editor: Kristina Boden
Format: 16mm, Video (60:00)
Distributor: Pacific Street Film Projects, Inc.

## NEAR DEATH

*Documentary*

Shot in the medical and surgical intensive care units at Beth Israel Hospital in Boston, this film considers the interrelationships among patients, families, doctors, nurses, and religious advisers as they confront the issues involved in deciding whether to continue life-sustaining treatment to dying patients.

Production Organization: Exit Films, Inc., Cambridge, MA
Year Produced: 1987
Executive Producer/Director: Frederick Wiseman
Cinematography: John Davey
Editor: Frederick Wiseman
Awards: Dupont-Columbia Award, Best Independent Documentary; International Forum/Berlin Film Festival, Critics Award; Royal Film Archive of Belgium, L'Age d'Or Prize
Format: Video (350:00)
One almost six-hour program on 4 (90:00) cassettes
Distributor: Zipporah Films

## ON SECOND THOUGHT

*Documentary*

In this two-part program, Harvard philosopher Robert Nozick explores the philosophy, value, and meaning of work, leisure, and contemporary institutions with Gloria Steinem, president of *Ms.* magazine, and Dr. Gerald Klerman, psychiatrist.

Production Organization: WGBH, Boston, MA
Year Produced: 1984
Executive Producer: Glenn Litton
Producer: Ann Peck
Production Assistant: Susan Presson
Writers: Robert Nozick, Ann Peck
Editor: Patricia Cahalon
Format: Video
2 (30:00) programs
Distributor: Not currently available

## OUT OF ORDER

*Documentary*

In Out of Order, six former nuns tell why they entered and why they left religious life: three to become teachers, one an artist, one an insurance agent, and one a private investor.

Production Organization: Documentary Research, Inc., Buffalo, NY
Year Produced: 1982
Producers/Directors/Editors: Diane Christian, Bruce Jackson
Cinematography: Bruce Jackson
Festivals: Melbourne Film Festival; Houston International Film Festival; Dorothy Arzner Film Festival; American Film Festival; Museum of Modern Art
Format: 16mm, Video (89:00)
Distributor: First Run/Icarus Films

## PURSUIT OF HAPPINESS

*Documentary*

Shot in vérité style, Pursuit of Happiness follows the lives of several Americans as they consciously or unconsciously search for this "inalienable right."

Production Organization: Global Village, New York, NY
Year Produced: 1984
Coproducers/Codirectors: John Reilly, Julie Gustafson
Editor: Nicole Fanteaux
Awards/Festivals: Chicago International Film Festival, Gold Plaque; Toronto Film Festival; Atlanta Film and Video Festival, Prize Winner; American Film and Video Festival, Honorable Mention
Format: Video (60:00)
Distributor: Global Village

## SHADOWS OF THE NUCLEAR AGE: AMERICAN CULTURE AND THE BOMB

*Documentary Radio Series*

Shadows of the Nuclear Age examines the impact of the nuclear age on American social, ethical, and economic values.

### Program 1

**Seven Minutes to Midnight**

gives an overview of the impact of recent breakthroughs in the technology of nuclear weapons and the proliferation of nuclear materials.

### Program 2

**Hiroshima: The Decision to Use the Bomb**

discusses the Truman Administration's decision to drop the bomb; the role of bureaucratic momentum, military necessity, and cold war politics, and public reactions to the bomb and its aftermath.

### Program 3

**The Story of the H-Bomb**

examines the development of the early arms race, with particular attention to The Baruch Plan and the decision to build the hydrogen bomb.

### Program 4

**The Years of Testing**

traces the history of nuclear testing, fallout, air raid drills, bomb shelters, and the effects of these on Americans in the 1950s.

### Program 5

**The Missile Crisis**

recounts the Kennedy years, the Cuban missile crisis, and the move toward arms control and a test ban.

### Program 6

**The Road Not Taken: Protest and the Bomb**

examines the attitudes behind public efforts to end the arms race.

### Program 7

**Nuclear Hollywood**

analyzes the different ways that nuclear war has been presented in film from the cold war to the present.

### Program 8

**Nuclear Anxiety: Coping with the Eve of Destruction**

explores the way Americans are affected by the possibility of nuclear destruction and looks at the means we have for facing the dangers of nuclear war.

### Program 9

**Memos and Megatons—How We Talk about the Bomb**

considers the language of modern war, nuclear deterrence, and bureaucratic decision-making.

### Program 10

**The Literature of Apocalypse**

presents leading literary figures and critics discussing the concept of war in modern fiction, poetry, and drama, as well as the role of the literary artist in relation to war.

### Program 11

**Swords and Plowshares—The Economy of the Arms Race**

examines the effects of a growing military sector and high levels of military spending.

100

*Program 12*
**Ethics and Options for a
Threatened Planet**
discusses what values, ethics, and
laws are relevant in the nuclear age.

*Program 13*
**Where Do We Go from Here? The
Great Nuclear Debate**
explores the feasibiltity of various
plans to end the arms race.

Production Organization: SANE Education
Fund, Philadelphia, PA
Year Produced: 1980
Executive Producer: Stephen Shick
Producer: David Freudberg
Associate Producer: Michael Marchino
Research Director: Diana Roose
Project Director: Robert K. Musil
Format: Audiocassette
13 (30:00) programs
Distributor: Consider the Alternatives Radio

## VISIONS OF SOCIAL ORDER: FOR THE LOVE OF WORK

*Documentary*

For the Love of Work presents the
life and thought of Karl Marx,
explaining such ideas as alienation,
exploitation, the dialectic, material-
ism, human nature, technology, and
revolution. Cohosts Sidney Hook
and Tibor Machan discuss and
debate differing perspectives on
Marx's ideas.

Production Organization: Palmer R.
Chitester Fund, Erie, PA
Year Produced: 1986
Executive Producer: Robert J. Chitester
Producer/Director: Eben Wilson
Writers: Eben Wilson, Tibor Machan,
Robert J. Chitester
Cinematography: Bob Ames, Gordon Hickie
Editor: Nicolette Bolgar
Co-Hosts: Tibor Machan, Sidney Hook
Format: Video (58:00)
Distributor: Palmer R. Chitester Fund

*Children's
and Family
Programming*

## ASHPET: AN AMERICAN CINDERELLA

*Drama*

Based on an Appalachian version of *Cinderella*, this drama is set in the rural South during the early years of World War II. (see also Soldier Jack and Mutzmag)

Production Organization: Folktale Film Group, Delaplane, VA
Year Produced: 1990 (first broadcast as part of *Tales From the Brothers Grimm*)
Executive Producer: Mimi Davenport
Producer/Director: Tom Davenport
Writer: Roger Manley
Cinematography: Tom Kaufman
Editor: Randall Horte
Narrator: Louise Anderson
Cast: Kelly Mancini, Susan Tolbert, Brilane Bowman, Louise Anderson, Nancy Robinette, Mitchell Riggs, Tim White
Awards: Houston International Film Festival, Gold Award; National Educational Film and Video Festival, Gold Apple; American Film Festival, Finalist; Sinking Creek Film Festival, Honorable Mention; CINE Golden Eagle; Baltimore International Film Festival, Bronze Medal; Columbus (OH) International Film Festival, Gold Award; New York Exposition of Short Films & Videos, Juror Award; American Library Association, Notable Film for Young Adults; International Film & Television Festival of New York, Bronze Medal; Rosebud Award, Washington, DC
Print Material: Study Guide available
Format: 16mm, Video (45:00)
Distributor: Davenport Films

## BLIND TOM: THE STORY OF THOMAS BETHUNE

*Drama*

Blind Tom is the story of the 19th-century black musician, Tom Bethune, a blind slave who, even after Emancipation, spent his life under the "guardianship" of an enterprising southern general who earned a small fortune through Tom's performances.

Production Organizations: KCET and The Beem Foundation, Los Angeles, CA
Year Produced: 1986
Executive Producer: Bette Cox
Producers: Jack Terry, Deke Simon, Pamela Elder
Director: Mark Travis
Writer: Kathleen McGhee Anderson
Editor: Arthur Klein
Cast: Bonnie Bartlett, Missy Gold, Ben Piazza, Fran Bennett, Jessie Ferguson, Vaughn Tyree Jelks, Darius Lawrence
Awards: International Children's Film and Television Festival, Ruby Slipper Award, Best Television Special, Children's Jury; National Educational Film and Video Festival, Gold Apple, Social Studies Category; NAACP Image Award, Best Children's Special; National Black Programing Consortium, Prized Pieces Competition, Children's/Teen Category; Local Emmy, Creative Technical Crafts
Print Material: Study Guide available
Format: Video (28:48)
Distributor: Barr Films

## BOOKER

*Drama*

This drama focuses on a critical period in the early life of pioneering black educator and writer Booker T. Washington (1856–1915). The story traces his family's transition from slavery to freedom at the end of the Civil War and the young Booker's desire to learn to read in an environment where blacks had few opportunities for education.

Production Organization: New Images Productions, Berkeley, CA
Year Produced: 1983 (first broadcast on *Wonderworks*)
Executive Producer: Avon Kirkland
Producer: Whitney Green
Director: Stan Lathan
Cinematography: Jon Else
Editor: Stephen Stept
Writers: John Allman, Charles Johnson
Cast: Levar Burton, Shelley Duvall, James Bond III, Marian Mercer, Shavar Ross, C.C.H. Pounder, Marian Mercer, Thalmus Rasulala
Awards/Festivals: Banff Television Festival, Best of Festival, Children; Houston Educational Film Festival, Silver Award; Birmingham International Education Film Festival, Best of Festival; Odyssey Institute Media Awards Competition, First Prize, Educational/After School; National Educational Film Festival, Best Film, Social Science; Black Filmmakers Hall of Fame, Best of Festival; Los Angeles Herald Tribune, Selected among "Ten Best" TV programs; American Film Festival, Honorable Mention, Profiles; Writers' Guild of America, Best Script, Children's Category
Format: 16mm, Video (40:00)
Distributor: Coronet/MTI Film and Video (for Disney Educational Productions)

## DON'T EAT THE PICTURES: SESAME STREET AT THE METROPOLITAN MUSEUM OF ART

*Drama*

Don't Eat the Pictures introduces children to many treasures of the New York Metropolitan Museum through the adventures of members of the Sesame Street gang, who find themselves accidentally locked up in the museum overnight.

Production Organization: Children's
Television Workshop, New York, NY
Year Produced: 1983
Producer: Dulcy Singer
Directors: Lisa Simon, Arlenne Sherman,
Tony Geiss
Writer: Tony Geiss
Editor: Matty Powers
Cast: James Mason, Fritz Weaver, Paul
Dooley, the cast of Sesame Street
Award: International Children's
Programming Festival, Prix Jeunesse
Format: Video (60:00)
Distributor: Random House Home Video

## EAST OF THE SUN, WEST OF THE MOON

*Radio Series (Documentary and Drama)*

Through stories, songs, interviews, and special features, East of the Sun, West of the Moon brings history, literature, anthropology, linguistics, folklore, music, and philosophy to children 8–12 years old.

### Program 1
**Origins**
focuses on word derivations, music history, and etiological myths.

### Program 2
**Frontier Days**
tells of the opening of the American West and explores the ways in which we learn about the past.

### Program 3
**Kings, Queens, and Castles**
introduces aspects of medieval Europe through a mix of dramatized and documentary segments.

### Program 4
**Hail to the Chief**
studies the nature of political power, the need for government, and the meaning of the U.S. Constitution.

### Program 5
**The Seasons**
explores how people around the world interpret a common experience, the weather, through folklore and myth.

### Program 6
**Sail Away**
concentrates on maritime history, the European encounter with the new world, and stories, poems, and myths that have resulted from human contact with the sea.

Production Organizations: The Children's
Audio Service, Chapel Hill, NC, with the
Southern Educational Communications
Association, Columbia, SC
Years Produced: 1986–1990
Project Director: Jeanne Phillips
Executive Producer: Charles Potter
Segment Producers: Candace Barrett Birk,
Jack Ellis, Stephen Erickson, Stuart Leigh,
David Leveille, Helene Potter, David
Rapkin, D. Roberts, Judith Walcutt, Faith
Wilding
Host: John Lithgow
Print Material: A booklet on how to produce
your own radio show is available from The
Children's Audio Service, 808 Woodland
Avenue, Chapel Hill, NC 27516, 909-933-
0300
Format: Audiocassette
6 (89:00) programs that can also be used as
8 (29:00) programs
Distributor: Southern Educational
Communications Association, Radio
Division

## THE FIG TREE

*Drama*

Set in rural Texas in 1905, this film is an adaptation of Katherine Anne Porter's story about a nine-year-old girl whose eccentric great aunt helps her come to terms with the cycles of nature and the inevitability of human mortality.

Production Organizations: KERA-TV,
Dallas, TX and Lumiere Productions, NY
Year Produced: 1987 (first broadcast on
*Wonderworks*)
Executive Producers: Patricia Perini, Calvin
Skaggs
Producer: Terry Benes
Director: Calvin Skaggs
Adaptation: Stephanie Keys
Cinematography: Frank Prinzi
Editor: Jay Freund
Cast: Teresa Wright, Doris Roberts, Olivia
Cole, William Converse-Roberts, Karron
Graves
Format: 16mm, Video (60:00)
Distributor: Wonderworks/WQED

## HISTORIAN AS DETECTIVE

*Radio Series (Drama and Documentary)*

This series, created for adolescents, uses drama and commentary to recreate important moments in history and to depict investigative methods used by historians.

### Program 1
**The Papers of Benjamin Franklin**
presents three segments from Franklin's life (1706–1790): his arrival in Philadelphia as a runaway teenager from Boston; his split over the American Revolution with his son William, Governor of New Jersey, who remained loyal to England; and his close relationship with his illegitmate grandson, Temple.

*Program 2*

**The Writings of Francis Parkman**
dramatizes the efforts of historian
Francis Parkman (1823–1893) to
recreate the seventeenth- and eighteenth-century struggle between
England and France for North
America.

*Program 3*

**Historians in Wartime Service/
D-Day Deceptions**
traces the successful Allied plan to
mislead the Nazi armies as to the
timing and location of the D-Day
invasion.

Production Organization: WYNE-FM,
Brooklyn, NY
Year Produced: 1985
Coproducers: Phillip Lewis, Irwin Gonshak,
Gary Defrancesco, Cindy Raabe
Writer: Irwin Gonshak
Print Material: Discussion Guides available
Format: Audiocassette
3 (30:00) programs
Distributor: New York City Board of
Education, WYNE-FM

# LONG AGO AND FAR AWAY

*Dramatic Series*

Long Ago and Far Away is a series
for children 6 to 9 years old that presents dramatic productions based on
children's books, folktales, and fairy
tales from around the world.

The Endowment supported the
acquisition and broadcast rights for
the first two seasons; partial production of The Fool of the World for
the third season; and partial production of three shows in the fourth season: Merlin and the Dragons, The
Emperor's New Clothes, and Uncle
Elephant.

*Program 1*

**Abel's Island**
Abel, an articulate and sophisticated
mouse, struggles to escape from an
island after a torrential rainstorm
leaves him stranded there.

Awards: Emmy nominee, Best Animated
Television Program; Action for Children's
Television Award, Outstanding Program;
CINE Golden Eagle; American Film and
Video Festival, Red Ribbon; Houston
International Film and Video Festival, Gold
Medal/First Prize for Animation
Production Organizations: Michael Sporn
Animation, Inc., New York, NY, and
Italtoons Corporation/SSR-RTSI
Year Produced: 1988
Producer/Director: Michael Sporn
Adaptation: Maxine Fisher, Michael Sporn
(from the book by William Steig)
Voices: Tim Curry, Lionel Jeffries, Heidi
Stallings
Format: (30:00) Cel animation
Distributors: Italtoons Corporation
Random House Video (home video), ask for
39-489870-02

*Program 2*

**As Long as He Can Count the Cows**
When a boy's teacher tries to con-
vince his family in Bhutan that he
should have glasses, they are not
persuaded that he needs them.

Awards: International Children's
Programming Festival, Prix Jeunesse;
German UNESCO Commission, Cologne,
Special Prize and Prize in the Category of
Information
Production Organization: Wide Film
Service, Danmarks Radio, and Dandia,
Denmark
Year Produced: 1985
Producer/Director: Finn Clasen
Adaptation OR Writer: Rumle Hammerick
and Tim Cenius
Narrator: Brian Paterson
Cast: Ugey Dorji, Dawa Penior, Wangchuk
Wangdi, Dago Tshering, Chopen, Tshering
Dorji, Tashi Dori, Narjy
Format: (30:00) Live-action
Distributor: Coronet/MTI Film and Video

*Program 3*

**Beauty and the Beast**
A merchant's daughter volunteers to
live in the enchanted castle of the
Beast to save her father's life.

Awards: Chicago International Festival of
Children's Films, First Prize, Animation/
Short Videotape; National Educational Film
and Video Festival, Bronze Apple; CINE
Golden Eagle; Parents Choice Award
Production Organization: Lightyear
Entertainment
Year Produced: 1988
Producer: Joshua Greene
Director: Mordicai Gerstein
Adaptation: Mordicai Gerstein (inspired by
the original 18th-century
French story by Madame Leprince de
Beaumont)
Music: Ernest Traost
Narrator: Mia Farrow
Format: (30:00) Cel animation
Distributor: Lightyear Entertainment (home
video)

*Program 4*

**Bill and Bunny**
Bill and his family welcome the birth
of his baby sister Bunny but have to
come to terms with the fact that she
is different.

Award: International Children's
Programming Festival, Prix Jeunnesse, Best
Children's Program
Production Organization: Svenska
Filminstitutet, Sweden
Year Produced: 1984
Producer: Lisbeth Gabrielsson
Director: Jan Glasberg
Adaptation: Gunilla Bergstroms (from her
own book)
Narrator: Kim Loughran
Format: (30:00) Cel animation
Distributor: Coronet/MTI Film and Video

**106**

*Program 5*

**Bill the Minder**

This program relates the adventures of a boy who becomes a minder, or babysitter, for his two young cousins.

Award: London Film Festival, Outstanding Film of the Year
Production Organization: for Bevanfield Films, England, in association with Link Licensing Limited
Year Produced: 1985
Producer: Mary Swindale
Director: Timothy Forder
Writer: Timothy Forder (based on the books by W. Heath Robinson)
Narrator: Peter Chelsom
Format: (30:00) Cel animation
Distributor: No U.S. distributor, contact Link Licensing Limited

*Program 6*

**The Boy in the Oak Tree**

A young boy lives for years in a nest at the top of an oak tree to avoid eating his peas and mashed potatoes.

Award: International Children's Programming Festival, Prix Jeunesse
Production Organization: Sveriges Television, Malmo, Sweden
Year Produced: 1987
Producer: Bert Sundberg
Director/Writer: Ake Sandgren
Cinematography: Lasse Björne
Cast: Richard Blom, Per Eggers, Sonja Hejdeman, Chess (the dog)
Format: (30:00) Live-action, dubbed in English from the Swedish
Distributor: No U.S. distributor, contact Sveriges Television

*Program 7*

**Circus Dreams**

Three episodes explore the world of the traveling circus: a boy finds a magical pet; a sympathetic elephant returns a whale to the sea; and a woodcutter joins the circus after his forest is cut down by developers. (see also The Happy Circus)

Award: César Award (French Oscar)
Production Organizations: La Maison de Cinéma de Grenoble, Antenne 2, and Folimage-Valence, for the French series *Le Cirque Bonheur*
Year Produced: 1986
Executive Producer: Jean-Pierre Bailly
Conceived by: Jacques-Remy Girerd with Annie Fratellini
Director: Vincent Bidault, Jean-Pierre Chaligne, Guy Chanel
Directors/Writers: "Circus Dream" by Franck Flanquart and Pierre Scarella, "The Elephant and the Whale" by Jacques-Remy Girerd, "Timber the Woodsman" by Alexandre Fletchet
Narrator: Tammy Grimes
Format: (30:00) Model animation
Distributor: No U.S. distributor, contact Fremantle International

*Program 8*

**The Emperor's New Clothes**

This is an animated adaptation of Hans Christian Andersen's classic story.

Production Organizations: Michael Sporn Animation, Inc.; Italtoons Corporation; and WGBH, Boston, MA
Year Produced: 1990
Producer/Director: Michael Sporn
Adaptation: Maxine Fisher (from the tale by Hans Christian Andersen)
Voices: Barnard Hughes, Kevin McCarthy
Format: (30:00) Cel animation
Distributor: Family Home Entertainment (home video)

*Program 9*

**The Fool of the World and the Flying Ship**

This classic Russian folktale concerns a Czar who announces he will give his daughter's hand in marriage to the first man who brings him a flying ship. A good-natured simpleton succeeds and marries the princess.

Production Organizations: Cosgrove Hall Productions, Ltd., England and WGBH, Boston, MA
Year Produced: 1990
Producer: Chris Taylor
Director: Francis Vose
Adaptation: John Hambley (from a classic Russian folktale)
Voices: John Woodvine, Robin Bailey, Jimmy Hibbert, Barbara Wilshere, Alan Rothwell, Miriam Denham, Martin Jarvis, Edward Kelsey
Narrator: David Suchet
Format: (60:00) Model animation
Distributor: WGBH

*Program 10*

**Frog and Toad Are Friends and Frog and Toad Together**

These films present the adventures of the blustery Toad and patient Frog with a behind-the-scenes look at how the filmmaker creates and works with the puppets.

Awards/Festivals: Frog and Toad Are Friends: CINE Golden Eagle; ALSC Notable Children's Film; Birmingham International Educational Film Festival; National Educational Film and Video Festival; Frog and Toad Together: CINE Golden Eagle; International Film and Television Festival of New York; Parent's Choice Award; Los Angeles International Animation Festival; ALSC Notable Children's Film; Chicago International Festival of Children's Films; National Educational Film & Video Festival; Chicagoland Film Festival; Birmingham International Educational Film Festival
Production Organization: Churchill Films, Los Angeles, CA
Year Produced: Frog and Toad are Friends (1986), Together (1987)

Producer/Director/Adaptation: John Matthews (from books by Arnold Lobel)
Voices: Hal Smith, Will Ryan
Narrator: Arnold Lobel for Frog and Toad Are Friends
Format: (two parts, 30:00 each) Model animation
Distributor: Churchill Films, Inc.

## Program 11
### The Happy Circus

Three episodes explore the world of dreams and fantasy: a boy trapped in a subway stumbles into a magical adventure; a seal leaves the circus to find its true vocation; and two children find excitement when they sneak out of their house at night. (see also Circus Dreams)

Award: César Award (French Oscar)
Production Organizations: La Maison de Cinéma de Grenoble, Antenne 2, and Folimage-Valence, for the French series *Le Cirque Bonheur*
Year Produced: 1986
Producer: Jean-Pierre Bailly
Director/Writers: "The Small Multicolored Circus" & "The Two Little Nightwalkers" by Jacques Remy-Girerd; "The Baby Seal" by Pierre Veck
Narrator: Tammy Grimes
Format: (30:00) Model animation
Distributor: Coronet/MTI Film and Video

## Program 12
### Hungarian Folk Tales

This program presents three classic Hungarian folktales: "Johnny Raven," "Pinko," and "The Hedgehog". (see also More Hungarian Folktales)

Production Organization: Magyar Televizio
Year Produced: 1985
Producer: Ferenc Mikulas
Executive Director: Marcell Jankovics
Directors: Joszef Haui, Maria Horvath, Zsusanna Krioskovics, Zoltan Madarasz
Adaptation: Marcell Jankovics (based on three classic Hungarian folktales)
Narrator: Tammy Grimes
Format: (30:00) Cel animation
Distributor: No U.S. distributor, contact Hungarian Television Enterprises

## Program 13
### Jazztime Tale

is an original story which takes place in 1919, at the height of the Harlem Renaissance. Two girls, one black and one white, meet by accident, become friends, and see the first performance of their friend, the young "Fats" Waller, in a vaudeville show.

Production Organizations: Michael Sporn Animation, Inc. for Italtoons Corporation and WGBH, Boston, MA
Year Produced: 1991
Executive Producers: Guiliana Nicodemi, Sandy Cohen
Director: Michael Sporn
Writer: Maxine Fisher
Editor: Ed Askinazi
Narrator: Ruby Dee
Format: Video (30:00) Cel Animation
Distributor: Italtoons Corporation

## Program 14
### The Man Who Planted Trees

A peaceful shepherd changes the face of a desolate mountain region and the lives of its inhabitants by planting thousands of trees.

Awards: Academy Award, Best Animation; International Animated Film Festival, Grand Prize; Ottawa International Animation Festival, Grand Jury Award
Production Organization: Société Radio-Canada, Canadian Broadcasting Corporation Montreal
Year Produced: 1987
Producer/Director/Design & Animation: Frederic Back
Adaptation: Frederic Back (from the book by Jean Giono, translated by Jean Roberts)
Executive Producer: Hubert Tison
Narrator: Christopher Plummer
Format: (30:00) Rendered animation
Distributor: Direct Cinema Limited

## Program 15
### Merlin and the Dragons

A bedtime story from the magician Merlin dispels the doubts of young King Arthur about his ability to rule.

Production Organizations: Lightyear Entertainment, New York, NY for WGBH, Boston, MA
Year Produced: 1990
Producer: Joshua Greene
Directors: Dennis J. Woodyard, Hu Yihong
Writer: original story by Jane Yolen based on *Vita Merlini*, *Historia Brittonum* by Nennius, and *Historia Regnum Brittaniae* by Jeoffrey of Monmouth
Narrator: Kevin Kline
Format: (30:00) Cel animation
Distributor: Lightyear Entertainment (home video)

## Program 16
### More Hungarian Folk Tales

Four traditional Hungarian folktales are recounted in this program: "The Poor Man's Vineyard," "First the Dance, Then the Feast," "The Wandering of the Needle, the Dog, the Egg, and the Rooster," and "The Astronomer, the Thief, the Hunter, and the Tailor," (see also Hungarian Folktales)

Production Organization: Magyar Televizio
Year Produced: 1985
Producer: Ferenc Mikulas
Executive Director: Marcell Jankovics
Directors: Joszef Haui, Maria Horvath, Zsusanna Krioskovics, Zoltan Madarasz
Adaptations: Marcell Jankovics (based on three classic Hungarian folktales)
Music: Kalaka Hungarian Folk Group
Narrator: Tammy Grimes
Format: (30:00) Cel animation
Distributor: No U.S. distributor, contact Hungarian Television Enterprises

**108**

## Program 17
### Noah's Ark
Preparing to clear the world by flood, God instructs Noah and his family to build a huge ark and take on board one pair of every species of animal.

Awards: National Educational Film and Video Festival, Silver Apple; Action for Children's Television Award; CINE Golden Eagle
Production Organization: Lightyear Entertainment
Year Produced: 1989
Producer: Joshua M. Greene
Directors: Richard T. Morrison, Steven Majaury
Adaptation: Barbara Brenner (based on the Book of Genesis and on Peter Spier's book, *Noah's Ark*)
Animated at: Shanghai Animation Studio
Narrator: James Earl Jones
Music: Stewart Copeland
Format: (30:00) Cell animation
Distributor: Lightyear Entertainment (home video)

## Program 18
### Oh, Mr. Toad!
Mr. Toad, the pompous aristocrat from *Wind in the Willows*, is humbled when the weasels kidnap him and hire an impersonator to take his place.

Production Organization: Cosgrove Hall Productions, Ltd., England
Year Produced: 1988
Producers: Mark Hall, Brian Cosgrove
Director: Jackie Cockle
Writer: Brian Trueman (inspired by Kenneth Grahame's *Wind in the Willows*)
Voices: Sir Michael Hordern, Peter Sullis, Richard Pearson, David Jason
Format: (two parts, 30:00 each) Model animation
Distributor: DLT Entertainment, Ltd.

## Program 19
### Pegasus
is the story of the fabulous winged horse, as told by Uranea, youngest of the Muses.

Production Organization: WGBH Educational Foundation, Boston, MA
Year Produced: 1991
Executive Producer: Arne Holland
Producers: Joshua M. Greene
Director: Marek Duchwald
Writer: Doris Orgel
Narrator: Mia Farrow
Format: Video (30:00) Cell animation
Distributor: Lightyear Entertainment, L.P.

## Program 20
### The Pied Piper of Hamelin
A mysterious stranger saves the medieval town of Hamelin from a plague of rats by luring them away with his magic pipe, but then puts his pipe to a different use.

Awards: International Children's Programming Festival, Prix Jeunesse, Best Children's Program; British Academy of Film and Television Arts, Best Children's Program
Production Organization: Cosgrove Hall Productions, Ltd., England
Year Produced: 1980
Producers: Brian Cosgrove, Mark Hall
Director: Mark Hall
Adaptation: Rosemary Anne Sisson (from the poem by Robert Browning)
Narrator: Robert Hardy
Format: (30:00) Model animation
Distributor: Media Guild

## Program 21
### Rarg
The blissful inhabitants of Rarg discover they exist only in the dream of a man named Edwin Barnes, and must find a way to stop Barnes from waking up when his alarm clock rings.

Awards: British Animation Festival, Best Children's Animated Film; Chicago International Film Festival, Silver Plaque; British Academy of Film and Television Arts, nominated for Best Short Animated Film
Production Organization: Hit Communications.
Year Produced: 1989
Producer: Chris O'Hare
Director/Writer/Animation: Tony Collingwood
Voices: Nigel Hawthorne, Michael Gough, Ronnie Stevens
Format: (30:00) Cell animation
Distributor: No U.S. distributor, contact Hit Communications.

## Program 22
### The Reluctant Dragon
A shepherd's son befriends a dragon, who is more inclined to compose poetry than attack the frightened villagers.

Award: British Academy of Film and Television Arts, Best Animation
Production Organization: Cosgrove Hall Productions, Ltd., England
Year Produced: 1987
Producer: Mark Hall, Brian Cosgrove
Director: Bridget Appleby
Adaptation: Willis Hall (based on the book by Kenneth Grahame)
Voices: Martin Jarvis, Simon Callow
Format: (30:00) Model animation
Distributor: No U.S. distributor, contact D.L.T. Entertainment, Ltd.

## Program 23
### The Silver Cornet
Filmed in rural England, this film tells of a young boy's determination to learn to play a cornet he has found in the barn.

Production Organization: Yorkshire Television, England
Year Produced: 1985
Producer: Joy Whitby
Director: Peter Tabern
Writer: Neil Innes
Cast: Adam Sedgwick, Elizabeth Mickery, Neil Phillips, Steve Morley, John Whittock, Ian Bleasdale, Mike Kay
Format: (30:00) Live-action
Distributor: Coronet/MTI Film and Video

## Program 24
### The Sleeping Princess

This program retells the story of a young princess who, after being put to sleep for one hundred years by a wicked fairy, is awakened by the kiss of a brave prince

Production Organization: BBC, England, for the series *Jackanory Playhouse*
Year Produced: 1976
Producer: Angela Beeching
Director: Paul Stone
Adaptation: Kay McManus (based on "Sleeping Beauty" as told by the Brothers Grimm)
Cast: Bernard Cribbins, Sylvia Syms, Gabrielle Hamilton, Vivian Pickles, Peggyann Clifford, Georgina Kean, Peter Settelen
Format: (30:00) Live-action
Distributor: No U.S. distributor, contact Lionheart Television

## Program 25
### Svatohor

In this Russian folktale, Svatohor (Saint Mountain) is a young hunter who must complete seemingly impossible tasks to save the czar from his enemies and win the hand of his daughter, Maria.

Production Organization: Czechoslovak Television, Bratislava
Year Produced: 1984
Producer/Director: Ivan Renc
Adaptation: Ivan Renc (based on a Russian folktale)
Cinematography: Vladimir Malik
Narrator: Tammy Grimes
Format: (30:00) Model animation
Distributor: No U.S. distributor, contact Ceskoslovenska Televizia

## Program 26
### The Talking Parcel

Parrot, accompanied by a girl named Penelope and a comic Cockney toad, must rescue H.H. Junketbury and the land of Mythologia from the talons of the evil cockatrices.

Production Organization: Cosgrove Hall Productions, Ltd., England
Year Produced: 1978
Producer: Brian Cosgrove, Mark Hall
Director: Brian Cosgrove
Adaptation: Rosemary Anne Sisson (from the book by Gerald Durrell)
Voices: Lisa Norris, Freddie Jones, Mollie Sugden, Roy Kinnear, Edward Kelsey, Windsor Davies, Sir Michael Horden, Peter Woodthorpe, Harvey Ashby
Format: (two parts, 30:00 each) Cell animation
Distributor: Media Guild

## Program 27
### Uncle Elephant

After a young elephant loses his parents at sea, Uncle Elephant comes to comfort him with tricks, stories, and songs.

Production Organization: Churchill Films, Inc., Los Angeles, CA, and WGBH, Boston, MA
Year Produced: 1991
Producer/Director: John Matthews
Adaptation: John Matthews (from a book by Arnold Lobel)
Voices: Not known yet
Narrator: Not known yet
Format: (30:00) Model animation
Distributor: Churchill Films, Inc.

## Program 28
### The Wind in the Willows

This is the story of an unusual group of friends: the wise Badger, the innocent Mole, the generous Rat, and the reckless Toad.

Awards: British Academy of Film and Television Arts, Best Children's Program; International Emmy
Production Organization: Cosgrove Hall Productions, Ltd., England
Year Produced: 1983
Producer: Mark Hall, Brian Cosgrove
Director: Mark Hall
Adaptation: Rosemary Anne Sisson (based on the book by Kenneth Grahame)
Voices: Richard Pearson, Ian Carmichael, David Jason, Sir Michael Hordern
Format: (90:00) Model animation
Distributor: Thames Video Collection (home video), ask for *Wind in the Willows, Volume 1*

Series Production Organizations: WGBH, Boston, MA, in partnership with the International Reading Association, the Association for Library Services to Children, a division of the American Library Association, and the Library of Congress, Center for the Book
Years Produced: see individual listings
Series Executive Producer: William Brennan (for Season I)
Series Project Director/Editor: Carol Greenwald (for Season I)
Executive-In-Charge of Series: Kate Taylor
Series Producer: Sandy Cohen
Series Project Director: Brigid Sullivan
Host: James Earl Jones
Series Awards: National Education Association Award, Advancement of Learning through Broadcasting; Action for Children's Television, Achievement in Children's Television Award; National Catholic Association of Broadcasters and Communicators, Gabriel Award, Best National Children's Program; International Film and Television Festival of New York, Gold Medal; Connoisseur Magazine, Connie Award, Best National Children's Series; International Reading Association, Broadcast Media Award
Print Material: Educational materials available: Discussion and Activity Guide (32-pages, including lesson plans, written by Dr. Susan Hepler, children's literature specialist and co-author of *Children's Literature in the Elementary School*); student newspaper; booklists; poster
Format: Video
Programs 1–8,11–16,18–23,25 (30:00);
Programs 9,10,17,24 (60:00);

Program 26 (90:00)
Distributors: See individual listings or contact: Amy McMahon, Long Ago and Far Away, WGBH (617-492-2777, x4346)

## MARION'S MEN: THE LIFE AND TIMES OF THE SWAMP FOX

*Dramatic Radio Series*

This series of radio dramas examines the life of Francis Marion, who commanded troops that practiced guerrilla action against British forces in South Carolina during the revolutionary war.

Production Organization: Radio Arts Productions, New York, NY
Year Produced: 1984
Executive Producer/Director: Charles Potter
Writer: Ralph Pezzullo
Narrator: Timothy Jerome
Cast: Chris Sarandon, Timothy Jerome, Paul Hecht, Merwin Goldsmith
Format: Audiocassette
8 (30:00) programs on 4 cassettes
Distributor: Radio Arts Productions

## MUTZMAG

*Drama*

Mutzmag is a traditional Appalachian folktale about a thirteen-year old girl and her two half-sisters, whose poverty and mother's death prompt them to leave their mountain shack in search of better fortune. (see also Soldier Jack and Ashpet)

Production Organization: Davenport Films, Delaplane, VA
Year Produced: 1991
Producers: Tom Davenport, Mimi Davenport
Director: Tom Davenport
Associate Director: Sarah Toth
Writers: Tom Davenport, Sarah Toth, Gary Carden
Cinematography: Douglas Miller

Editor: Thom Sheperd
Cast: Robbie Sams, Bart Whitman, Stephanie Jones
Print Material: Study Guide available
Format: Video (60:00)
Distributor: Davenport Films

## OUT OF TIME

*Drama*

Out of Time tells the story of two contemporary farm children who are mysteriously hurled back in time and trapped in the environment of the Baltimore harbor of 1851 until they can find the historical truth that will return them to the twentieth century.

Production Organization: Educational Film Center, Annandale, VA
Year Produced: 1984 (first broadcast on NBC)
Executive Producer: Ira H. Klugerman
Producer: Donald Fouser
Director: Michael Schweitzer
Writers: Ruth Pollak, Ira Klugerman, Patrick Prentice
Cinematography: Tony Louis Cutrono
Cast: Adam Baldwin, Amy Locane, R.D. Robb
Format: Video (two versions, drama only 47:26, drama plus historical postscript 58:50)
Distributor: Family Express Video

## POETIC LICENSE: AN INTRODUCTION TO POETRY FOR A YOUNG AUDIENCE

*Documentary and Drama*

Through the experiences of a group of children who have taken over an abandoned television studio, viewers aged 8 to 12 are exposed to famous poetry and encouraged to write their own poems.

Production Organization: ViceVersaVision
Year Produced: 1985
Producer/Director: Brooks Jones
Editors: Brooks Jones, Mary Jay Michel
Writers: Thomas Babe, James Thurman, Brooks Jones
Format: Video (30:00)
Distributor: Not currently available

## RAINBOW'S END: AN INTRODUCTION TO THE HUMANITIES FOR DEAF CHILDREN

*Documentary*

Through a visit to the National Archives and a meeting with Thomas Jefferson, viewers and the on-camera cast of children and adults are exposed to concepts relating to the Declaration of Independence and the Constitution. The program is intended for deaf and hearing audiences of children, ages eight to twelve.

Production Organizations: D.E.A.F. Media, Inc., Berkeley, CA
Year Produced: 1985
Executive Producer: Susan Rutherford
Associate Producers: Michael Cunningham, Louise Lo
Director: Robert Zagone
Dramatic Director: Freda Norman
Writer: Rico Peterson
Format: Video (30:00)
With sign language, closed captioning, and voice-over
Distributor: D.E.A.F. Media, Inc.

## SOLDIER JACK

*Drama*

In this adaptation of an Appalachian tale, a soldier returning from World War II captures Death in a magical sack. (see also Ashpet and Mutzmag)

Production Organization: Folktale Film Group, Delaplane, VA
Year Produced: 1987
Executive Producer: Mimi Davenport
Producer/Director: Tom Davenport
Writers: Sarah Toth, Julian Yochum, Marcia Lynch, Tom Fuller
Cinematography: Arnie Sirlin, Tom Kaufman
Editors: Marcia Lynch, Randy Horte
Narrators: Gary Slemp, Julian Yochum
Cast: Michael Heintzman, Kate Weber, Mark Jaster, Diane Couves, Nancy Robinette
Awards: International Festival of Children's Film, Best Live Action Film; New York Film and Video Festival, Best Film for Young Adults; Chicago International Film Festival, Best Short Subject; The American Film Institute and Billboard Magazine's American Video Conference, Best Short Fiction
Print Material: Study Guide available
Format: 16mm, Video (40:00)
Distributor: Davenport Films

## SONGS JUMPING IN MY MOUTH

*Radio Series (Drama and Documentary)*

Songs Jumping in My Mouth is a series of thirteen programs designed for six- to ten-year-old children in which three animal characters introduce aspects of history, culture, and ideas. (see also Word Stories)

### Program 1
### Why?

This program explores children's "why" questions and introduces the trio of animal characters—Hootenanny Granny, Ndovu, and Fe Fy Fly.

### Program 2
### How Things Came to Be

The animal trio wrestles with the origin of things and children give their original explanations.

### Program 3
### Mama's Talk and Daddy's Walk

Hootenanny Granny remembers the unusual ancestors in her family tree as children describe their own family traditions.

### Program 4
### What's in a Name?

Unusual naming traditions and how children feel about their names are the focus of this program.

### Program 5
### Word Play

Funny words, mispronounced words, and word origins lead to a contest between Fe Fy Fly and Hootenanny Granny.

### Program 6
### Rhythm and Rhyme

Listeners are introduced to city jump rope champions and the rhythms of traditional and current childlore.

### Program 7
### I Am What I Eat

Ndovu gives a party and Fe Fy Fly shares recordings of children's questions about family table customs.

### Program 8
### Past and Present Frogs

Nationally known storytellers share frog tales while children describe their own experiences with frogs.

### Program 9
### Imaginary Creatures

Ndovu meets the legendary hoop snake and children describe the creatures of their imagination.

### Program 10
### Inventions

Children learn about significant inventions and describe things they would like to invent.

### Part 11
### Marking Time

The animals celebrate a birthday and children describe personal milestones.

### Part 12
### Sharing with Others Across Time—Past

An antique music box links the past to the present as children describe family keepsakes.

### Program 13
### Sharing with Others Across Time—Future

The trio makes a time capsule for the future.

Production Organization: WETA, Washington, DC
Year Produced: 1983 (first broadcast on WETA-FM, then released on NPR)
Producer/Director/Writer: Pamela Brooke
Hosts: Yeardley Smith, Kelly Smith
Print Material: Discussion Guide available
Format: Audiocassette
13 (30:00) programs
Distributor: The Radio Road Gang, Inc., attn: Pamela Brooke

## A STORY, A STORY: TRADITIONS IN STORYTELLING FOR CHILDREN

*Drama*

These two animated programs are for children six to eight years of age. The first is based on Gail Haley's Caldecot Medal-winning book, *A Story, A Story*, which recounts an African folktale; the second is Pete Seeger's *A Foolish Frog*.

Production Organization: Weston Woods
Institute, Inc., Weston, CT
Year Produced: 1985
Executive Producer: Morton Schindel
Producer: Terri Payne Butler
Project Director: Bena Kallick
Director: Jerry Hughes
Writer: Robert Brush
Narrator: Neil Innes
Awards: The Foolish Frog: American Film
Festival, Red Ribbon; Columbus (OH) Film
Festival, Chris Certificate
Format: Video (18:00)
A Story, A Story (10:00); The Foolish Frog
(8:00)
Distributor: Weston Woods

## TALES OF THE UNKNOWN SOUTH

*Dramatic Series*

Aimed at young people ages 14 to
18, Tales of the Unknown South
dramatizes three short stories by
American authors.

*Program 1*
**Ashes, by Julia Peterkin,**
concerns an independent back-
woods woman, who is threatened
with eviction when a new landowner
decides to construct a home near her
old and unsightly log cabin.

*Program 2*
**The Half-Pint Flask, by DuBose
Heyward,**
tells of a visitor to the Sea Islands off
the coast of South Carolina who un-
wittingly disturbs the superstitious
population by removing a half-pint
dispensary flask from the top of a
grave.

*Program 3*
**Neighbors, by Diane Oliver,**
was inspired by an event that took
place in Charlotte, North Carolina,
in 1957 when a friend of the author's
became the first black student to at-
tend the previously all-white
Harding High School.

Production Organization: South Carolina
Educational Television Network, Columbia,
SC
Year Produced: 1984
Executive Producer: Peter Anderson
Producer/Writer: Benjamin Dunlap
Directors: Jim McMahan, Randy Brinson,
Jim Eddins
Editors: Elaine Cooper, Pat Kay
Cinematography: Bob Gilbert, Buck
Brinson, Everett Davis, Joe Bowie
Host: James Dickey
Cast: Ashes: Rosanna Carter, Dean
Whitworth, Danny Nelson, Timisha Barnes;
Half-Pint Flask: John Malloy, Richard
Leighton, Estelle Evans; Neighbors: Sandra
Mills Scott, Frances Foster, Mel Winkler,
David Guider
Awards: Samuel G. Engle International Film
and Television Drama Competition, First
Place Award; Chicago Film Festival, Gold
Plaque; Ohio State Award; Parents Choice
Award; American Film Festival, Finalist;
SECA Awards, Certificate of Merit; INPUT,
Program Selection; Ashes: CINE Golden
Eagle; The Half-Pint Flask: CINE Golden
Eagle
Print Material: Viewer's Guide available
Format: Video (117:00)
Ashes (38:00); Half-Pint Flask (45:00);
Neighbors (33:00)
Distributor: South Carolina Educational
Television Marketing

## TRAITOR IN MY HOUSE

*Drama*

Traitor in My House is a Civil War
drama based on chronicled events in
the life of Elizabeth Van Lew, a Virginia aristocrat who ran a secret,
pro-union espionage operation
throughout the war. The story is
told from the point of view of her
teenaged niece.

Production Organization: Educational Film
Center, Annandale, VA
Year Produced: 1989 (first broadcast on
*Wonderworks*)
Executive Producer: Stephen L. Rabin
Producers/Writers: Laverne Y. Berry,
Rosemary Puglia-Ritvo
Director: Nell Cox
Cinematography: Bryan England
Editor: Gloria Whittemore
Cast: Mary Kay Place, Charles Dutton,
Harris Yulin, Angela Goethals
Format: Video (50:00)
Distributor: Educational Film Center

## THE WEB (YOUNG PEOPLE'S RADIO THEATRE): MASTERPIECES OF NINETEENTH-CENTURY AMERICAN LITERATURE— PART 1

*Radio Series (Drama and
Documentary)*

These fifty-four half-hour radio programs are the first of a two-part
series that dramatizes twenty-six
classics of nineteenth-century
American fiction for young people.
Each program is accompanied by a
brief commentary on the social, cultural, and intellectual milieu from
which the work emerged. (Note:
The number in parentheses indicates
the number of half-hour episodes
devoted to each literary work)

*Little Women*
by Louisa May Alcott (8)
*Occurrence at Owl Creek Bridge*
by Ambrose Bierce (1)

*The Sheriff's Children*
by Charles Chesnutt (1)

*Desiree's Baby*
by Kate Chopin (1)

*The Open Boat*
by Stephen Crane (1)

*Life in the Iron Mills*
by Rebecca Harding Davis (1)

*Blake (or) The Huts of America*
by Martin Delany (4)

*The Revolt of Mother*
by Mary E. Wilkins Freeman (1)

*The Return of a Private*
by Hamlin Garland (1)

*The Yellow Wallpaper*
by Charlotte Perkins Gilman (1)

*The Man without a Country*
by Edward Everett Hale (2)

*Iola LeRoy (or) The Shadows Uplifted*
by Frances Ellen Watkins Harper (3)

*Young Goodman Brown*
by Nathaniel Hawthorne (1)

*My Kinsman, Major Molineux*
by Nathaniel Hawthorne (1)

*The Cop and the Anthem*
by O. Henry (1)

*Mammon and the Archer*
by O. Henry (1)

*Editha*
by William Dean Howells (1)

*Rip van Winkle*
by Washington Irving (1)

*Washington Square*
by Henry James (4)

*The Country of the Pointed Firs*
by Sarah Orne Jewett (4)

*The Celebrated Jumping Frog of Calaveras County*
by Mark Twain (1)

*Billy Budd*
by Herman Melville (2)

*Bartleby, The Scrivener*
by Herman Melville (2)

*The Gold Bug*
by Edgar Allan Poe (1)

*The Purloined Letter*
by Edgar Allen Poe (1)

*The Adventures of Huckleberry Finn*
by Mark Twain (8)

*Uncle Tom's Cabin*
by Harriet Beecher Stowe (7)

Production Organization: WGBH
Educational Foundation
Year Produced: 1984
Executive Producer: Everett Frost
Producers: Wendy Schwartz, Francis Shrand
Writers/Producers/Directors: Erik Bauersfeld, Robert Billings, Perru Carter, Jim Cook, Don Fouser, Everett Frost, Midge Mackenzie, Marvin Manvell, Lee Ellen Marvin, Anthony Maulucci, Melvin Moore, David Ossman, Linda Patton, Jordan Pecile, Faith Wilding, Yuri Rasovsky, James Spruill
Cast: Series hosts and performers include Julie Harris, James Earl Jones, Lily Tomlin, Jane Alexander, Elma Lewis
Format: Audiocassette
26 programs in 54 (30:00) episodes
Distributor: Not currently available

## THE WEB (YOUNG PEOPLE'S RADIO THEATRE): MASTERPIECES OF NINETEENTH-CENTURY AMERICAN LITERATURE— PART 2

*Radio Series (Drama and Documentary)*

These thirteen half-hour radio dramas comprise the second part of a series of adaptations of nineteenth-century American literature (see previous listing). (Note: The number in parentheses indicates the number of half-hour episodes devoted to the literary work)

*The Red Badge of Courage*
by Stephen Crane (4)

*The Silent Partner*
by Elizabeth Stuart Phelps (4)

*The Turn of the Screw*
by Henry James (4)

*The White Heron*
by Sarah Orne Jewett (1)

Production Organization: WGBH
Educational Foundation
Year Produced: 1985
Executive Producer: Everett Frost
Associate Producers: Judith Walcutt, David Leveille
Writers/Producers/Directors: Erik Bauersfeld, Everett Frost, David Ossman, Faith Wilding
Format: Audiocassette
13 (30:00) programs
Distributor: Not currently available

## THE WEB (YOUNG PEOPLE'S RADIO THEATRE): MYTHOLOGY SERIES

*Radio Series (Drama and Documentary)*

Designed for teenagers and a general audience, this series introduces the myths of ancient Greece and Rome by dramatizing episodes from the classic tales of ancient dieties, heroes, and heroines. Each program also contains a five-minute commentary following the drama.

*Program 1*
**Echo and Narcissus**

*Program 2*
**Deucalion and Pyrrha**

*Program 3*
**Prometheus and Pandora (Part I)**

*Program 4*
**Prometheus and Pandora (Part II)**

*Program 5*
**Demeter and Persephone**

*Program 6*
**Hermes and Apollo**

*Program 7*
**Daphne and Apollo**

*Program 8*
**Artemis and Actaeon**

*Program 9*
**Phaethon**

*Program 10*
**Theseus and the Minotaur**

*Program 11*
**Daedalus and Icarus**

*Program 12*
**Cupid and Psyche (Part I)**

*Program 13*
**Cupid and Psyche (Part II)**

*Program 14*
**Orpheus and Eurydice**

Production Organization: WGBH
Educational Foundation
Year Produced: 1984
Executive Producer: Everett Frost
Associate Producer: Wendy Schwartz
Writers/Producers/Directors: Everett Frost,
Charles Potter, Wendy Schwartz, Vanessa
Whitburn, Faith Wilding
Awards: Gabriel Award; Odyssey Award;
Ohio State Award; endorsed by the National
Educational Association
Format: Audiocassette
14 (30:00) programs
Distributor: Not currently available

# WORD STORIES

*Radio Series (Drama and
Documentary)*

In this six-part radio series, three
animal characters introduce children
to the history and lore behind ordinary words. (see also Songs Jumping
in My Mouth)

*Program 1*
**Word Play**
is an introduction to the variety of
words in the English language.

*Program 2*
**Word People**
explains the nature of an eponym, or
a word that comes from a person's
name.

*Program 3*
**Word Stories**
traces the history of how some
words came to be.

*Program 4*
**Word Changes**
explains how words change over
time, and how they can start out
meaning one thing and end up
meaning another.

*Program 5*
**Word Travels**
explores how words travel when
people do.

*Program 6*
**Word Inventions**
examines the idea and practice of
creating words.

Production Organization: The Radio Road
Gang, Inc., Washington, DC
Year Produced: 1989
Producer/Writer: Pamela Brooke
Sound Recordists: Donna Fox, William
Brown III
Engineer: Michael Zook
Music: George Fulginiti-Shakar, Cathy Fink,
Tom Jones, Marcy Marxer, Rico Petrucelli
Music Performed by: D.C. Youth Ensemble
Narrator: Vincent Prevost
Cast: Dianne Bye, Michael Howell, George
Fulginiti-Shakar, and children
Print Material: Companion book of family
activities available
Awards/Festivals: International Radio
Festival of New York, Gold Medal; Ohio
State Award; NHK Japan Prize, Special Jury
Commendation; Parents Choice Honor
Award
Format: Audiocassette
6 (30:00) programs on 3 cassettes, sold only
as a set
Distributor: The Radio Road Gang, Inc.,
attn: Pamela Brooke

*General*
*Humanities*

## SLOW FIRES: ON THE PRESERVATION OF THE HUMAN RECORD

### *Documentary*

Slow Fires: On the Preservation of the Human Record examines the disintegration of millions of books, newspapers, documents, photographs, drawings and maps due to the acidic content of most paper produced since the mid-nineteenth century.

Production Organization: American Film Foundation, Santa Monica, CA
Year Produced: 1986
Executive Producer: Frieda Lee Mock
Producer/Director: Terry Sanders
Writers: Ben Maddow, Terry Sanders
Cinematography: Erik Daarstad
Editor: William T. Cartwright
Narrator: Robert MacNeil
Awards/Festivals: CINE Golden Eagle;
Directors Guild of America; Festival
International du Film sur l'Art, Montreal;
Salerno Film Festival, Grand Prix
Print Material: Transcript available
Format: 16mm, Video (two versions, 30:00
and 60:00)
Distributor: American Film Foundation

## SOUNDINGS

### *Radio Series (Interview/Discussion)*

Soundings is a weekly cultural affairs series that features conversations with scholars and visitors at the National Humanities Center. In existence since 1980, the series includes nearly 600 programs.

Production Organization: National
Humanities Center, Research Triangle Park,
NC
Year Produced: 1980–91
Producer/Writer/Editor: Wayne J. Pond
Host: Wayne J. Pond
Print Material: For a complete list of
programs, please write or call the National
Humanities Center, 7 Alexander Drive,
Research Triangle Park, NC 27709, 919-549-
0661
Format: weekly (30:00) radio series,
available to NPR stations via satellite, to
commercial stations on LP discs, to non-
broadcast audiences on audiocassettes
($5.00 each)
Distributor: National Humanities Center

# Distributor
# List

## DISTRIBUTORS

*(Film, Video, and Audiocassette)*

Adams County Historical Society
Box 102
Hastings, NE 68902
402-463-5838

Adams-Jefferson Project of Carleton
    College
Carleton College
Northfield, MN 55057
507-663-4000

Adult Learning Service, PBS
1320 Braddock Place
Alexandria, VA 22314-1698
1-800-257-2578
1-703-739-5360

James Agee Film Project Library
316 East Main Street
Johnson City, TN 37601
1-800-352-5111

AIMS Media
6901 Woodley Avenue
Van Nuys, CA 91406-4878
1-800-367-2467
818-785-4111
FAX: 818-376-6405

The Almi Group
1900 Broadway
New York, NY 10023
1-800-888-8166
212-769-6400

The Altschul Group
1560 Sherman Avenue
Suite 100
Evanston, Il 60201
1-800-323-5448
708-328-6700 (in Illinois)

Ambrose Video Publishing, Inc.
1290 Avenue of the Americas
New York, NY 10104
1-800-526-4663
212-265-7572
FAX: 212-265-8088

American Film Foundation
P.O. Box 2000
Santa Monica, CA 90406
213-459-2116

The Annenberg/CPB Collection
(see Intellimation)

Appalshop Films
306 Madison Street
Whitesburg, KY 41858
1-800-545-SHOP
606-633-0108 (in KY)

James Ault Films
71 Fifth Avenue, Suite 1100
New York, NY 10003
212-673-1878

Jane Balfour Films, Ltd.
Burghley House
35 Forbes Road
London NW5 1AD, England
011-44-7l-267-5392
FAX: 011-44-71-267-4241

Ball State University
University Libraries
Educational Resources-Public
    Services
Muncie, IN 47306
(Note: in-room use only)
317-285-5444

Barr Films
12801 Schabarum Avenue
P.O. Box 7878
Irwindale, CA 91706-7878
1-800-234-7878
818-338-7878

Mordecai Bauman
49 West 12th Street
New York, NY 10011
212-242-2280

Beller, Hava Kohav
118 Riverside Drive
Apt. #14A
New York, NY 10024
212-288-3387

Bill Jersey Productions
(see Jersey)

Blackside, Inc.
486 Shawmut Avenue
Boston, MA 02118
617-536-6900

Bullfrog Films, Inc.
Oley, PA 19547
1-800-543-FROG
215-779-8226
FAX: 215-370-1978
for UPS delivery: RD3, Dautrich
Road, Reading, PA 19606

Cabin Creek Center for Work and
    Environmental Studies
58 West 42nd Street
New York, NY 10019
212-677-1312

California Newsreel
149 Ninth Street, Room 420
San Francisco, CA 91403
415-621-6196

Capitol Entertainment
    and Euro Films
attn: Ted Goldberg
4818 Yuma Street, NW
Washington, DC 20016
202-363-8000

Caridi Entertainment
250 West 57th Street, Suite 831
New York, NY 10107
212-581-2277

Center for Ozarks Studies
attn: Robert Flanders
S.W. Missouri State University
Springfield, MO 65804
417-836-5755

Center for Southern Folklore
P.O. Box 40105
1216 Peabody
Memphis, TN 38104
901-525-3655

122

Centre Productions, Inc.
1800 30th Street, Suite 207
Boulder, CO 80301
1-800-824-1166
303-444-1166

Ceskoslovenska Televizia
TELEXPORT
Slovak Department
Osmolovova 28
CS 845 45 Bratislava
Czechoslovakia
TLX: 84992272 CST C

Charles B. Potter
(see Potter)

Charles Fries Entertainment
6922 Hollywood Boulevard
Los Angeles, CA 90028
213-466-2266

Palmer R. Chitester Fund
EBCO Park
2810 West 21st Street
Erie, PA 16506
814-868-1739

Dr. Chung-wen Shih
(see Shih)

Churchill Films, Inc.
12210 Nebraska Avenue
Los Angeles, CA 90025-9816
1-800-334-7830
213-207-6600 (in CA)

Cinelit
St. Paul, Minnesota
612-290-0149

The Cinema Guild
1697 Broadway, Room 802
New York, NY 10019
212-246-5522
FAX: 212-246-5525

Cine Research Associates
32 Fisher Avenue
Boston, MA 02120
617-442-9756

Cleveland Museum of Natural History
Education Division
Wade Oval Circle
Cleveland, OH 44106
216-231-4600

Colonial Williamsburg Foundation
A-V Distribution Section, Box C
Williamsburg, VA 23187
1-800-446-9240
804-220-7148

Consider the Alternatives Radio
5808 Greene Street
Philadelphia, PA 19144
215-848-4100

Corinth Films
34 Ganseveroot Street
New York, NY 10014
212-463-0305

Coronet/MTI Film and Video, Inc.
108 Wilmot Road
Deerfield, IL 60015
1-800-621-2131
708-940-1260 (call collect)
FAX: 708-940-3600

Joanna Costantini
33165 Mulvey Road
Fraser, MI 48026
313-293-0252

Crystal Productions
1812 Johns Drive
or Box 2159
Glenview, IL 60025
1-800-255-8629
FAX: 708-657-8149

Cypress Productions, Inc.
135 West 26th Street
New York, NY 10001
212-691-8565

Danmarks Radio
TV-Byen
DK 2860 Soborg, Denmark
TLX: 85527386

Davenport Films
Rt. 1, Box 527
Delaplane, VA 22025
703-592-3701

D.E.A.F. Media, Inc.
2600 Tenth Street
Berkeley, CA 94710
415-841-0163
415-841-0165 (TDD)

Devillier Donegan Enterprises
4401 Connecticut Avenue, N.W.
Washington, DC
202-686-3980

D.L.T. Entertainment, Ltd.
31 West 56th Street
New York, NY 10019
212-245-4680
FAX: 212-315-1132

Direct Cinema Ltd.
P.O. Box 10003
Santa Monica, CA 90410
1-800-525-0000
310-396-4774
FAX: 310-396-3233

Documentary Educational
  Resources
101 Morse Street
Watertown, MA 02172
617-926-0491
FAX: 617-926-9519

Documentary Research, Inc.
96 Rumsey Road
Buffalo, NY 14209
716-885-9777

Doreen Moses
(see Moses)

Educational Film Center
5101F Backlick Road
Annandale, VA 22003
703-750-0560

The English Speaking Union
640 Sutter Street, #600
San Francisco, CA 94102
415-673-7313

Moctezuma Esparza
3330 Cahuenga Boulevard, Suite 500
Los Angeles, CA 90068
213-269-8251
213-969-2896

Equinox Films, Inc.
200 West 72nd Street
New York, NY 10016
212-799-1515

The Film Company
511 Second Street, NE
Washington, DC 20002
202-547-5016

Family Express Video
37630 Interchange Drive
Farmington Hills, MI 48331
313-347-4630

Family Home Entertainment
  (home video)
15400 Sherman Way, Suite 500
P.O. Box 10124
Van Nuys, CA 91410-0124
818-908-0303

Filmakers Library
124 East 40th Street, Suite 901
New York, NY 10016
212-808-4980

Films for the Humanities
  and Sciences
P.O. Box 2053
Princeton, NJ 08540
1-800-257-5126
609-452-1128

The Film History Foundation
650 Fifth Street
Suite 202
San Francisco, CA 94107
415-777-3453

Films, Inc./PMI
5547 North Ravenswood Avenue
Chicago, IL 60640-9979
1-800-323-4222
312-878-2600

First Run/Icarus Films
153 Waverly Place, 6th Floor
New York, NY 10014
1-800-876-1710
212-727-1711
212-243-0600

Flower Films
10341 San Pablo Avenue
El Cerrito, CA 94530
415-525-0942

Folger Shakespeare Library
Museum Shop
201 East Capitol Street, SE
Washington, DC 20003
202-544-4600

Fogg Fine Arts Film Library
P.O. Box 315
Franklin Lakes, NJ 07417
201-652-1989

Foundation for African Prehistory
427 Grinder Hall
University of Florida
Gainesville, FL 32611
904-392-7499

Fremantle International
660 Madison Avenue
New York, NY 10021
212-421-4530
FAX: 212-207-8357
or
MC4, 2 rue de Belgrade
38000 Grenoble, France
011-33-76-50-32-99

Global Village
431 Broome Street
New York, NY 10013
212-431-7261

Globe Radio Repertory
5220 University Way, NE
Seattle, WA 98105
206-527-2480

Great Plains National Instructional
  Television Library
P.O. Box 80669
Lincoln, NE 68501
1-800-228-4630

Great Projects Film Company, Inc.
584 Ninth Avenue
New York, NY 10036
212-864-0811

Hava Kohav Beller
(see Beller)

HBO Video (home video)
1100 Avenue of the Americas
New York, NY 10036
212-512-7400

Hearts and Hands Media Arts
372 Frederick Street
San Francisco, CA 94117
415-664-9623

Hit Communications
The Pump House
13-16 Jacob's Well Mews
London W1H 5PD, England
011-44-1-224-1717
FAX: 011-44-1-224-1719

Home Vision (home video)
Films Inc./PMI
5547 North Ravenswood Avenue
Chicago, IL 60640-1199
1-800-323-4222
312-878-2600

**124**

Hungarian Television Enterprises
1051 Budapest
Munnich Ference Ucta 18, Hungary
011-36-11-116-447

Independent Broadcasting
 Associates, Inc.
111 King Street
Littleton, MA 01460-1527
508-486-9180

Indiana University
Audio-Visual Center
Bloomington, IN 47405-5901
1-800-552-8620 (out of state)
1-800-942-0481 (in Indiana)
812-855-2103 (Film Library, local)
FAX: 812-855-8404

Intellimation
The Annenberg/CPB Project
130 Cremona
P.O. Box 1922
Santa Barbara, CA 93116-1922
1-800-LEARNER
805-968-2291

International Film Bureau, Inc.
332 South Michigan Avenue
Chicago, IL 60604-4382
1-800-432-2241
312-427-4545

Italtoons Corporation
32 West 40th Street
New York, NY 10018
212-730-0280
FAX 212-730-0313

Jack J. Roth
(see Roth)

James Agee Film Project Library
(see Agee)

James Ault Films
(see Ault)

Jane Balfour Films, Ltd.
(see Balfour)

Janson Associates
Plaza West
88 Semmens Road
Harrington Park, NJ 07640
1-800-952-6766
201-784-8488

Bill Jersey Productions
c/o Quest Productions
attn: Joy E. Ramos
2600 10th Street
Berkeley, CA 94710
415-548-0854

The Jewish Heritage Film Project
150 Franklin Stret, #1W
New York, NY 10011
212-925-9067

Joanna Costantini
(see Costantini)

Judi Moore Smith-Latta
(see Smith-Latta)

KCET-TV
4401 Sunset Boulevard
Los Angeles, CA 90027
213-666-6500

Kaleidoscope Media Service
attn: Judith L. Strasser
P.O. Box 1123
Madison, WI 53701
608-238-7976

Keener Productions
3177 Lindo Street
Los Angeles, CA 90068
213-851-2167

Lara Classics Inc.
9 Merrill Street
Cambridge, MA 02139
617-491-7387

Learning in Focus
4 Chatsworth Avenue
Larchmont, NY 10538
914-833-3390

Les Films René Malo
1207 Saint Andre
Fourth Floor
Montreal, Quebec
Canada H2L 3S8
518-844-4555

Robert S. Levi
28 East 10th Street
New York, NY 10003
212-924-0739

Light-Saraf Films
131 Concord Street
San Francisco, CA 94112
415-469-0139

Lightyear Entertainment
 (home video)
Empire State Building
3650 Fifth Avenue, Suite 5101
New York, NY 10118
212-563-4897
FAX: 212-563-1932

Link Licensing Limited
United Newspapers Building
23-27 Tudor Street
London EC4Y OHR, England
011-44-1-353-7305
FAX: 011-44-1-583-3479

Lionheart Television
1762 Westwood Blvd.
Suite 320
Los Angeles, CA 90024
213-470-3939

Long Bow Group, Inc.
55 Newton Street
Brookline, MA 02146
617-277-6400

Mass Productions
1510 Guerrero
San Francisco, CA 94110
415-648-3789

Media Guild
11722 Sorrento Valley Road, Suite E
San Diego, CA 92121
619-755-9191

The Metropolitan Washington
   Ear, Inc.
35 University Boulevard East
Silver Spring, MD 20901
301-681-6636

Mississippi Authority for
   Educational Television
attn: Sandra Russell
3825 Ridgewood Road
Jackson, MS 39211
601-982-6565

Moctezuma Esparza
(see Esparza)

Modern Poetry Association
60 West Walton Street
Chicago, IL 60610
312-280-4870

Monterey Movie Company
   (home video)
5142 North Clareton Street
Suite 270
Agoura Hills, CA 91301
818-597-0047

Mordecai Bauman
(see Bauman)

Doreen Moses
911 R Street, NW #201
Washington, DC 20009
202-483-7071

Murray Street Enterprise
47 Murray Street
New York, NY 10007
212-619-1475

Mystic Fire Video
P.O. Box 1092
Cooper Station, NY 10276
212-677-5040

National Humanities Center
Alexander Drive or P.O. Box 12256
Research Triangle Park, NC 27709
919-549-066l

National Public Radio
2025 M Street, NW
Washington, DC 20036
202-822-2000

National Radio Theatre
5520 South Cornell, #3-5
Chicago, IL 60637
708-684-6961

Nebraska Educational Television
   (NETV)
attn: Jim Danielson
P.O. Box 83111
Lincoln, NE
1-800-228-4630
402-472-3611

The Newark Museum
49 Washington Street
   or P.O. Box 540
Newark, NJ 07101
201-596-6655

New Day Films
121 West 27th Street, Suite 902
New York, NY 10001
212-645-8210

The New Film Company, Inc.
7 Mystic Street, Dept. D
Arlington, MA 02174
617-641-2580

The New York Center for
   Visual History
625 Broadway
Twelfth Floor
New York, NY 10012
212-777-6900

New York City Board of Education
WYNE-FM
112 Tillary Street
Brooklyn, NY 11201
718-935-4480

New Yorker Films
16 West 61st Street
New York, NY 10023
212-247-6110

NightOwl Productions
P.O. Box 433
Vineyard Haven, MA 02568
508-693-6414

Northside Films
181 Bedford Avenue
Brooklyn, NY 11211
718-384-5268

Pacific Arts Video
11858 La Grange Avenue
Los Angeles, CA 90025
1-800-538-5856

Pacific Street Film Projects
579 Broadway
Hastings-on-Hudson, NY 10706
914-478-1900

Pacifica Program Service/
   Radio Archive
3729 Cahuenga Boulevard West
North Hollywood, CA 91604
1-800-735-0230
818-506-1077

Palmer R. Chitester Fund
(see Chitester)

Parabola Video
656 Broadway
New York, NY 10012
212-505-6200

PBS Video
1320 Braddock Place
Alexandria, VA 22314-1698
1-800-344-3337
1-800-424-7963

**126**

PBS, Adult Learning Service
(see Adult Learning Service, PBS)

Penn State Audio-Visual Services
University Division of Media and
    Learning Resources
Special Services Building
Pennsylvania State University
University Park, PA 16802
1-800-826-0132
814-865-6314

Charles B. Potter
838 West End Avenue, #6-D
New York, NY 10025
212-866-1123

Producer Services Group
7461 Beverly Boulevard
Penthouse
Los Angeles, CA 90036
213-937-5020

Pyramid Film and Video
Box 1048
Santa Monica, CA 90406-1048
1-800-421-2304
213-828-7577

Professor Theodore Rabb
c/o History Department
Princeton University
Princeton, NJ 08544
609-258-4994
FAX: 609-258-5387

Radio America
499 South Capitol Street, SW
Suite 417
Washington, DC 20003
202-488-7226

Radio Arts Foundation
838 West End Avenue, #6D
New York, NY 10025
212-866-1123

Radio Road Gang, Inc.
attn: Pamela Brooke
624 A Street, NE
Washington, DC 20002
202-544-2791

Random House Home Video
400 Hahn Road
Westminster, MD 21157
1-800-726-0600 (customer service)
1-800-733-3000 (orders only)

Realizations, Inc.
338 West 11th Street
Apt 5D
New York, NY 10003
212-929-6125

R. M. Associates, Inc.
250 West 57th Street
New York, NY 10019
212-262-3230

Robert S. Levi
(see Levi)

Jack J. Roth
24301 Bryden Road
Beachwood, OH 44122
216-464-2238

SVS, Inc. (Sony Video)
1700 Broadway, 16th Floor
New York, NY 10019
212-757-4990
1-800-523-0823
(c/o Movies Unlimited)

San Diego State University
KPBS-TV
San Diego, CA 92183
619-265-6431

Dr. Chung-wen Shih
2500 Virginia Avenue, NW
Washington, DC 20037
202-333-9133

Silvercloud Video Productions, Inc.
attn: John Crouch
1321 East King Road
Tucson, AZ 85719
602-326-7647

Smeltzer Films
403 Dimm Street
Richmond, CA 94805
415-235-1357

Judi Moore Smith-Latta
4744 Silverstone Drive
Silver Spring, MD 20904
301-384-2859

Smithsonian Institution Press
Video Division
470 L'Enfant Plaza
Suite 7100
Washington, DC 20560
202-287-3738

South Carolina Educational
    Television Marketing
Drawer L, 2712 Millwood Avenue
Columbia, SC 29250
1-800-553-7752
803-737-3390 (in SC)

Southern Educational
    Communications Association
Radio Division
P.O. Box 50008
2628 Millwood Avenue
Columbia, SC 29250
803-799-5517

Straight Ahead Pictures, Inc.
Box 395
Conway, MA 01341
413-369-4784

Sveriges Television
S-105 10 Stockholm, Sweden
011-46-87840000
FAX: 011-46-87841500

Tell Me a Story
attn: Marjorie Leet
1234 Filbert Street
San Francisco, CA 91909
415-474-7727

Thames Video Collection
Dept. 8747
P.O. Box 3012
Wallingford, CT 06494
(no phone number available)

Third World Newsreel
335 West 38th Street, 5th Floor
New York, NY 10018
212-947-9277

Time-Life Video
Customer Service
1450 West Parkham Road
Richmond, VA 23280
1-800-621-7026

Unicorn Projects, Inc.
3023 Tennyson Street, NW
Washington, DC 20015
202-543-6656

University of California
Extension Media Center
2176 Shattuck Avenue
Berkeley, CA 94704
415-642-0460 (preview or rent)
415-642-5578 (purchase)

University of Michigan
Film and Video Library
400 4th Street
Ann Arbor, MI 48103-4816
1-800-999-0424
313-764-5360

University of Texas at Austin
Film Library, Box W
Austin, TX 78712
512-471-3572

University of Washington Press
P.O. Box 50096
Seattle, WA 98145
206-543-8870

University of Wisconsin-Milwaukee
Golda Meir Library
P.O. Box 604
Milwaukee, WI 53201
414-229-4785
414-229-5527 (Media Department)

Vermont Public Radio
Box 89.5
Windsor, VT 05089
802-674-6772

ViceVersaVision
Box 3239
Noroton, CT 06820
203-655-9800

Vineyard Video Productions
Elias Lane
West Tisbury, MA 02575
508-693-3584

Voces Unidas Bilingual
    Broadcasting Foundation
KUBO-FM
P.O. Box 1243
Salinas, CA 93902

Vox Productions
2335 Jones Street
San Francisco, CA 94133
415-673-6429

WGBH Educational Foundation
125 Western Avenue
Boston, MA 02134
617-492-2777

WIPB-TV
P.O. Box 1708
Muncie, IN 47308
317-285-1249

WQED (Metropolitan Pittsburgh
    Public Broadcasting)
4802 Fifth Avenue
Pittsburgh, PA 11521
412-622-1300

WQED-FM
4802 Fifth Avenue
Pittsburgh, PA 11512
412-622-1436

WRFG Radio
attn: Harlan Joye
P.O. Box 5332
Atlanta, GA 30307
404-523-3471

WSBE-TV
50 Park Lane
Providence, RI 02903
401-277-3636

Western Public Radio
Building D, Fort Mason Center
San Francisco, CA 94123
415-271-1161

Weston Woods
Weston, CT 06883-1199
1-800-243-5020
203-226-3355 (in CT call collect)

Wheelright Museum of the
    American Indian
704 Camino Lejo
P.O. Box 5153
Santa Fe, NM 87502
505-982-4636

Wonderworks/WQED
4802 Fifth Avenue
Pittsburgh, PA 11521
412-622-1300

World Music Institute
attn: Becky Miller
49 West 27th Street #810
New York, NY 10001
212-545-7536

Zipporah Films, Inc.
1 Richdale Avenue, #4
Cambridge, MA 02140
617-576-3603

ISBN 0-16-038136-3